"Ramesh Richard rightly observes conviction, a '*sacred* oughtness' bo quickly we may forget our calling in Thankfully, readers will find genuine help and biblical insight from a seasoned preacher who has walked these steps before. This is a theme very dear to my heart addressed by one who has demonstrated this gift and calling all over the world."

Ravi Zacharias, author and speaker

"The gospel hasn't changed in nearly two thousand years. It's still the transforming power of Jesus Christ! In this book, Dr. Ramesh Richard shows how to preach the gospel humbly, prayerfully, biblically, expectantly. May God change lives as you proclaim that Good News!"

Luis Palau, world-renowned evangelist and author of High Definition Life

"My good friend Ramesh has provided every communicator who has a heart for the lost with tools to proclaim the gospel message with power."

Tony Evans, senior pastor, Oak Cliff Bible Fellowship

"The clarity, simplicity, and power of Ramesh Richard's seven-step approach to constructing sermons has well served students and pastors in many settings and nations. Now to have this most approachable method of sermon construction applied to evangelistic preaching is truly good news not only for pastors wanting ready assistance but also for lost souls needing eternal security."

Bryan Chapell, president, Covenant Theological Seminary

"I believe this resource will strengthen your effectiveness as an evangelistic preacher and give you more boldness as you approach your task in the power of the Holy Spirit."

Daniel Southern, president, American Tract Society

"Long awaited, here is the foundational text for evangelistic preaching written by a master teacher of the art. Applying the lessons of this book will enhance the ministry of anyone called to preach the Word of God."

Robert E. Coleman, distinguished professor of evangelism and discipleship,
Gordon-Conwell Theological Seminary

"Ramesh is one of God's choice gifts to the body of Christ. I applaud his work on equipping others to effectively deliver the gospel message."

Dennis Rainey, president, FamilyLife

"A masterpiece from a master evangelist! Ramesh Richard has written an indispensable work for all those who passionately seek to save the lost. This book provides a clear and compelling case for presenting the gospel with content, conviction, and class. It is a must-have for both beginners and seasoned veterans alike. It's a great book that deserves the widest reading."

James Ryle, president, TruthWorks Ministries

"This book is not just a theoretical discussion of evangelistic preaching, but a practical book, filled with ideas all of us can use. I found it refreshing because the author so clearly communicates his own passion and firsthand experience in sharing the Good News."

Erwin W. Lutzer, senior pastor, The Moody Church

"Ramesh Richard's book comes at a very opportune moment. During forty years of evangelistic preaching, I've never seen the harvest potential I see today. During these days of worldwide uncertainty, people are searching for answers to life's most basic problems. There's a great need for men and women who can communicate clearly, biblically, and in the authority of the Holy Spirit the life-changing message of the gospel of Christ. Ramesh Richard teaches us how to do that. I pray that this timely book will be read widely and be used to bring multitudes into the kingdom of God. I encourage anyone who has a desire to communicate the gospel to the world around them to read *Preparing Evangelistic Sermons*. This book is for pastors, evangelists, and laypersons with a heart to communicate the good news of God's love for a lost and dying world."

Sammy Tippit, international evangelist

"I have sat in the audience as Ramesh has powerfully and clearly proclaimed Jesus and his love. His ministry is a model of what he writes about in this book. Thank you, Ramesh, for the inviting way in which you show us that we don't have to sacrifice the truth of God's Word to connect with the hearts of non-Christians. This is a wonderful, valuable, practical resource for anyone who wants to proclaim the hope of Jesus Christ to empty, needy hearts. My only regret is that you didn't write this thirty years ago!"

Crawford W. Loritts Jr., associate director, Campus Crusade for Christ, USA

"Ramesh Richard has earned the right to write on evangelism in sermons. He has demonstrated for an entire generation the common union of evangelistic fervor and biblical and scholastic excellence. His book should be foundational and encouraging to all who mount the sacred desk."

Tommy Nelson, senior pastor, Denton Bible Church

"Ramesh, I am now able to define ministry 'success,' verify my effectiveness, and live a more stress-free life. Wow, great work, Doc!"

Mike Silva, president, MSE, Inc.

"An evangelistic speaker must interact with both the biblical text and his audience. *Preparing Evangelistic Sermons* challenges you to speak in a relevant way and preach his Word, not your words. I am grateful for Ramesh's heart for lost people and his desire to impart what he has learned through experience."

R. Larry Moyer, president and CEO, EvanTell, Inc.

"In today's culture, effective communication is crucial for the delivery of the message. Ramesh Richard takes the greatest message *ever* given and takes the reader on an insightful journey of how to connect with the listener's head and heart. In a multicultural world, adrift from the moorings to absolutes, you'll want to read this book if your passion is to passionately and powerfully share the message of Jesus Christ with a world that so desperately needs to hear, comprehend, and embrace it."

Bob Reccord, president and CEO, North American Mission Board, SBC

"Ramesh Richard is a brilliant teacher and can put that same skill to words on paper. He is a true lover of people, which makes him the perfect 'evangelist.' He pursues God's heart like few men I've ever met. Take these three qualities and you have the recipe for a book that will set your heart afire with the desire to 'go and do likewise.'"

Joe White, president, Kanakuk Kamps

Preparing Evangelistic Sermons

A Seven-Step Method for Preaching Salvation

Ramesh Richard

BakerBooks
Grand Rapids, Michigan

© 2005 by Ramesh Richard

Published by Baker Books
a division of Baker Publishing Group
P.O. Box 6287, Grand Rapids, MI 49516-6287
www.bakerbooks.com

Printed in the United States of America

All rights reserved. No part of this publication may be reproduced, stored in a retrieval system, or transmitted in any form or by any means—for example, electronic, photocopy, recording—without the prior written permission of the publisher. The only exception is brief quotations in printed reviews.

Library of Congress Cataloging-in-Publication Data
Richard, Ramesh, 1953–
    Preparing evangelistic sermons : a seven-step method for preaching salvation / Ramesh Richard.
       p.   cm.
    Includes bibliographical references.
    ISBN 0-8010-6574-7 (pbk.)
    1. Preaching. 2. Evangelistic work—Sermons. 3. Missions—Sermons. I. Title.
BV4211.3R53 2005
251'.3—dc22   2005013247

Unless otherwise indicated, Scripture is taken from the HOLY BIBLE, NEW INTERNATIONAL VERSION®. NIV®. Copyright © 1973, 1978, 1984 by International Bible Society. Used by permission of Zondervan. All rights reserved.

Scripture marked ESV is taken from The Holy Bible, English Standard Version, copyright © 2001 by Crossway Bibles, a division of Good News Publishers. Used by permission. All rights reserved.

Scripture marked Message is taken from *The Message* by Eugene H. Peterson, copyright © 1993, 1994, 1995, 2000, 2001, 2002. Used by permission of NavPress Publishing Group. All rights reserved.

Scripture marked NASB is taken from the New American Standard Bible®, Copyright © 1960, 1962, 1963, 1968, 1971, 1972, 1973, 1975, 1977, 1995 by The Lockman Foundation. Used by permission.

Scripture marked NRSV is taken from the New Revised Standard Version of the Bible, copyright 1989, Division of Christian Education of the National Council of the Churches of Christ in the United States of America. Used by permission. All rights reserved.

Dedicated to

"Pastor"

The Rev. Dr. Samuel T. Kamaleson,
whose formidable impact
during impressionable teen years
provided a ministry template for
penetrative proclamation,
peripatetic ministry, and
pastoral training
worldwide

Contents

Introduction   9

Part 1: Foundation
1. The Inner Calling of the Preaching Evangelist: Personal and Spiritual Compulsion   17
2. The Outer Calling of the Preaching Evangelist: Biblical Conviction and Motivation   37

Part 2: Framework
3. A Theological Framework for Evangelistic Preaching   59
4. A Definition of Evangelistic Preaching   71

Part 3: Method
5. Textual Evangelistic Preaching: Integration with the Scripture Sculpture Process   85
6. Sources and Samples of Textual Evangelistic Preaching   93
7. Text-Driven Topical Evangelistic Preaching   123
8. Audience-Driven Topical Evangelistic Preaching   135

Part 4: Special Issues
9. Support Materials: Illustrating the Evangelistic Sermon   151
10. The Evangelistic Invitation   173

Appendix 1: Relevant Terms in Evangelistic Preaching   191
Appendix 2: A Synopsis of the Scripture Sculpture
   Process   193
Appendix 3: Shades of Evangelistic Presentation   209
Appendix 4: A Sample Pre-evangelistic Sermon   217
Appendix 5: The Evangelistic Invitation: A Preparation
   Checklist   229
Appendix 6: A Checklist for Evaluating the Textual or Topical
   Evangelistic Sermon   233

A Concluding Challenge: A Preaching Audit   237
Notes   245

Introduction

> My gracious Master and my God,
>   Assist me to proclaim,
> To spread through all the earth abroad
>   The honors of thy name.
>
> —Charles Wesley

I failed. Last week in Argentina, I failed my own criteria for evangelistic preaching.

The evening went well. Our hosts exceeded our stipulation of a 50 percent non-Christian audience. Having declared it an evening of cultural interest, the mayor was present. In friendly Argentine style, the place was filled with pre-meeting conversation and the promise of exotic after-event snacks. Economic crises had well prepared an audience to hear my presentation, "Finding Meaning in a World of Chaos."

Everything was right. Except I failed at a critical point. I ramped up to the people's need for finding meaning outside the existential situation. They laughed, cried, and shook their heads in agreement, variance, and empathy. Yet I failed.

I failed in my presentation of Jesus's substitution. I introduced the concept and explored its meaning but did not possess an effective illustration the audience could embrace quickly or easily or clearly.

In evangelistic preaching especially, the illustration is as important as the point—to present the concept, to contemporize a two-thousand-year-old event, to clarify its meaning, to reinforce its significance, and to invite a response.

Fortunately, the Holy Spirit succeeded despite my failure. The One who precedes me and follows my preaching found a way into the hearts of sinners. He convicted the unbelievers of guilt in regard to sin, righteousness, and judgment to regenerate them (John 16:8).

I count on the Holy Spirit to succeed in spite of my failure rather than count on my failure to permit the Holy Spirit to succeed. As in every other endeavor in our faith—whether in the Christian journey or in Christian ministry—so in evangelistic preaching. Do the best you can and trust God for his plan! We shall do the best we can, for God has already worked, is working, and will work the rest of his plan in converting sinners.

Doing our best in evangelistic preaching—that's what this book is about. Doing our best thinking about our best preparing, our best praying, our best preaching toward effective evangelistic proclamation and leaving the rest to God.

Did you notice I didn't count the number of people who attended the evangelistic event or those who responded to the evangelistic invitation as markers of success? Instead, I assessed the impact of the meeting based on whether our hosts had done their honest hard work in getting a good percentage of non-Christians there and whether I had been faithful to my personal calling as well as the rather clear criteria for effective evangelistic preaching.

So ask only two questions to gauge the success of an evangelistic sermon: Have you been faithful to the evangelistic mandate, exploiting your giftedness to meet people's salvation needs in the opportunities God has opened for your utility? Have you met the criteria for an effective evangelistic sermon? Then leave the rest to God.

Do your best to get as many non-Christians there as possible. I don't count how many people come, but I sure attempt to find out the percentage of unbelievers in attendance. I find it very difficult to evangelize believers.

Do your best in keeping the meeting non-Christian-friendly—for example, no repetitive and long congregational singing.

Do your best in picking a theme that is relevant to your audience.

Do your best in finding and placing an adequate number of appropriate illustrations in your talk.

Do your best in expounding the content of the gospel specifically or weaving it through the talk.

Do your best in inviting people to transfer their trust to the Lord Jesus as their only God and Savior.

Do the best you can, and trust God to work his plan in rescuing the lost. You will see how he moves some across the line, from death to life, from non-seeker to seeker, from seeker to believer. How he moves some toward the line, from ignorant or defiant to seeker. How he also moves believers toward greater appreciation of their own salvation or deeper motivation to evangelize the lost.

Converting the sinner is God's role. Communicating the gospel is yours. Since he is working his harvest plan, let him take care of the effectiveness of the meeting. He makes the meeting effective; we make it efficient. As a mere laborer in *his* harvest, you take care of the details of a well-executed evangelistic event.

Struggling with my failure that night, I asked God for a pertinent and powerful illustration to present the aspects of the gospel. I found one I could use in any place where financial crises threaten a country, for Argentina faced the worst crisis in its economic history. All currency was devalued; all deposits were frozen; all banks were closed. It didn't matter what you had in the bank, or thought you had in the bank, your account statements always showed zero.

Personal anxiety spilled over in street marches and behind closed doors of homes, offices, and shops. Public anger about people scavenging for food around garbage cans—a sight unseen until then in a once rich country—dominated coffeehouse conversations. All trust in any institution had eroded. Greater faith didn't mean greater bank accounts. The only hope and help for an individual was to find a benefactor who would give him money through a foreign bank that couldn't be corrupted by local restrictions and regulations. The donor would absorb the cost of graciously giving the individual what he didn't deserve.

All sorts of evangelistic parallels to Argentina's dire circumstance emerged quickly. Whatever your good works, they show up as a grand goose egg. You have no credit! Faith, no matter how sincere and great it is, does not help your bank account grow. The object of faith needs to be valid for faith to be vital. Further, your only hope is a gracious giver who will absorb the cost of a gift you must simply receive and can't contribute toward. Will you receive God's provision of a gift that cannot be corrupted, stolen, or defiled by you or anyone else?

That night Enrique understood God's provision very well. A middle-aged accountant to some of Argentina's top companies, he depended on his own faithfulness and excellence as a husband and father. He decided that his creditworthiness counted as a zero before God, that he needed the provision of God's benefactor, Jesus, to absorb the penalty of personal corruption by dying on the cross instead of him. Jesus's resurrection guaranteed the deposit of God's salvation in Enrique's account if he would receive the gift. Enrique, in Castilian-accented English, clearly professed, "I accept God's provision in his Son on my behalf. I depend on what Jesus would want me to depend on to get me into God's heaven." He remarked, "I thought about the question of my death even as you spoke tonight. I thought about how making economic provision for my wife's and children's future showed that I had done more good than bad things in my life. I now depend on Jesus to give me eternal life." I sent him away to do more good but to not depend on it as proof of eternal salvation. That perpetual salvation was deposited in the unshakable bank of heaven in a currency that could not be devalued, because Jesus had guaranteed it with his own death and resurrection.[1]

I found further illustrations for the two other high-powered events of last week. They too helped me . . . illustrate, for illustrations are for the purpose of illustrating the message, not for entertaining. I think I did the best I could within my limitations, and God worked the rest of his plan. Dozens crossed over from the kingdom of darkness to the kingdom of God's dear Son.

From colaborer you move to spectator, watching people's responses at the evangelistic invitation with amazement, gratitude, joy, and even terror as God uses stumbling, bumbling human beings to work the rest of his plan for people's salvation: he rescues people from the power of darkness and transfers them into the kingdom of his beloved Son, in whom they have redemption, the forgiveness of sins (Col. 1:13–14).

This book focuses on your responsibility in preaching salvation. The first half discusses biblical and theological convictions an evangelist *must* possess. Notice the necessity of these convictions. People behave not according to their beliefs but according to their values. They live their convictions; they apply their values. I shall identify and comment on basic theological convictions that drive evangelistic preaching.

The second half of the book deals with homiletical method in evangelistic preaching. By God's plan and in his economy, I have had the privilege of teaching preaching to hundreds of seminary students and thousands of pastoral leaders worldwide. Sometimes I can't tell the difference between fourth-year seminary students and semiliterate pastors! I have learned much from the intellectual tensions of the former and the experiential tensions of implementing effective preaching of the latter.

I kept notes from these informal teachers of mine for twenty-five years and put together the Scripture Sculpture[2] process of expository preaching. I suggest that you regularly work through that process of preparing and preaching expository sermons. Where you choose to expound a text in evangelistic preaching, I will show you how to integrate the Scripture Sculpture process. We will also deal with other major kinds of evangelistic preaching—thematic and topical.

In God's pleasure, I have been privileged to present the Good News one on one, one on many, and via major media thrusts. During many of these times, God has exceeded my expectations in responses, consistently confirming that my calling is greater than my gifts and the gifts are larger than the person. While spiritual empowerment cannot be transferred, spiritual endowment can be recognized, gifts may be developed, and inclinations can be turned into strategies. If you possess the gifts and inclinations, I trust that my insight and experience will provide the opportunity for your growth and utility in the Ultimate Economy.

Welcome to *Preparing Evangelistic Sermons*!

PART 1

FOUNDATION

1

THE INNER CALLING OF THE PREACHING EVANGELIST

Personal and Spiritual Compulsion

> No one takes this honor upon himself; he must be called by God.[1]
>
> —Hebrews 5:4

"I have always wanted to be one. I don't do it for the pay, nor the exposure, nor the fun. I do it because I am committed. I pay the price of extreme workouts three to four hours a day, the tedious practice of learning moves, the long hours of keeping in shape between seasons . . . even when nobody is watching."

I heard those words on a radio interview.[2] You would think they were spoken by an athlete on a professional team. In one sense they were. She belonged to a miniscule filler act for the Dallas Cowboys, once America's football team. The speaker belonged to their well-endowed, uninhibited, overexposed cheerleading squad—which still shocks and dismays this immigrant—though she did say she didn't do it for the exposure. She did it because she was committed to the game, the team, and the city. Compared to the large sum the main entertainment squad—the Cowboys used to identify themselves as an "entertainment company"—gets paid, these hardworking cheerleaders receive a measly fifty dollars a game. Yet they are committed in the very core of their being to their team's mission. At this sorry season, the Dallas Cowboys themselves could gain from that sort of internal compulsion.[3] The players recently have been avoiding the white powder delineating the goal line for fear that it is weaponized with anthrax or sarin. Our whole city pines for a return to a winning season soon.

Internal compulsion reveals a necessity for, a conviction about, even an obligation toward, the need for evangelistic preaching for human salvation. Our message seems harsh, the results are not guaranteed, the audience is sometimes unfriendly, and the pay is small. But the news *must* be delivered, the message *must* be proclaimed "whether the time is favorable or unfavorable" (2 Tim. 4:2 NRSV).

As in every pursuit, it's not whether you obsess over an object, but whether it is a valid fixation. All validity, and especially Christian validity, depends on the worth of the object and the weight of the activity. In evangelistic preaching, the worth of the object and the weight of the activity are without measure. You are after the glory of God that is enhanced by the rescue of human beings from eternal lostness. Evangelistic preaching as a passion *in* your life, as an expression of your love for the Lord Jesus, the passion *of* your life, is valid, justifiable, and compelling.

In this lethargic, hesitant age that diagnoses vigorous and rigorous commitment to any cause as a psychological disorder, even the drivenness of a cheerleader in lightweight entertainment is as refreshing as the inner compulsion that must possess the servant of the Lord Jesus Christ—the only true heavyweight of the universe. He is worthy as the passion *of* your life—refer to his Great Commandment. His work is worthy as your passion *in* life—refer to his Great Commission. Let your necessary consent to the Great Commission in evangelistic preaching flow from your sufficient assent to his Great Commandment—your love of God overflowing into love for your non-Christian neighbor.

Evangelistic preaching is first and foremost, then, driven by internal conviction, a compulsion, even a propulsion, which has often been described as "calling."[4] One's calling is describable but not definable, stateable but not provable, more easily understood by those who experience it than by those who do not. I have elsewhere noted and evaluated the use of the word *calling* as a substitute for pretty much any vocation—business, law, medicine.[5] Yet we must regard Christian calling as a sacred "oughtness."[6] It cannot be trivialized to refer to an occupation or vocation. Any professional occupation can be an acceptable service to God, a spiritual act of worship that can be turned into a necessary means of evangelistic witness, but evangelism is the end. Evangelism motivates your inner being. You "occupate to vocate," says an African-American friend. In the last few weeks, I have met Christians called in this surreptitious sense. One is a "work station steward" at the headquarters of insurance giant State Farm, another serves on the senior legal team at the major signal-processing firm Texas Instruments, and yet another has begun a ministry arm of his real estate company. They excel in expertise and output, but their work is not their calling. In the theological sense of calling, they use their professions as platforms to introduce people to Jesus's salvation or as a means to recruit people to Jesus's service.

It is in a narrow sense that evangelistic preaching is a sacred calling, because you are called to call people to call on the Lord Jesus for salvation. You may be a pastor, professor, or plumber, but if you sense a personal giftedness in evangelism combined with a heart sensitivity to non-Christians, you can focus toward learning to preach evangelistically. If you possess the gifts and the heart, don't worry about the preaching aspect of an evangelistic ministry. Just like the many who have been taught, you can learn the evangelistic preaching process.

One's sacred oughtness, or ministry calling, especially toward evangelistic preaching, can be expressed in the following equation:

Oughtness = Sentness + Willingness

Your sense of *oughtness* arises from a *sentness* accompanied by your *willingness* in developing and doing your evangelistic preaching. Since you know God has called you, you know who you are and what you are about—the reaching and rescuing of human beings with God, for Jesus, to salvation.

Sacred Oughtness

You can't escape the sacred oughtness. You can neglect it, suppress it, even abandon it, but you can't break away from it. It gnaws at your soul, seeps in through your activities, makes a background noise in your conscience. You can't run away from it, even though like Jonah you tend to run away in disobedience. Instead, like the Lord Jesus, who sensed he *must* go through Samaria to reach one person, a tabloid-headline-prone woman (cf. John 4:4), you sense a ministry necessity.[7] Jesus transfers that oughtness to us. Notice the plural pronoun accompanied by necessity when Jesus says, "As long as it is day, *we must* do the work of him who sent me" (John 9:4). That's why Paul writes, "Yet when I preach the gospel, I cannot boast, for I am *compelled* to preach. Woe to me if I do not preach the gospel!" (1 Cor. 9:16).

If you are highly committed to evangelistic preaching, you must be deeply convinced that anything other than pursuing God's calling will be less than the best. You wouldn't give a serious thought, at your saner moments, to looking back after laying your hands on the plow. If you look back, you'll only remark, "You mean God did that through me?" How risky to have walked that scraggy edge of a ministry cliff to survive with perfect hindsight about "the one who is faithful who called you (not only to salvation and sanctification, but also to service) and who also brought it to pass" (1 Thess. 5:24, author's interpretation). There is no full-blown empirical proof that explains your convinced oughtness, only an interior sense of summons and necessity, observable but not describable by others, contagious but not infectious, for it is too personal.

Your sacred oughtness in evangelistic ministry addresses the same challenges as any kind of demanding ministry vocation. Highlight some of these to which you are liable to succumb, or that you are presently experiencing, and add a few more for good measure:

discouragement (my easiest inclination)
pride (my biggest danger)
fatigue
burnout
lack of results
lack of resources
criticism
apparent lack of opportunities
lack of board understanding
lack of staff cooperation
busyness
distraction
staleness
plateauing
awareness of limitations
ignorance of dangers, inadequacies, the future
sense of uselessness
boredom
despondency
feeling overwhelmed
seasonal transitions
developmental peculiarities
opposition
bureaucracy

lack of initiative
conflicted motives
false and selfish ambition
self-doubt
imbalance
task-focused rather than people-focused living
rigidity
multifaceted temptations
failure
discontentment
imbalance between life's segments
family struggles
grief
illness
death
unbelief

Yet a sacred internal sense of "mustness," an intentional oughtness, will possess you and provide for

- purposeful involvement, coherent strategizing, and consistent follow-through
- criteria for choices among good opportunities, mixed motives, conflicting activities, and distractions
- balance between people and task focuses, for calling is always toward people—the ends—with tasks as means
- steadiness and even excellence in fulfilling responsibilities in the three segments of life: personal, familial, and vocational
- perseverance under difficult circumstance regardless of fatigue, limitations, opinion, opposition, or results
- sensitivity to divine initiatives, to what God is placing on your mind and heart
- courage to find and implement wisdom

- high utility of ministry gifts, a willingness to change methods, and an awareness of limitations

All of the above are pursued with a humble heart set toward God, a mind set toward a vision, and compatible missional behavior.[8] How humble can God get, placing some of his plans in your obedience, inviting you to embrace his burden for the lost and implement it as uniquely yours? As evangelistic preachers, we are gratefully overwhelmed by that realization as well.

In the course of a dinner conversation about friends, even as I thought about ending this section, I heard the phrase "ministry calling" several times. "Youth," "reconciliation," "fathers and sons," etc. The conversation moved on to the esteemed leader of twentieth-century evangelicalism, Billy Graham, whose impact related to simply "doing one thing." Oh, yes, there are several things under that one thing, but Mr. Graham's sacred oughtness related to his one thing, winning the world to Christ.

Divine Sentness

If you examine biblical models who reveal the contours of the sacred compulsion, you will find that their personal oughtness arose from a sense of divine "sentness." It resulted in a divine propulsion.

Sentness begins with God's *identification* of you.[9] He calls you by name not only to offer his salvation but also to designate you as his servant. In a broad sense, apostolic calling in Scripture can apply to anyone sent for the achievement of some objective. In the technical sense, the verb *sent* is used of Jesus sending out his disciples. It could also be used of dispatching a message, not only the sending of persons.[10] In evangelistic preaching, the sentness applies to Jesus dispatching his disciples with a message toward his objective. At the climax of the book of Acts, Paul asserts, "Therefore I want you to know that God's salvation has been sent to the Gentiles, and they will listen!" (Acts 28:28). How was God's salvation *sent* to the Gentiles? It was taken by one who was sent.

Divine sentness also relates to the biblical understanding of *appointment* to ministry.¹¹ Paul declares, "I thank Christ Jesus our Lord, who has given me strength, that he considered me faithful, *appointing me to his service*" (1 Tim. 1:12). Paul frequently begins his epistolary charges with the phrases "a servant of Jesus" or "by the will of God." Jesus had called him and willed his ministry. While you can't enter into Paul's assured announcement as an *apostle* of Christ Jesus (Rom. 1:1; 11:13; 1 Cor. 9:1; 15:9; 2 Cor. 1:1; 11:5; Gal. 1:1; Eph. 1:1; Col 1:1; 1 Tim. 1:1; 2 Tim. 1:1), you can definitely connect with his broader assertion of being a *servant* of Jesus (Rom. 1:1), by the will of God (2 Cor. 1:1; Eph. 1:1; Col 1:1; 2 Tim. 1:1), set apart for the gospel of God (Rom. 1:1), even to the nations. Paul states three personal functions in his appointment to the gospel: "a herald and an apostle and a teacher" (2 Tim. 1:11). You can enter into only the looser meaning of *apostle* (i.e., one who is sent but is not one of the twelve apostles of the Lord Jesus [cf. Matt. 19:28; Acts 8:1; 14:14]), but you can connect to any level of herald and teacher of the true faith to the nations (1 Tim. 2:7).

Actually, we find this ministerial "entry and connection" problem with any biblical character—whether in the Old Testament or New Testament, David or Peter. We must therefore exhibit care in how we draw from them into our own experience. They were unique, not only like each of the six and a half billion of us living today, but also in their unique roles in the unshakable economy. Our challenge is to distinguish between their uniqueness and ordinariness in ministry. They were unique in their assignments but not in their humanness. Human beings just like us, in their own understanding and implementation of God's role for their lives, they disbelieved, reflected, argued, and surrendered to their divine appointments.

The fact of the matter is that some of these "select" from whom we distance ourselves did not feel very much like the elite we make them out to be. Often, these called and chosen didn't see God's point in choosing and sending them. We too can enter into that very human sentiment of reserve, awareness of limitation, weakness, the "can't do" spirit.¹²

- Moses stammered: "Who am I, that I should go to Pharaoh?" (Exod. 3:11).

- Gideon doubted: "But Lord . . . how can I save Israel? My clan is the weakest in Manasseh, and I am the least in my family" (Judg. 6:15).
- Saul and David brought up the "smallest and the least" objections (1 Sam. 9:21; 18:18).
- Solomon hesitated: "I am only a little child and do not know how to carry out my duties" (1 Kings 3:7).
- Isaiah confessed his sin: "Woe to me . . . I am ruined! For I am a man of unclean lips, and I live among a people of unclean lips" (Isa. 6:5).
- Jeremiah felt like Solomon: "I do not know how to speak; I am only a child" (Jer. 1:6).
- A racially prejudiced Jonah ran away from his appointment (Jon. 1:1–3).

We enter and connect with these stalwarts not in terms of their prophetic and apostolic roles, but under the umbrella of God's calling of *individuals* to serve his purposes. Elijah, the miracle-working prophet, sometimes courageous and at other times discouraged, was "a man just like us" (James 5:17). The Bible doesn't stipulate that God should come to every man in the same way. Most of us have not seen Isaiah's or Paul's commissioning visions, but God's use of errant human beings to bring his message to humans in need of salvation is surprisingly consistent across all biblical stewardships. God's normal course includes humans, whom he calls, prepares, and uses for his service.

Perhaps, and rightly so, we don't sense the appointment connection with Paul's apostolic selection.[13] However, I don't think you would feel as distant from timid Timothy. He seems to be more human than Paul, a lot more like us. Hence, Paul reminds Timothy of his appointment for service: "Fan into flame the gift of God, which is in you through the laying on of my hands" (2 Tim. 1:6). But you might still distance yourself from the Timothy who was handpicked by Paul! You might remark, "If I could be hand-touched by an apostle, I would sense more of a divine appointment." Notice that Timothy was given to timidity, withdrawal, shame, and weakness in spite of this "elite" status. Paul had to remind him about his heritage, his faith, his ministry gifting, his usefulness, and the general endowment of the spirit of power, of love, and of self-discipline (2 Tim. 1:7).

Could you possibly regard Silas as a peer in the divinely personal appointment? Since he was already a leader, he was chosen by the apostles but also appointed by mere elders (Acts 15:22). He accompanied Paul beyond the relational split with Barnabas (Acts 15:37–40).

Even though Timothy and Silas are not apostles of Jesus Christ, Paul includes them in epistolary salutations while writing inspired texts: "Paul and Timothy, servants of Christ Jesus" (Phil. 1:1) or "Paul, Silas and Timothy" (1 Thess. 1:1; 2 Thess. 1:1). Together with the apostle Paul, from whom you should sense a hallowed distance, the less exceptional Timothy, with whom you may existentially connect, and the more ordinary Silas, who was a leader like you among the brothers (Acts 15:22), you too can preach the Son of God, Jesus Christ (2 Cor. 1:19).

Again, you would have had a difficult time convincing any of these "giants" that they were more gifted, called, and hopeful than you are. Yes, certainly enter into their hesitation, but live off your own appointment today. For when all is said and discussed, I want you to read, underline, and memorize our Lord's words of choice and selection that apply to you and me without equivocation and circumscription: "You did not choose me, but I chose you and appointed you to go and bear fruit—fruit that will last" (John 15:16). Write those words out on the tablet of your heart. Implicit in God's appointment is a bestowment of his resources needed to fulfill your appointment.

That divine appointment is active, not dormant. If you are anything like me, you smile in amazement and lose sleep over the fact that God has appointed you at all. Though not always caught up in the excitement, your amazement over God's calling never ceases. Inside, you know that if God only knew you like you know yourself, he wouldn't choose you, only to realize that in fact he knows you *better* than you know yourself. That amazes you as well. May your appointment resonate with Paul's deep thankfulness (1 Tim. 1:12).

Personal Willingness

If a sacred oughtness theologically parallels God's calling, and divine sentness arises from God's appointment, the ministry equation is completed by our personal willingness to be entrusted with God's ministry. Calling, we noted earlier, goes beyond God's identification and is reinforced by his invitation to you. Once accepted, he thrusts you into usefulness. Calling, then, is also an invitation to embrace the assignment and its responsibilities. There we find the tension in the humility of God in choosing us to serve. God does not need to include us to accomplish his plans, but our need to be included beckons us, so we willingly embrace his appointment. Check out this paraphrase of a sentiment attributed to church historian Kenneth Scott Latourette: "I do not fear that God's work will not get done, but I have every fear that it will get done without me." So receive his trust of you in ministry.

Quite different from appointment, entrustment requires cooperation in the calling. You could sense the summons of divine sentness and the necessity of oughtness, but if there is no willingness, God's calling is unactuated, and God's mission through your life goes unimplemented.

If we examine the verbal nuances of *calling*, we see that God is doing the calling in the active sense, with humans being "the called" in the passive sense (e.g., Rom. 8:28–29). That distinction clearly applies to soteriological calling and its effects.[14]

In the practical sense of ministry, however, divine calling takes on a further nuance. We certainly don't call ourselves into the ministry. We have been "acted upon" in our receipt of gifts and tasks. Yet ministry calling cannot parallel the passive voice, for there is no personal calling without our embrace of the calling. We still have to discharge our gifts and tasks in faithfulness, accountability, and utility. We don't minister *ourselves,* nor do we minister *on* and *for* ourselves. Instead, the conceptual and practical equation for what we propose in terms of ministry calling runs thus: our participation is personal; our consent is given; our permission has been secured in God's calling. But the action is not caused by us.

If our "appointment and choice" is used in the active sense (cf. *klerao*—active voice), we would still have to obtain, possess, or receive that appointment and choice. If *I* didn't receive it, it wouldn't be *my* appointment. My willingness to receive it actuates God's calling in *my* life.

That's why I include willingness in the ministry equation Oughtness = Sentness + Willingness. Your willingness turns God's summons into personal necessity, into a voluntary acceptance of your gifts, roles, and tasks. God doesn't force you into the corner, into his calling, into his commission. He calls to gain your assent in propelling you into service. In fact, your love relationship moves you into a willing position to turn the call into a calling. You accept the general invitation to participate in his work. Ministry calling is not merely an endowment by God, nor are you a mere recipient. You function as an instrument entrusted with a unique, specific role in his economy. You have given God the permission to "play" you. You can't make his sounds, but you can garble the sound of his music.

You are the instrument, the courier, the mouthpiece. The Lord says to Ananias about Paul, "Go! This man is my chosen [required an appointment] instrument [required Paul's willingness] to carry my name before the Gentiles and their kings and before the people of Israel" (Acts 9:15). That's what we are—instruments, implements, tools, vessels, couriers for his Good News to the nations. But willing instruments at that.

In our organization we draw a strategic visual called "the proclamation bugle." God is the blower, the player, the artist; I am just his mouthpiece. The mouthpiece doesn't create music or noise. Expert buglers can make music just with the mouthpiece, and with any mouthpiece! But when the mouthpiece is joined to the rest of a compatible musical instrument, the sounds are glorious. It's very difficult to play the instrument without the mouthpiece, and as such, we humans play a deliberate role in God's work. And mouthpieces, especially if they use reeds, are changeable and exchangeable. Who are we? Nothing but servants to be used, not kings to be revered. Indeed, reeds and servants should be replaced after wear and tear.

Your only option is to be a *willing* instrument. God will get his work done through you but not by you. Ministry is by God, through you! "We are therefore Christ's ambassadors, as though God were making his appeal *through* us" (2 Cor. 5:20). In our willingness, we roughly equal the freewill offerings of the Old Testament. You may enjoy reading Ezra in the context of the free, extra, and joyous gifts people brought to the temple—not a forced offering, but a freewill offering prescribed in the Pentateuch to be without defect (Num. 29:29), "as an aroma pleasing to the Lord" (Num. 15:3) and in proportion to divine blessings (Deut. 16:10). Once you have consented, you are responsible to keep the instrument of your life ready, shining, and available for use.

The calling to ministry is his, but the willing to ministry is yours. The prompting is his, but the obeying is yours. The entrustment is divine, but the execution is human—according to gifting, understanding, and opportunity. Once you have made his calling yours, you can't escape, withdraw, or quit. Evangelistic preaching is all about Jesus through you.

The Mystery of Ministry

The mystery of ministry extends from the Trinity, by the incarnation, to you. In some mysterious sense, God rests the administering of his Good News on our integrity and faithfulness with omnipotent confidence and expectation. This entrustment of his message and task is not for safekeeping alone, but for fruitful investing and purposeful dispensing—these three aspects of entrustment carry parabolic precedent in Scripture (cf. Matt. 25:14ff.; Luke 19:11–27). You are a trustee of the gospel, as if you have been appointed to hold God's property, to take care of it and use it for the benefit of those entitled to it. But you have to be willing to receive his appointment, to discharge all the duties of your ministry calling, including the work of an evangelist (2 Tim. 4:5).

God's confidence in us certainly seems misplaced. Again, I occasionally think, *If God only knew me like I know myself, he wouldn't trust me with his gospel! How stupid can God get?* But then my thoughts get saner. *That's exactly why it takes God to trust me with his gospel. God does know me better than I know myself. And be-*

cause he is God, he can indeed trust me without fear of mishap in his program. His confidence is assured because he is God and not because I am anybody on whom he depends for the success of his plan. It is through God's mercy that we have our ministry (2 Cor. 4:1). God's seemingly mistaken confidence doesn't take away from the responsibility we feel in stewarding the treasure or from the integrity we must evidence in managing his trust.

Paul had not only the gospel itself entrusted to him (1 Tim. 1:11) but the *preaching* of the gospel too (Titus 1:3). Others, Paul says, "saw I had been entrusted with the task of preaching the gospel to the Gentiles, just as Peter had been to the Jews" (Gal. 2:7). Not only did he personally sense the stewardship, but *others* perceived this personal entrustment as well. I wonder what evidences Paul gave that revealed his stewardship to observers. Fervent enthusiasm? Faithfulness to the message? A focus on geographical areas where Christ had not been named? Finishing the course he had started?

So, while we don't enter the personal callings of our biblical models, we do understand their personal frailties. They too could transgress from real stewardship of the ministry to engage in thievery—owning rather than utilizing the endowment. They too could become unreliable in fulfillment. They could become lazy or fearful and bury their talents. They too could neglect gifts. Just like us. They were not tempted in unique ways, since they faced the same kinds of trials we face today. Therefore, the entrustment of the gospel risked the same jeopardy with them as it does with us.

But a personally received holy trust is an easy bond between us and the apostles. A sense of willing stewardship was not and cannot be unique to them. While their personal commissioning, especially in their geographic and audience specificity, may not transfer to us, the internal sense of being entrusted with the gospel follows the *a fortiori* argument. If the apostle Paul himself felt the stewardship of the gospel, how much more should we mere evangelists seek to steward our sacred oughtness to proclaim the Good News as wisely and widely as possible?

Consider, for instance, Paul's move from the "I" to the "we" of entrustment. First Thessalonians 2:4 reads, "We speak as men approved by God to be entrusted with the gospel." A powerful motivating sequence indeed. They were already *approved* to be entrusted. God couldn't and wouldn't have entrusted the gospel to them unless he had approved of them in the first place. This personal condition of God's approval to entrust us with his work does transfer across the human spectrum of ministry stewardship.

Like Paul, we are entrusted with

- the gift of the gospel (1 Thess. 2:4; 1 Tim. 1:11)
- the task of preaching the gospel (Gal. 2:7; 2 Tim. 1:11; Titus 1:3)
- the ministry of reconciliation (2 Cor. 5:18)
- the presentation of "the word of God in its fullness" (Col. 1:25)

The only issue is if we are *willing* to receive and manage his trust. Entrustment conjures all the dimensions of stewardship under the One who retains ownership until he returns (Luke 19:13). Those so entrusted are expected to be as follows:

1. Recipients of gifts and tasks: In Matthew 25:15, the master *gives* each person according to his ability. Paul asks, "What, after all, is Apollos? And what is Paul? Only servants, through whom you came to believe—as the Lord has assigned to each his task" (1 Cor. 3:5).
2. Faithful in fulfillment: "It is required that those who have been given a trust must prove faithful" (1 Cor. 4:2).
3. Accountable for investment: "He sent for the servants to whom he had given the money, in order to find out what they had gained with it" (Luke 19:15).
4. Useful in service: "Each one should use whatever gift he has received to serve others, faithfully administering God's grace in its various forms" (1 Pet. 4:10).

I read a newspaper headline announcing a massive bequest to a poetry magazine: "An ailing heir who tried but failed to have her poems published in a small literary journal has given that journal an astonishing bequest that is likely to be worth more than $100 million." At times the assets of this ninety-year-old magazine have been less than one hundred dollars, but it has never missed printing an issue. When the editor heard about the bequest, he couldn't quite grasp it or understand it, and he now has to hire advisers to handle the gift! His response: "Evidently she did not take the rejections to heart. . . . There just isn't anything to compare it [the donation] to. We will be the largest foundation in the world devoted to poetry. It's a huge responsibility, as I'm realizing every day more and more." The editor had not met the giver but understood that she was pleased with the way his magazine handled previous donations.[15] With all that the present four-member staff can envision with a hundred million dollars in resources, the editor declared that the overall mission of the magazine will remain the same.

Every sentiment that overwhelmed the editor can be echoed in your response to the trust of God's gospel—far more valuable than any quantifiable gift, with an impact that will possibly cross centuries of time and boundaries of space. You too are inclined to be faithful with little or much, for what you have doesn't influence your mission. But the increasing understanding, availability, and opportunity of God's trusts generate a daily realization of your huge responsibility. Your calling is an entrustment that you are willing to receive and implement fully and always (cf. 1 Cor. 15:58).

Conclusion

Leadership mentor Jim Collins of *Built to Last* and *Good to Great* fame delineates a critical difference between creators and reactors.[16] His first distinction between creator and reactor corroborates the evangelist's personal compulsion in evangelistic preaching. A creator is internally driven but externally aware. A reactor is externally driven without intrinsic passion.[17]

It is true that millions are dying every day without the gospel, that billions of people have not had a chance to hear the name of Jesus, and that all of them will be heartily welcomed by hell, Satan, and his demons forever. However, any red-blooded Christian knows those dastardly scenarios, and most don't do a thing about eternal condemnation.

Why?

Eternal condemnation, or its obverse, the promise of eternal life, is good for ministry vision but not for personal mission. Personal mission must arise from the inside, generate keen gratitude for your gifting, cause astonishment over unpredicted positive responses, claim sleeping hours for ruminating over seizing opportunities. If you are committed to evangelism, you will never get over God's choosing and sending of you.

Oughtness = Sentness + Willingness. In ministry generally, and particularly in evangelistic ministry, you need at least one of the two components operating in implementing oughtness.[18] Sometimes, when willingness fails, your sentness carries you through. And at other times, your willingness revitalizes your sentness. You reflect Paul's sentiments of personal motivation: "If I preach voluntarily, I have a reward; if not voluntarily, I am simply discharging the trust committed to me" (1 Cor. 9:17). Or you copy the servants in Jesus's parable: "So you also, when you have done all that you were commanded, say, 'We are unworthy servants; we have only done what was our duty'" (Luke 17:10 ESV). But in the working together of the duties of love that include the love of duties toward the Beloved One, you can "discharge all the duties of your ministry" (2 Tim. 4:5). Your calling will be not merely efficient but also effective.

At these precise and powerful points, you are fulfilling your calling. Sentness and willingness pervade your inner core to impel, compel, and propel evangelistic proclamation. Nothing else is needed than a maturing understanding, a growing conviction, and increasing confirmation of divine appointment and entrustment. In this mix, you sense the following:

Pleasure. And which one of us can operate without the smiling, shining face of God upon us? If I am not willing to be sent, I will not sense his pleasure.

Power. Not a self-generated power of "possibility thinking," nor even the unchangeable power of the gospel, but an internal propulsion, since the God who called us will sustain us in the willing faith steps we take to fulfill his ministry. If I am not willing to be sent, I will not sense his empowerment in executing his entrustment.

Profitability to the master, from being used by God to do his will. Only if you are willing will you make yourself available for use—servile use—as a means to the larger end of human salvation, even though you are an end in yourself as a human being. You will be making yourself available for usefulness to reach another end—a human being who does not know Jesus. It means that our earthly life is expendable for another's secure eternity. We are not trying to add value or significance to ourselves in this endeavor, but seeking to be helpful to others, thus bringing profit to the master and to people too.

Participation in the spectrum of involvement in God's multi-level, multilayered purposes. For instance, if you were not willing, you would have no desire to acknowledge, develop, and use your cluster of spiritual gifts. You would ignore your gift set and would not attempt to find connections between gifts and opportunities. Allow me to ponder if presently unknown eternal rewards for earthly labor attach not only to the kind and quantity of work but also to the degree of heart-willingness in participating with God's priorities.

Persistence. If I am not willing to be sent, I will not finish the course set for me to run. Paul clarifies his focused perseverance in evangelism: "However, I consider my life worth nothing to me, if only I may finish the race and complete the task the Lord Jesus has given me—the task of testifying to the gospel of God's grace" (Acts 20:24).

Your decision to serve Christ is freely made, but it converts into a claim. Listen to Paul's *obligation* terminology, which mixes sentness and willingness to result in the sacred oughtness: "And for this purpose, I was appointed a herald and an apostle—I am telling the truth, I am not lying—and a teacher of the true faith to the Gentiles" (1 Tim. 2:7). He punctuates the middle of this lofty and specific appointment with strong oath language—"I am telling the truth, I am not lying"—not only to affirm the sphere of his purpose and the content of his proclamation but also to reveal strong *personal* responsibility. God's calling on me, says Paul, is *my* calling in his program.

In a friend's pastoral study hang graduation diplomas and some photo reminders of family but also a powerful portrait of a "proclamation calling." In this portrait entitled "The Legacy" (1999), artist Ron Dicianni portrays a black-suited, white-shirted, open-Bibled preacher earnestly delivering a sermon from a pulpit. Behind the preacher in faint outline, as if from the heavenly world, are Moses with his tablet, Jeremiah clutching some scrolls, and John the Baptist. To the preacher's right are three figures: the Lord Jesus himself with his hand on the preacher's shoulder; a man, probably Peter, with a fishing net; and another man with a shepherd's staff. At the far right and far left, toward the back, are two angels standing and facing one another holding flaming torches.

I will let the artist describe the rationale for this powerful painting:

> With that passion [of Jesus quoting in Luke 4 from Isaiah 6:1], those we know as ministers, long to follow in the footsteps of the Master to fulfill the same mission. They know they have been "sent" and not just to a job, but to a "calling." It doesn't take long, however, for many of them to realize the size of the shoes they are filling, as well as the difficulty of the task. Discouragement, doubt, and meager results, sometimes give a servant the temptation to quit. Many have. Too many think about it. Is there a secret to survival? I believe there is. It may be found in the remembrance of Who has commanded you, and in whose footsteps you follow. It is also found in the realization that you are not called to be successful, just obedient![19]

Can you sense sacred oughtness, internal conviction, divine calling in the artist's description without additional comment from me? My pastor friend regularly reminds himself that he stands in a long line of divine appointments. He was certainly unique in his person, yet in terms of ministry, he too had received a divine appointment like the others. God's legacy of appointment and entrustment continues today. The only One who knows your failings, faults, and frailties more than you know them yourself has appointed you to serve and has entrusted you with the gospel. He will undergird your forays into the unlikeliest of opportunities. He will own your ministry. How shocking is that to you and me? Never get over your calling! No one takes the honor of preaching evangelistically on himself. He must be called by God.

2

THE OUTER CALLING OF THE PREACHING EVANGELIST

Biblical Conviction and Motivation

> You are not the oil, you are not the air—merely the point of combustion, the flashpoint where the light is born. You are merely the lens in the beam. You can only receive, give, and possess the light as a lens does.[1]
>
> —Dag Hammarskjöld

"Uncorrected poor vision is one of the most pressing problems in the developing world. The World Health Organization estimates that 180 million people—90 percent of them in poor countries—suffer serious visual impairments." In a place like Ghana, getting glasses can take a week's travel and several months' wages. Now an Oxford

University physicist has developed a novel remedy—eyeglasses that allow wearers to correct their own vision with no need for an optometrist. He calls them "adaptive glasses."[2]

> Their lenses are filled with silicone oil and form a chamber bounded by polyester film. Turning a small frame-mounted pump changes the amount of oil in the lenses and, therefore, the power of the glasses. Users adjust the oil levels on each side until they can see clearly, a process that takes about 30 seconds.
>
> The glasses do not correct astigmatism, but they are effective against nearsightedness and farsightedness.[3]

I wrote a "wow" in the margin of that joyous news item. I also saw the many obvious connections between the article and evangelistic preaching. People, billions of individuals, desperately need help in their spiritual blindness: "The god of this world has blinded the minds of the unbelieving" (2 Cor. 4:4 NASB). Just like the idea of fluid-filled lenses has existed since the eighteenth century, the notion of Jesus being the correction for spiritual astigmatism has existed for two thousand years. Paul implicitly reveals the solution to blindness: "The god of this world has blinded the minds of the unbelieving so that they [the spiritually blinded, unbelieving, and perishing] might not see the light of the gospel of the glory of Christ" (2 Cor. 4:4 NASB). That is, when the light of the glory of Christ descends on the blind, Christian conversion happens.

In addition, I was intrigued with the physicist's journey toward the solution: "I started working on this idea [fluid-filled lenses] for glasses in the mid-80's out of curiosity. . . . Then I realized, if I could make something that could help a billion people, I ought to just go out and try to do it."

As a teenager, through the encouragement of pastors, parents, and peers, I too started out early, working on the idea of Jesus as the solution to human blindness. Presently, I am introduced to sophisticated audiences as a "spiritual philosopher," but I don't know that I have ever ceased simply serving as an open-market proclaimer. I so wish I could have recordings of what I proclaimed in those early years in people-dense Moore Market and on the sands of now tsunami-ravaged Triplicane Beach in Chennai (at that time, Madras), South India. I will have to wait for heaven to discover my homiletical flaws, but perhaps that youthful boldness to proclaim, that heated fervency for the lost, that biblical urgency in addressing the problem of the masses living in spiritual blindness, has not been entirely lost. Like the Oxford physicist, I too realized that if I could do something that could help a billion people, I ought to just go and try to do it.

However, exploring the metaphor of the adaptive glasses took a far more personal twist. It was *I* who frequently experienced missional visual impairment. Spiritual astigmatism in my own life had been addressed at conversion, but my problem of nearsightedness needed ongoing correction. I get so involved in the existentially immediate, so distracted by the circumstance, so occupied with the urgent, that I lose sight of the critically important, the highest rung in the ladder of Christian responsibility to humanity—bringing news of Jesus to the lost everywhere as widely, wisely, and winsomely as possible. And all without delay. I need to wear those spiritually self-adjusted glasses myself. I need to turn the wheel on the pump of my Christian glasses to release the fluid, find the best level of adjustment, close the sealing valve, and remove the adjusters in order to see more clearly. When my spiritual sight of the lost becomes impaired, I need to go through that sequence again. I shall not become comfortable with my loss of vision nor retreat from the expense of involvement. I'll put the adjusters back on my Christian glasses so I can possess the power of sight concerning people about to be forever lost.

I'd like to equip you with those adjusters. I want you to see the unbeliever's situation more clearly, whether the one spiritually blind person around you or the many billions of people who need spiritual sight immediately.

Three decades after I began proclaiming the Lord Jesus, by God's graces of gifting, confirmation, provision, and favor, I still find ways to clean dirtied lenses, to become better able to see the blind, and to speak the healing of salvation to them.

Let's move from internal awareness—the oughtness of sentness and willingness of the previous chapter—to external awareness. I differentiate between inner calling, or oughtness, of chapter 1 and outer calling. Inner Calling = Sentness + Willingness. That sacred oughtness arises from a duty to sentness accompanied by the loving response of willingness. It's neither a love of duty itself nor a love of love itself, but a duty of love to the One who loves you and sends you.

On the other hand, outer calling can be expressed in the following way:

Outer Calling = Gifts + Realities

Aside from the willingness of obedience lie some outer biblical realities that claim every believer regardless of personal responsiveness. Here are some outer realities, some biblical convictions to regain prescriptive power for your glasses, some biblical motivations to clarify evangelistic sight in the inevitable erosion of vision concerning the ultimate needs of lost people amid the pressures and pleasures of life.

Biblical Conviction: The Spiritual Situation of the Unbeliever

Lostness and Savability

A biblical sample of the current but correctable status of nonbelievers renders pause for the preacher as well as possibilities for the nonbelievers. These convictions stimulate involvement and beckon our investment in the evangelistic ministry. People who have not yet called on the Lord Jesus are

sinners *but* can be justified (Gal. 3:22–23)
guilt ridden *but* can be forgiven (Acts 13:38)
dead *but* can be made alive (Eph. 2:2–5; Col. 2:13)
asleep *but* can be awakened (Eph. 5:14)
unsaved *but* can be saved (Acts 16:30–31)
enslaved *but* can be freed (John 8:34–36)
cursed *but* can be redeemed (Gal. 3:13–14; 1 Pet. 1:18)
sick *but* can be healed (1 Pet. 2:24)

lost *but* can be found (Isa. 53:6; Luke 15)

blind *but* can be cured (John 9:35–41)

unrighteous *but* can be declared righteous (Rom. 3:23–26)

eternally condemned *but* can be acquitted (John 3:18)

spiritually hungry and thirsty *but* can be nourished (John 6:35)

empty and destructible *but* can be possessors of full life (John 10:10)

burdened and weary *but* can find rest (Matt. 11:28)

imprisoned by the dominion of darkness *but* can be rescued (Col. 1:13)

That contrarian word, the divine *but*, provides salvation hope for unbelievers in spite of their present and sorry situation. God designs and builds the longest spiritual suspension bridge known, needed, and possible—from earth to heaven. Heaven's "*but* bridge" is woven with several strands so that nonbelievers can indeed be brought to God's heaven if the strong cables are anchored at both ends. Fortunately, that condition has been met in heaven and history.

Heaven's end of God's *but* bridge, the farther side, is anchored in God's eternal choice. That eternal choice is not only a past event but a present and future event, for eternity comprises all aspects of time.

The earth's side of God's *but* bridge needed an anchor too. God certainly could not anchor it in fickle, sinful, human beings. So he sent his one and only Son to anchor the suspension bridge of salvation on the earth by his death and resurrection. Presently, the Holy Spirit shuttles as "the traveling wheel" between heaven's side and the earth's side. He lays successive parallel strands—one of which is evangelistic proclamation—to build salvation's suspension bridge for each person, drawing individuals to call on Jesus and experience God's *but* action.

Darkness and Blindness

Earlier we cited Paul's declaration concerning the spiritual blindness of unbelievers (2 Cor. 4:4). Blinded minds, rooted in Satan's doings, deeply impede unbelievers' understanding of the gospel.

Their problem is a constitutional defect, a genetic condition from birth, a spiritual challenge of the first order. Add an intellectual dimension to their spiritual predicament too. Paul brings together Satan's activity, hardness of heart, and clouded understanding to describe nonbelievers. They live "in the futility of their thinking. They are darkened in their understanding and separated from the life of God because of the ignorance that is in them due to the hardening of their hearts" (Eph. 4:17–18). Not only are they in the dark, they wear spiritual "glasses" that filter Jesus's message in ways that Jesus would not approve. Worldview, religion, and culture—*the human matrix*—prescribe the power for the glasses unbelievers wear.[4] For example, every unbiblical "ism"—secularism, pluralism, modernism, postmodernism, posthumanism—works as a formidable prism by which the gospel is confused in the minds of unbelievers. Their hardened hearts cannot accept what their darkened minds cannot approve. Of course, every part of a non-Christian human matrix is not evil or bad or antagonistic to truth, for the proponents of these alternate matrixes stand in a continuum of response to God's revelation in nature, conscience, and history. While no alternate is salvific, some are conceptually closer to a Christian view of reality (e.g., other monotheisms and Christian cults) than others (e.g., atheism and pantheism). All matrixes are made up of individuals who are deeper and wider than their intellectual prisms and are redeemable from these prisons by the liberating truths and person of Jesus. However, every question a nonbeliever asks about salvation is tainted, every objection contaminated, every motive spoiled, every argument polluted, every tactic ruined by a Satan-inspired blindness, a heart-hardened darkness. No wonder it takes God himself to draw, awaken, and incline the heart and mind to believe on the Lord Jesus and be saved—through our preaching.

Biblical Motivation: The Instrumental Necessity of Evangelistic Preaching

We noted that the *but* bridge of heaven that God, the master bridge builder, builds is anchored in himself. The parallel strands of salvation's suspension bridge between the eternal choice of heaven and the cross of Jesus on earth are laid by the Holy Spirit. According to Romans 10:14–15, the successive strands for a person to savingly call on the Lord Jesus are constituted in the following sequence:

1. A sending of the preacher
2. A preaching of Jesus
3. A hearing about Jesus
4. A believing on the One

For one to *call on* Jesus takes *believing*, which takes *hearing*, which takes *preaching*, which takes a preacher *being sent*. The Holy Spirit of God lays the cable at each one of these levels. He orchestrates the sending of the preacher, empowers the preaching of the gospel, moves the individual from exposure to salvific hearing, and inclines his heart toward believing on the One. Then the Lord richly blesses any caller (Jew or Gentile) with salvation (Rom. 10:13).

At the very instant of a believing call on Jesus for salvation, the prospect of the unbeliever changes from condemnation to eternal life. He crosses over from death to life and steps onto God's secure *but* bridge to begin the rest of life's journey.

Our role in the Holy Spirit's strand laying concerns the effective presentation of Jesus in the hearing of unbelievers. We responsibly prepare to present salvation's message effectively, for they cannot hear without a preacher. Turning that hearing into calling by believing lies in the Holy Spirit's court of responsibility, not ours. Yet in God's economy throughout history, he has utilized our presentation as a necessary step toward unbelievers' salvific hearing. Of course, though many may hear, preaching doesn't consummate in belief unless the Holy Spirit draws people, awakens the hearers' hearts, and influences their will to believe. Yet the Holy Spirit doesn't make them believe or give them the faith to believe. The Holy Spirit romances, arouses, and inclines their personal embrace of Jesus even through our preaching. *Personal* belief on Jesus, a faith appropriation, provides for *personal* salvation.

The *instrumental* necessity of preaching varies from the *efficient* necessity of preaching. Preaching doesn't cause salvation any more than a hammer causes a wooden fence, a lens causes light, or a pen causes a book. Yet the general reality is clear: there is no wooden fence without tools, no reflection without lenses, no writing without writing instruments, and no human salvation without our preaching of Jesus.

Preaching and preachers are necessary—but only as instruments. We don't produce fruit; we only bear fruit. Branches are instruments of bearing fruit in connection with the vine.

Why are we convinced of our instrumental necessity? In the previous chapter, we looked at the sacred oughtness that is comprised of appointment and obedience, entrustment and accountability, sentness and willingness. That inner calling provides the motivation, while the outer calling prompts a responsibility that includes your acknowledgment, utility, development, and investment of giftedness as evidence of your willingness. Following are some biblical motivations that undergird the preacher's instrumental necessity in the salvation process.

The Person of Jesus as Exclusive for Human Salvation

Four aspects of Jesus's person and salvation control the evangelist's motivated involvement in preaching. I derive all these from Peter's simple declaration in one of the first evangelistic messages preached: "And there is salvation in no one else, for there is no other name under heaven given among men by which we must be saved" (Acts 4:12 ESV).

1. "There is salvation in *no one else*" points to the *uniqueness* of Jesus. There is no salvation outside the person of Jesus.

2. "There is salvation in no one else, for there is *no other name*" points to the *exclusivity* of Jesus. There is no salvation without the *name* of Jesus in preaching, hearing, and believing.

3. "There is salvation in no one else, for there is no other name *under heaven given among men*" points to the *universality* of Jesus. There is no salvation for the *whole* world of human beings without the person and name of Jesus.

4. "There is salvation in no one else, for there is no other name under heaven given among men *by which we must be saved*" points to the *sufficiency* and *necessity* of Jesus. The person and name of

Jesus is the sufficient and necessary means of definite human salvation.[5]

If we aren't convinced of the uniqueness, exclusivity, universality, sufficiency, and necessity of Jesus in human salvation, the life-changing content in evangelistic preaching will be blunted.

The Destiny of the Lost without Jesus

Those who do not call on Jesus experience lostness forever, a separation from God's life eternally. Hell militates against every muscle, grates against even the crustiest fibers in my being. Like C. S. Lewis, "there is no doctrine I would more willingly remove from Christianity than this if it lay in my power."[6] The unbeliever does not need to do anything to be lost forever. The most beloved Bible verse of all time, which narrates the incomparable love of God for the world (John 3:16), implies the obvious: one believes on Jesus to *not* perish, but whoever does not believe on the Son is already perishing and continues to perish (cf. 2 Cor. 2:15; 4:3). The wrath of God that already is upon him, "remains on him" (John 3:36). Physical death only confirms an unbeliever's eternal lostness and hurls him into an eternal hell.

The nature of hell as *literal*—"a real place where people suffer eternal fiery torments"—or *metaphorical*—"an anguished state of existence eternally separated from God"[7]—can be reduced to mere theoretical discussion or cause intense angst in the heart of the evangelist. America's most brilliant thinker, the theologian of the heart orated, "The wrath of God burns against them, their damnation does not slumber; the pit is prepared, the fire is made ready, the furnace is now hot, ready to receive them; the flames do now rage and glow."[8] Just as our best thoughts about heaven would be inadequate to explore its grandeur, our worst thoughts about hell, whether in imaginative art or caricatured media, would scarcely touch the realities of its horror. Hell is at least literal, but more than literal. The literal "fire" view can comprise the metaphorical "anguish" view as you consider the precedent of the Mosaic "burning bush that didn't burn" and the horrific narrative of Lazarus and the rich man in eternally conscious, quarantined situations. However, both views carry the irrevocable, binding permanence of eternity.[9]

Though I write these words while listening to a cheery Boston Pops orchestral performance with private headphones in a convenient climate-controlled library carrel, a holy hush has descended on my soul. Hell indeed is ghastly and dastardly, horrible and sickening. I contemplate the billions, present, past, and future, near and far, in reachable and unreachable situations, who shall not hear the name of Jesus. If half of all who lived in history are alive right now, then at least half of hell's population is alive right now. In China recently, a friend remarked how his adoptive land and my birth land comprised over a third of the world's population. And he then made the population of hell more stark: "Twenty percent of hell's eventual population live right now in just China and India." I took the facts farther into Asia, where half of the world lives within five hours flying from Hong Kong. My only assurance at this time arises from God's justice that will keep anyone from hell who should not be there. Yet that also means that no one will be in heaven who should not be there. Theologically convinced about the reality of eternal lostness of large numbers of people, I must deliver the Good News of Jesus personally, effectively, widely, and quickly. Was a "large numbers focus" part of Paul's urgent declaration to "win as many as possible" (1 Cor. 9:19) "by all possible means" (1 Cor. 9:22)? Perhaps the savable will be salvaged. While pondering the destiny of the lost to an eternal hell, the promise of an eternal heaven for *them* unleashes my evangelistic involvement as well. Could God use me to depopulate hell and thereby increase the population of heaven? "Even the fear of the Lord that is going to fall on the unsaved is a legitimate incentive for service in seeing the lost saved (2 Cor. 5:11)."[10] If we aren't convinced of the eternal lostness and abandonment of those without Christ, the burning bosom needed for evangelistic preaching has been quenched.

The Power of the Gospel

I have mentioned the power that a simple willingness to serve gives to ministers. That power is not autonomic or automatic, a self-talking, a self-willing, a psyching-up of the self to serve God. That power is a God-inspired, God-inaugurated, and God-intensified confidence in him alone. It's not the believing in yourself much like an athlete needs to take to the field, for no amount of believing in yourself will endow the power of God upon your ministry. However, one of the outer realities that nurtures evangelistic ministry relates to the gospel *in itself* as power—the power of God for salvation to everyone who believes. "I am not ashamed of the gospel, because it is the power of God for the salvation of everyone who believes: first for the Jew, then for the Gentile" (Rom. 1:16). That verse may be the theme of the entire grand book of Romans and carries a subjective nuance in the phrase "I am not ashamed." To paraphrase Paul, "I am not ashamed. In fact, I trust and am confident of the gospel" because of its outer reality—the power of God for human salvation. The fact that the gospel saves everyone who believes empowers and unleashes me in the evangelistic ministry.

The power of the gospel to *change* a life is a result of salvation. Look up the list regarding the spiritual situation of the unbeliever earlier in this chapter (pp. 40–41). The movement from the left side of the list to the right side results from the power of the gospel to exchange the theological status and even the existential situation of human beings. For example, "guilty" is not only a divine verdict but also a personal feeling. When unbelievers embrace the gospel, both the theological verdict and personal feeling of guilt are changed to "forgiven." Yes, they are theologically forgiven by God, but they also *sense* being forgiven by God. "To us who are being saved it [the word of the cross] is the power of God" (1 Cor. 1:18) in an ongoing, transforming, and liberating way.

Radical life change through dramatic conversion reveals the most obvious present manifestations of the power of God. You'll find these testimonies all over the place—former drug addicts, murderers, prostitutes, persecutors, gluttons, liars, homosexuals, and HIV-positive patients who have been thoroughly changed. I recall the couple who went to bed each night with a gun by each one's side because they were afraid of one killing the other and how powerfully the gospel changed them. I recently received a note that read:

> Thank you. I just finished crying through the end of your book. I'm not sure if that is the reaction you wanted out of your readers... but

that is what you got from me. I cried from your Seeker section, until I got on my knees and swore to Jesus and accepted him into my life.

I never before realized why I always went from one thing to the next. . . . Nothing I do has meaning. . . .

My life changed about 9 days ago. . . . You recommend telling the person who guided me to this book about my experience. Since I can only think of you for that, I'd like to tell you thank you. . . . For now, I'm going to start talking to God. I've never talked to God before. And I think it is a start.

Let the promise of personal change by God's power that is intrinsic to the gospel message convince you to persevere in evangelistic communication with fervent focus. Entire communities, even cultures, have been changed by the power of the gospel.

The Futility of Alternate Salvation Messages

We know that alternate religious claims do not offer salvation. But what about secular messages that seek to provide meaning without reference to God. Leadership messages, motivational thoughts, advertisements for successful living, directions for self-improvement, and witty and wise sayings regularly arrive in my inbox. Most I discard, for after a while they sound alike, since the authors begin to borrow from each other! Some I keep for illustrative value. One word can be written on any message without Christ—*empty*. Paul uses radical phrases like "empty deceit" or "hollow deception" or "foolish talk" or "human tradition" of all messages "not according to Christ" (Col. 2:8 NRSV).

For example, examining the beauty business and the promises of the cosmetic industry, the *Economist* speaks about a possible backlash against extravagant marketing claims. Women have been willing to buy into the illusion of the advertisements. "Kids look older younger" as people "strive to model themselves on some form of idealised human being," as modern beauty becomes "redefined as health, self esteem, and empowerment" in order to find "hope in a jar."[11] Unfortunately, while the jar will become empty to hearten the cosmetic business, hope too will be emptied of content.

Learn to think that evangelism results in the ultimate *and* immediate good of the unbeliever, that evangelism itself is part social action. Paul writes, "For I am not seeking my own good but the good of many, so that they may be saved" (1 Cor. 10:33). Consider taking that good to include earthly good in experiencing the implications of eternal life, of having found Christ's promise of abundant life in the present. You do not have to apologize for being an evangelist, as though you only bring some future, heavenly message irrelevant to unbelievers' present situations. You are really engaged in providing the greatest gift for their comprehensive good, beginning immediately on earth.

In contrast to the emptiness, uselessness, and even deceitfulness of any message, offering any kind of salvation, anywhere in the world,

> Paul's preaching was not futile but purposeful and effective because it was about Christ who had died and had been raised to life again. . . . Thus the purposefulness and effectiveness of Paul's apostolic ministry appear to be directly related to his divine mission to take the good news of God's salvation "to the end of the earth" (Isa. 49:6) and so serve the eschatological purposes of God.[12]

Evangelistic preaching is instrumental but purposeful and effective, and it is necessary for human salvation. As one preaching salvation, you are distributing a message that provides fullness rather than futility, offering a powerful rather than whimsical hope, assuring an eternal rather than vanishing promise to humanity. Get involved in evangelistic preaching to present a dependable, life-changing message to all who embrace the Lord Jesus Christ as Savior.

The Commission of the Lord Jesus

While calling is personal and specific, it is a responsive and personal application of Jesus's commission that goes out to all Christians. Since the Great Commission is as much an external, theological reality as a spiritual obligation, it claims believers regardless of personal inclination, gifting, or maturity. The Great Commission is not a target to aspire to; it's a command, a strategy, and a task to be personally obeyed by individual Christians.

Found in the Bible five times (in the Gospels and in Acts), the commission of Jesus carries a specific evangelistic thrust in Luke 24. Between the death and resurrection of the Messiah and the upcoming clothing of Pentecost power, Jesus furnishes an outer reality for Christians to personally obey: "that repentance and forgiveness of sins should be proclaimed in his name to all nations, beginning from Jerusalem" (v. 47 ESV). So Peter (Acts 2:38; 3:19) and Paul (Acts 17:30) personally preach repentance, resulting in people experiencing the forgiveness of sins to keep from a judgment to come—early apostolic versions of the evangelistic invitation.

Jesus's commission continues until he returns. In fact, the promise of the Great Commission is in effect "to the very end of the age" (Matt. 28:20). Discussion about the "go" in the Matthean version—whether the participle is to be subsumed under "making disciples," paralleling "baptizing" and "teaching," or functions with an imperatival force preceding a straightforward imperative (i.e., "go" and "make disciples")—may take away from the evangelism component of discipleship making. If the King is issuing a separate command (my preference canonically, contextually, and culturally), then the evangelistic force of the commission is rather acute. Even if going is parallel to baptizing and teaching, an evangelistic going is the first component of the commission. "Son, go and work today in the vineyard," says the master in Matthew 21:28—possibly a grammatical and parabolic precursor to Matthew 28:19. In any case, the Great Commission has lasted twenty centuries already. With no predictable finish line, it sets its expectations of Christians rather high—an outer theological reality that must be personally taken into account. We simply follow the Master who himself will turn us into catchers of men (cf. Luke 5:10).

At the Tomb of the Unknown Solder in the Arlington National Cemetery, near Washington, DC, a guard is posted twenty-four hours a day. Every hour on the hour, 365 days a year, a new soldier reports for duty. When the new guard arrives, he receives orders from the one who is leaving. The words are always, "Orders remain unchanged." Regarding the command to spread the Good News of Christ, those words can still be declared: "Orders remain unchanged."[13]

The Work of the Holy Spirit

The work of the Holy Spirit in his cosmic and comprehensive role with unbelievers also encourages the instrumental necessity of your evangelistic preaching. While the Holy Spirit himself is the Father's and Son's gift to believers (John 14:16), the specific work of the Holy Spirit in relation to the world of unbelievers provides two-dimensional motivation.

1. His work in unbelievers is an *incentive* to your evangelistic preaching: the Holy Spirit is already working in the lives of unbelievers before you get there. From the beginning of time, having created the world (Gen. 1:26–27), and "striving with sinful human beings" (Gen. 6:3), he convicts the world of guilt in regard to sin, righteousness, and judgment (John 16:8–11).

Consequently, you enter into any evangelistic event with the confidence that the Holy Spirit has preceded and will succeed your presentation of the Good News. Invited to speak on the inerrancy of the Bible in sophisticated, Nobel-laureate-fertilizing Trinity College in Dublin, I was concerned about the question-and-answer time following my lectures and how to turn it into an evangelistic opportunity. I prepared well and hard, went through my notes (as well as my digestive system) several times, getting ready for the unpredictable question, the resistant attitude, the distinguished but disguised philosopher in the audience. It was then that God's Holy Spirit hit me with a biblical whisper.

"Do you know that I have preceded you with this audience?"
"Yes, Lord."
"Do you know that I will succeed you with this audience?"
"Yes, Lord."
"And I will be with you during the whole series."
"Yes, Lord."
"So don't take yourself so seriously!"
"Okay, Lord."

You are not alone before potential jeerers. The Holy Spirit already has been softening some, showing them their deep need for salvation in the face of their own sin, their lack of righteousness, and their upcoming judgment. In that work lies some of your God-given confidence in approaching nonbelieving audiences.

Yet deeper than the precession and succession of the work of the Holy Spirit in unbelievers' lives is the very possibility of a meaningful spiritual conversation between you and nonbelievers. The theological side of the present spiritual situation of unbelievers lies in their intellectual need to discern between truth and error, an awareness of personal guilt and consequence, sourced in the inherent image of God imprinted in them.[14] This need and awareness are vivified by the Holy Spirit so that your gospel preaching doesn't bounce off unbelievers' hearts like Ping-Pong balls on a practice table. Unbelievers cannot positively process your presentation of the gospel unless the Holy Spirit has been working in their minds and lives to meaningfully receive your comments. Therein lies additional confidence concerning any sense you are making to their darkened and blinded minds.

The Holy Spirit's work in the nonbeliever also prohibits you from using your apparent lack of giftedness to excuse you from engaging in evangelism or evangelistic preaching. Timothy was to "do the work of an evangelist" (2 Tim. 4:5), though he may not have been called and gifted as an evangelist. Why? A theological and existential situation demanded this specific work: there are non-Christians around us whom the Holy Spirit is convicting of guilt in regard to sin, righteousness, and judgment. So though you may not be called or gifted to be an evangelist, an outer reality demands that you "discharge all the duties of your ministry" (2 Tim. 4:5). Those duties include the evangelistic preaching of the Word.

2. A second dimension of the Holy Spirit's evangelistic motivation must also be affirmed: the evangelist himself is the Holy Spirit's gift to the unbelieving world. Very definitely, *euangelistēs* denotes one who announces the gospel, who preaches the Good News to those who haven't heard the gospel. Ephesians 4:11 clearly classifies the gift of certain people as evangelists "standing between the two other groups [apostles/prophets and pastors/teachers]—sent

forth as missionary preachers of the gospel by the first, and as such preparing the way for the labors of the second."[15] The apostles and prophets laid the foundation for the church everywhere (cf. Eph. 2:20–21), while the evangelists and the pastors and teachers continue to build the superstructure of the church anywhere.

This gifting is evidenced not only in a heart toward evangelism and in talents of presenting the gospel but also in the authority and adequacy that emanates from being sent into the world as an announcer of the good tidings of great joy (remember sentness?). Second Corinthians 2:14–3:6, a section on proclaiming the gospel, reveals Paul's profound awareness of feelings of personal inadequacy (2 Cor. 2:16). Soon, however, Paul becomes aware of God's adequacy in ministry (2 Cor. 3:5), a true divine gift—"such confidence we have through Christ toward God" (v. 4 NASB)—in his evangelistic endeavors.

Why do I place a personal understanding of divine gifting in outer rather than in inner calling? Giftedness, to a certain extent, depends on others' recognition of and affirmative response to your use of your gift. Some people downplay their gifting and thereby become neglectful and falsely humble, or they do not rise to an opportunity. There are also those who have too high a view of their gifts, recognized only by self, spouse, and sibling, and are thereby deluded, prideful, or selfishly ambitious. I also place evangelistic gifting in outer calling because it is one of the more easily measurable spiritual gifts (others include giving and helps), for you'll know by people's responses if you possess the gift of evangelism.

The Reward of Heaven

Finally, the Bible also uses the reward of heaven as an outer calling to Christian service. Though not guaranteed, earthly reward is the usual result of conducting one's life and ministry well. In the fear of the Lord and in keeping God's precepts, there is great reward now (Ps. 19:9–11). To seek first God's kingdom and righteousness elicits God's supply for all our temporal needs (Matt. 6:33; Phil. 4:19). A full and fulfilled life often follows simple obedience to Christ. To know that none of our labor in the Lord is in vain (1 Cor. 15:58) gives us a powerful advantage and a divine privilege, never having to second-guess the worth of our work. A present sense of usefulness and fruitfulness could be viewed as great immediate reward.

However, eternal reward is the definite result of serving God. Numerous scriptural passages incentivize service with the promise of reward. "If the work that anyone has built on the foundation survives, he will receive a reward" (1 Cor. 3:14 ESV). Scripturally, heaven's reward is a recognition of service, not a wage, given in God's good pleasure (Luke 12:32; cf. Matt. 20:15), for any fruitful labor arises from an abiding connection to our source of power (John 15:5). Eternal rewards are strongly related to right motive (Matt. 6:1–18), not as much to quantity (Matt. 25:14–30) or mere busyness of engagement (1 Cor. 3:15, "burned-up work").

I place the reward of heaven in outer calling but at the latter end of this discussion, because the Bible includes reward as a motive for obedience. As much as it tries, the human heart may never be able to get away from a reward motive, so God simply recognizes what he himself has built into the heart—the desire for reward. But he severely limits the play of wrong motives by calling for them to be superseded by right motives (e.g., love of Christ) and by not disclosing the actual nature of his reward—its concrete content and precise time.

For example, all the crowns given in recognition for service are symbolic and intangible—the incorruptible crown (1 Cor. 9:25), righteousness (2 Tim. 4:8), life (James 1:12), glory (1 Pet. 5:4), etc.[16] Thus, we are unable to regard eternal rewards in a pure materialistic cause-and-effect meritocracy, as some other religions envision heaven. Next, private acts may be as rewarding and rewarded as public service (Mark 9:41; Luke 6:35). Rewards are always for faithful service, not for successful or visible or immediately admired service (Matt. 6:5), because God counts success, recognizes people, and sees hearts differently than we do. Equal faithfulness generates equal reward (Matt. 25:21, 23) and does *not* relate to quantifiable factors and public awareness of the ministry. That is, any public ministry opened for me will obtain the same (or maybe less) reward than my wife's private ministry. Also, the unpredictable, future time factor sanitizes confused motives by removing full understanding or expectation of eternal reward. We will not be meritocrats, manipulating heaven's graces into predictable reward like employees anticipating overtime wages. At that point, reward becomes a wage and grace becomes law. We are ignorant of both the time and the content of the rewards. Part of our reward may be tied to our willingness to intentionally delay gratification for unknown reward. Finally, Christ himself is our reward (Phil. 1:21; cf. Gen. 15:1). He will overwhelm us with the sight of his face (Rev. 22:4) and his glory (John 17:24). We will see him and be like him (1 John 3:2), and as coheirs, we will be glorified with him (Rom. 8:17–18). God's reward system also relates to our throne-sharing with Christ (Rev. 3:21), our gloriously appearing (Col. 3:4) with him upon his return, our reigning with Christ (2 Tim. 2:12), and our judging the world (1 Cor. 6:2). Eternal recognition by Christ, in fact, adds responsibilities in the kingdom in the present (Matt. 25:21).

In the context of our subject, I suggest a twist that connects eternal crowns to evangelistic preaching. Paul asks the Thessalonians, "For what is our hope or joy or crown of boasting before our Lord Jesus at his coming? Is it not you? Yes, you are our glory and joy!" (1 Thess. 2:19–20 NRSV). At the coming of Christ, Paul's endeavors that yielded Thessalonian fruit will turn Thessalonians themselves into his crown. "Paul contrasts this withering crown [a laurel wreath worn at banquets or given as a civic or military honor] to the Christians' imperishable one (1 Cor. 9:25; 2 Tim. 2:5), seeing his converts as his own garland (Phil. 4:1; 1 Thess. 2:19)."[17] Those whom we reach for Christ will be part of the reward we receive with rejoicing.

The hard, real question is, what is of eternal worth?[18] I dare you to find any work with greater eternal worth than evangelistic ministry, when mixed with right motive and action. To not lose out on rewards (cf. 1 Cor. 3:15; Rev. 3:11) or lose full reward (cf. 2 John 8), winning others for the kingdom beckons your intentional, instrumental engagement. In the future, "those who turn many to righteousness [will shine] like the stars forever and ever" (Dan. 12:3 ESV). Your evangelistic labor will not be in vain as long as your motives are more pure than tainted. You will never have to wonder if you are wasting your life. Would those whom you rescue from death be proof and part of the fruitfulness, the lasting fruitfulness, Jesus promises—"You did not choose me, but I chose you and appointed you to go and bear fruit—fruit that will last" (John 15:16; cf. Col. 1:10)? If so, his definite appointment and your probable fruitfulness mixes the inner and outer aspects of evangelistic calling. You will be rewarded for your response to God's appointment and for taking responsibility to implement his commission.

Conclusion

I seek and collect illustrations that stimulate evangelism. For example, last week in Africa, where potable water is scarce in the large cities, I saw a banner that read, "Water: one billion people are dying for it." That immediately prompts a connection to the billions dying for the Water of Life. The outer reality of thirst summons evangelistic preaching.

Another slogan read, "AIDS is preventable. Apathy is lethal." Of course, from present information and appearance, we don't know who is selected for heaven, for whom hell is preventable. Consequently, any form of evangelistic apathy is lethal for the unsaved. Questions of negligence and lethargy must be resolved by inner conviction.

So we now proceed to applying inner and outer calling to proclamation action. Evangelism desperately needs your focus and sacrifice in the preparation and delivery of evangelistic sermons. A newspaper feature noted how the New York City Parks Department has had trouble finding the 1,100 lifeguards it needs, since recruits must pass rigorous tests. They are looking for "professionals versed in nautical operations, emergency trauma medicine, endurance and hand-to-hand combat . . . already prepared for life-on-death situations, a responsibility that comes with the job."[19]

Once the inner and outer aspects of the evangelistic calling are in place, the rigor of professional preparation and experience for life-on-death situations begins. Let's move to your preparing and delivery of evangelistic sermons.

Part 2

Framework

3

A Theological Framework for Evangelistic Preaching

Support Search and Rescue . . . Get lost![1]
—A Coast Guard bumper sticker

A man attempting to train his dog, alas, had very little success. He was on the verge of despair when he happened across a very enchanting television evangelist. He unburdened his soul to the televangelist, who promptly asked him to leave the dog with him, and he would have it trained in a jiffy.

The next day the man returned and asked how the evangelist got on. The reply was positive, and the evangelist called the dog to give a demonstration.

He picked up a stick, threw it, and said, "Fetch." Instantly the dog took off, grabbed the stick, and returned. The evangelist said, "Drop," and the dog dropped the stick at his feet. He said, "Roll over," and the dog rolled over. By that time, the dog's owner was very excited and asked if he could have a go. "Sure," replied the evangelist.

"Heel," said the owner, and the dog lifted one paw, placed it on the man's forehead, and said, "I command this sickness to leave you."

Certainly this is an exaggerated but perceived stereotype of evangelists around the globe, especially of the television kind. We need to distinguish evangelistic preaching from deviant understandings and erroneous perceptions.

Defining evangelistic preaching is not difficult, though exploring its full scope is rather challenging for a textbook on homiletical method. An evangelistic sermon is framed by certain convictions and distinguished by specific features.

In the introductory section, we laid personal and biblical foundations for the preaching evangelist. God is pro-man in spiritual salvation. Man is anti-God in spiritual situation. We are called to stand in the spiritual gap. We now extend and emphasize those foundations to provide a theological framework for evangelistic preaching.

A Theological Framework for Evangelistic Preaching

The Evangelistic Stance of the Trinity in Evangelistic Preaching

Evangelistic preaching continues the saving initiatives of the Trinity on behalf of the unbeliever. We thoroughly ground such preaching in the doctrine, outlook, and relations of the Godhead in terms of the lost. Here is a trinitarian launch into evangelistic preaching:

1. The *Father's* basic attribute is hyphenated. When probed for the essential attribute of God, students invariably divide into two groups: those who see God's basic attribute as holiness versus those who see it as love. Instead, God's core attribute is holy-love (compare Isa. 6:3 and 1 John 4:8). His holiness keeps sinners from him. His love reaches out to them. As holy, he will judge all humanity. As love, he

wishes all people to be saved. His common grace sustains humanity in spite of their anti-God stance. His saving grace softens and eventually saves some people. Consequently, evangelistic preaching will point out the unbeliever's spiritual distance from God, but not without showing how God has bridged the eternal distance.

2. The *Son's* relation to human salvation is quadrangular, or to use an algebraic term, quadrinomial (four terms): (1) the uniqueness of his divine-human personhood, (2) the exclusivity of the condition of belief on him, (3) the necessity and sufficiency of his work on the cross, and (4) the universality of his invitation to all people. Thus, evangelistic preaching will proclaim the Lord Jesus Christ with these four dimensions implicitly or explicitly presented to the unbeliever.

3. The *Holy Spirit* harmonizes, as in music, a triad of ministry in salvation. The Holy Spirit's engaging sound strikes salvation's fundamental chord before a person's salvation in conviction, during his salvation in conversion, and after his salvation in confirmation. Hence, evangelistic preaching cooperates with the Spirit's ongoing work in an unbeliever.

The Evangelistic Situation of Humanity in Evangelistic Preaching

The following concepts have been treated in terms of the preaching evangelist earlier. Here, however, is a summary of the human situation that must frame all evangelistic preaching:

1. *People are eternally and perpetually lost without the salvation of the Lord Jesus Christ.* While election to salvation is based on God's free and gracious choice of heirs to salvation, God practices an eternal embargo that holds people responsible for their preferences. He permits in hell only those who would forever choose not to come to heaven. Accordingly, evangelistic preaching does not conceal the consequences of not embracing Jesus for earthly or eternal life.

2. *People are savable but unwilling to be saved.* If they were not savable, none would be saved. If they are presently unwilling, God works on their hearts to turn savability into salvation. An esteemed colleague and historian notes a pertinent point from America's

greatest and original theologian of Calvinist persuasion, Jonathan Edwards:

> As Edwards defines ability or power (i.e., the ability to do as one pleases) the sinner's difficulty is not in a proper inability to embrace the Savior, it is in a proper unwillingness to do so. That unwillingness is not because of a lack of ability to function willfully; it is because the will is without a holy, beautiful object to embrace. . . . The real difficulty is not in a person's inability to will or choose; it is his utter blindness to Christ. How can one choose what he does not perceive as extant?[2]

Therefore, evangelistic preaching counts on unbelievers' ability to embrace Jesus as Savior to be turned into a saving willingness as the Holy Spirit romances them. Evangelistic preaching takes seriously the human side of the dual evangelistic operation in placing the extant, beautiful object before unbelievers' ears as clearly and attractively as necessary.

3. *People must embrace the Lord Jesus as the only God who saves them from their lostness.* Their saving-faith response is not the *efficient* cause of salvation, that which makes salvation happen. Their willingness to believe did not cause God to offer salvation to them any more than a child's willingness to receive a Christmas gift caused his parent to give anything. Instead, one's saving-faith response is the *instrumental* condition of salvation, the means by which salvation is personally received. Though the willingness didn't cause the gift to be given, the child must receive the parent's gift in order to experience it. In view of that condition, evangelistic preaching invites unbelievers to trust the Lord Jesus Christ and personally experience salvation.

The Evangelistic Strategy of the Preacher in Evangelistic Preaching

Between the Trinity's stance and humanity's situation, evangelists position themselves in prayerful dependence on the God who called them to preach, to carefully prepare, and to proclaim the Lord Jesus to humanity. They must live in an milieu of prayer, constantly engage in preparation and enhancement of sermon material, and seize God-created opportunities for proclamation.

1. *Praying.* The dynamics of evangelistic preaching (over and against the mechanics of evangelistic preaching, which is our focus in this book) almost exclusively relate to the prayer life of the evangelist. As in all preaching, it is prayer that invites the Holy Spirit's filling for the task of proclamation. The complication of an unbeliever's presence in an audience drives us to our knees for additional provision of God's power for poise, God's favor for credibility, God's mind for creative rhetorical strategy with topic or text, God's gifts for sighting and using illustrations, and God's leadership of the preacher and guiding of the unbeliever during the invitation process. Evangelistic preaching demands prayer before, during, and after the preaching event and thus corresponds to God's work before, during, and after the preaching event.

2. *Preparing.* In a sense, the rest of this book deals with preparing evangelistic sermons. As an art and a science, evangelistic preaching builds on innate, God-given inclinations and calling and cultivates those gifts and talents into skills and habits to arrive at powerful and meaningful proclamation of the Lord Jesus Christ. You cannot go into the preaching occasion without preparation.

Preparation for evangelistic preaching is not less demanding than preparation for other preaching. In fact, it could turn out to be more intense, since unfamiliar audiences need to be taken into account. You have to study your audience's worldviews and lifeviews. You have to prepare for simplicity of terminology for good pedagogy; you have to sensitively prepare for appropriately placed illustrations. The sermon must exhibit unity between the sermon's purpose and the final invitation. That integration demands preparation.

You also have to theologically prepare to protect your sermon, to not guarantee what the Bible doesn't promise to unbelievers. I know one evangelist who increased a less than desired response to his final invitation by promising the "healing of all your diseases if you come forward."

You can't take evangelistic preaching lightly just because you need to preach more simply. Indeed, it takes a person who is very familiar with his theme to be strong enough to clarify the gospel to new, uninterested, or even hostile audiences.

However, I hasten to include a caveat here. Preparation for preaching may not be wholly understood as nor merely relegated to investment of time immediately preceding a specific sermon. You experience days and weeks when time and life hurtle by with urgent calls for your involvement in needy situations. Yet you can't postpone the upcoming preaching event. So do the best you can within the limitations you face, knowing that you have been preparing all along, over months and even years, for the evangelistic event. Of course, don't use busyness as a weekly ruse for lack of preparation, baptizing lack of planning and preparation with sanctified excuses. Let your explanation for not laying the groundwork or doing your homework for a strong sermon be the exception in preaching, whether regularly or evangelistically. If a divine "anointing" of a sermon includes God giving you energy to preach, a human "anointing" of a sermon relates to your honest and hard labor in preparation. Anoint your sermons with a heart set toward prayer and a mind (and schedule) set toward diligent study.

3. *Proclaiming*. You can pray and prepare, and in one sense you are continuously praying and preparing, but unless you proclaim the Lord Jesus Christ in terms of salvation, you are neither a preaching evangelist nor an evangelistic preacher. In God's provision of salvation to human beings, he has included evangelistic proclamation in the salvation sequence he has initiated. The Father's election, Christ's accomplishments, the Holy Spirit's role, evangelistic proclamation, and faith response seamlessly work together for a person's salvation. None of these cause salvation by themselves. In a multiple but distinguishable set of conditions, layered together, they effect salvation of human beings.

Consequently, there is no salvation without evangelistic proclamation by man or angel. For reasons best known to God alone, to be explained more fully in heaven, he has stipulated the proclamation of the gospel as a condition to yield the fruit of human salvation.

This strategy of evangelistic preaching comes from a range of biblical terms used for the activities of the preaching evangelist—to announce (*kēryssō*), to proclaim (*katangellō*), to speak (*legō, laleō*), to bear witness (*martyreō*), to teach (*didaskō*), to make known (*gnōrizō*), and so on. But the New Testament uses a key word that cannot refer to anything but evangelistic proclamation, a word that can be easily transliterated from Greek: *euangelizomai*. While the other words for proclamation can include a range of content—evangelistic or not (see Paul's overlap in Rom. 16:25)—*euangelizomai* cannot bear any other meaning than the content, quality, and strategy of preaching centered on the Good News concerning Jesus.[3]

Between those verbs, I arrive at the following strategy for preaching evangelists in evangelistic preaching:

In a *proclaimer's* strategy, they bear the burden of the breadth, faithfulness, and clarity of public proclamation. Paul writes, "Although I am less than the least of all God's people, this grace was given me: to preach to the Gentiles the unsearchable riches of Christ, and to make plain to everyone the administration of this mystery, which for ages past was kept hidden in God, who created all things" (Eph. 3:8). They imitate their Lord and join God's efficacious call of sinners to repentance widely, faithfully, and clearly.

In an *ambassador's* strategy, preaching evangelists carry the authority of the sender, the formality of the task, the gravity of the message, the urgency of delivery, and the dignity of representing the almighty God (2 Cor. 5:20). "We are therefore Christ's ambassadors, as though God were making his appeal through us. We implore you on Christ's behalf: Be reconciled to God." The *calling* of evangelists refers not only to their internal conviction and vocational responsibility but to their evangelistic strategy as well: calling unbelievers to be reconciled with God in all the urgency and boldness that requires hearing and response.

In a *lover's* strategy—not only Christ's love for them and their love for Christ but also Christ's love for those not yet reconciled (all three meanings embedded in the genitival phrase and in the context of 2 Cor. 5:14)—preaching evangelists care enough for the lost to be compelled to reach them, to appeal to them to be reconciled to God, to persevere while respecting unbelievers' right to continue to refuse Jesus.

Finally, and only analogously, verbal parallels with "announcing good news" (connects to a Hebrew word in 1 Kings 1:42) and evidence in the mood of an Old Testament event in 2 Kings 7 allow some degree of hermeneutical freedom. Famished and poverty-stricken lepers exclaim upon finding all they need to eat and more, "This is a day of good news and we are keeping it to ourselves. . . . Let's go at once and report this to the royal palace" (v. 9). May I include a *beggar's* strategy in evangelistic preaching as well? As a beggar, I ought to thankfully proclaim, joyfully announce, and humbly report of having found Christ's salvation to a spiritually poor and famished world from a position of weakness.[4]

Let's now move from a theological framework for evangelistic preaching to distinguish evangelistic preaching from roots and cousins of similar activity.

Some Theological Features of Evangelistic Preaching

While falling under the rubric of *evangelism*—verbally spreading the Good News of Jesus to unbelievers—evangelistic preaching needs to be theologically distinguished from other evangelistic activity. All evangelistic activity—for example, praying for unbelievers—is oriented to unbelievers, but evangelistic preaching is a special kind of evangelistic activity oriented to unbelievers. Since contrast is the mother of definition, let us examine what evangelistic preaching is not before proceeding to a definition.

1. Evangelistic preaching is not mere evangelistic *presentation*. All evangelistic preaching is evangelistic presentation, but not vice versa. Evangelistic presentations can be done in a wide variety of contexts, personal or public, usually in a one-on-one, face-to-face situation.

In a very distressing case that mesmerized our city in the summer of 2003, a woman was accused, convicted, and sentenced for hitting a man with her car on her way home from an alcohol-and-drug-fueled night with friends two years prior. Panicked and clouded in mind, she fled the scene with his body still lodged in her shattered windshield. Upon arriving home, she left the man locked in her garage, where authorities said he bled to death. After the sentence was read, the twenty-year-old son of the victim read a statement to those present in the court room: "There are no winners in a case like this," he said. "To [the guilty], I would like to say that I accept your apology. In return, I hope that you accept my forgiveness. I hope you accept the forgiveness of Jesus Christ."[5]

Assuming a degree of audience familiarity with the Good News of Jesus, this young man's offer of Jesus's forgiveness can be regarded as an attempt at evangelistic preaching. Had the opportunity been right in the public situation, a full-blown presentation of Jesus's death and resurrection could have been publicly developed with an invitation to trust the Lord Jesus right then and there. At that point, the presentation would have turned into preaching.

All evangelistic presentation ends up explicitly offering Jesus's salvation and at least implicitly inviting the person to embrace Jesus. Philip the evangelist made the most of the enquiry by the Ethiopian eunuch and modeled an excellent evangelistic presentation (Acts 8). We may also take our Lord's incredible and insightful self-introduction to the Samaritan woman in evangelistic dialogue as an example and motivation for evangelistic presentation (John 4). Components of these evangelistic presentations can be included in evangelistic preaching with confidence from the Master of redemption and communication.

While one evangelizes in evangelistic preaching, the obverse does not follow, because evangelism does not necessitate preaching as public proclamation, a rhetorical strategy, or the development of a theme from text or topic. In evangelism, you introduce people to Jesus Christ.[6] You begin with them but end the presentation with an invitation to trust Christ. You may evangelize in public, personal, or in private settings, but evangelistic preaching is always carried out in public settings with unbelievers in the audience. Evangelistic presentation, like a firefighter, sees sudden needs and seizes unexpected opportunities. At other times, such a presentation may be planned and executed in an informal situation with one or a few unbelievers. Spontaneous and opportunistic, there are no limitations on the context of evangelistic presentations. However, evangelistic preaching is always purposed and planned as a formal presentation to a group made up of a few or many unbelievers.

2. Evangelistic preaching is not pre-evangelistic witness, whether by presence, persuasion, or presentation. Pre-evangelistic witness attracts the attention of non-Christians. It prompts nonbelievers' interest in the gospel by our good works or right words in personal or public situations. Pre-evangelistic, verbal seed-sowing attempts to find reactions, queries, and openings for evangelistic presentations. In pre-evangelism, we introduce Jesus to unbelievers and proceed to evangelism, introducing them to Jesus if interest grows. Such pre-evangelistic seed-sowing is crucial before harvesting, especially among those who don't hold the Bible in authority or share the Christian worldview.

Pre-evangelistic witness by the *right words* points people to consider the Lord Jesus and is not evangelistic preaching nor even pre-evangelistic preaching. We will deal with pre-evangelistic preaching later. When our organization sends out a weekly pre-evangelistic "spiritual insight" email to thousands of non-Christians registered on our website, we seek to move them along the scale of knowledge from ignorance to an introduction to Jesus. Along with "a quote from God's Word" (not referred to as "a verse from the Bible"), this email stimulates responses that may be captured for evangelism by the perceptive counselor. Last week an Austrian foreign exchange student came over to our house. Noticing a Bible on our daughter's desk, the student began pummeling her with questions. She needed philosophical interchange at the "who created God?" and "aren't all religions the same?" level. Soon pre-evangelism moved to evangelism as we got to present the spiritual and moral distance between God and humanity and Jesus as the bridge. She listened and understood but did not embrace Jesus. Pre-evangelism went on to evangelism but did not result in personal conversion.

Pre-evangelistic witness by *good works* also points people to consider the Lord Jesus. Peter instructs wives to display conduct that will "win" their unbelieving husbands (1 Pet. 3:1). The Lord encourages a public demonstration of internal light so people will see our good works and glorify the heavenly Father (Matt. 5:16). These good works, on a small or large scale, generate questions concerning motive and intent. Christian good works, always done in the name of Jesus and always toward the needy, who carry the defaced image of God in them, will always intend to bring people to a consideration of Jesus as the answer for their ultimate need. Otherwise, good works would not be pre-*evangelistic*. Indeed, I make a case that social action that is not a means to evangelism may hardly be Christian and may be better carried out in the name of the United Nations or under the supervision of NGO (non-governmental organization) platforms. Christian good works are the first step in a multilevel apologetic strategy for reaching non-Christian neighbors.[7] Other religions exhibit faith-based initiatives to the poor as well. Pre-evangelistic witness through good works seeks to introduce Jesus to the beneficiary to eventually offer that person his salvation.

Conclusion

Surprisingly, I came upon a fitting story of active pre-evangelistic witness from a secular source. Rev. Yukio Saito, a Methodist minister, reaches out with a suicide hotline—fifty call-in centers, twenty-four hours a day, and more than seven thousand volunteers—in a "society driven to take their own lives."[8] He has devoted his life to persuading the isolated and despondent to spare themselves. His own conversion from Shintoism at the age of fifteen, during a huge identity crisis, led him "into the church for answers, and [he] became aware of a totally new life." The newspaper's standout quote from this pastor got my attention: "I became convinced a long time ago that saving lives was the most important work I could do." I'm quite certain that what the newsman saw simply as saving from suicide carries double meaning for the pastor. Saito moves on to presenting "the totally new life" in Jesus to lonely, hopeless, and desperate people. Those who have been romanced and saved by the Holy Spirit will, like Saito himself, eventually become aware of a totally new life. As biblical convictions intersect with personal compulsion and human need, I'd like us to echo Saito: saving lives is the most important work we can do. Pre-evangelistic physical and temporary salvation facilitates evangelistic presentation for spiritual and eternal salvation. We first go *in* the name of Jesus but eventually go *with* the name of Jesus.

Pre-evangelistic witness, then, pursues a strategy of attraction and prepares the way for Jesus to be introduced in concept (about his person) and to their consciousness (about his work) implicitly. It is not evangelistic preaching, though such preaching could be compressed into it.

So what is evangelistic preaching? It's time to pursue a working definition.

4

A Definition of Evangelistic Preaching

> This good news is news because others cannot know it unless someone tells them. The good news is good because hearing it brings about true freedom. It cannot be communicated coercively, for it must be received as good news rather than as compulsion. Its reception cannot be guaranteed because good news does not come naturally to us. It is a gift, grace.[1]
>
> —William Willimon

A stirring story of a preaching evangelist doing evangelistic preaching opens our shift from contrast to definition:

> [John Harper, a Scot] and minister of the Gospel, boarded the Titanic with his six-year-old daughter, Nana. He planned to travel to the Moody Church in Chicago, where he'd been invited to preach for three months. When the ship struck the fateful iceberg and began

to sink, Harper made sure his daughter was placed into one of the lifeboats. He then began what would be the last evangelistic work of his young life.

As the freezing waters began to fill the ship, Harper was heard shouting, "Let the women, children and the unsaved into the lifeboats." Survivors reported that Harper took off his own life jacket and gave it to another man. "Don't worry about me," he reportedly said, "I'm not going down, I'm going up!"

When the ship began to sink, more than 1,500 passengers jumped or fell into the icy waters. As they gradually drowned or froze to death, Harper was seen swimming from one passenger to another, pleading with them to accept Christ.

Only six of the 1,500 people struggling in the water were later rescued, including a man who later identified himself as Harper's last convert. This young man had climbed up on a piece of debris. Harper, who was struggling in the water near him, shouted out, "Are you saved?" "No," the man replied. Harper then shouted the words from Scripture: "Believe on the Lord Jesus Christ and thou shalt be saved." The man did not answer, and a moment later he drifted away on the waves.

A few minutes later, the current brought the two men back together. Again Harper asked, "Are you saved?" Once again, the answer was "no." With his dying breath, Harper shouted, "Believe on the Lord Jesus Christ and thou shalt be saved." He then slipped under the waves for the last time.

Then and there, the man he had witnessed to decided to turn his life over to Christ. Four years later, at a Titanic survivors meeting in Ontario, Canada, this man tearfully gave his testimony recounting how John Harper had led him to the Lord.[2]

John Harper, the preaching evangelist, engaged in evangelistic preaching in its simplest form as he concisely presented Jesus's salvation to desperate individuals in a frantic setting of deep upheaval as urgently as he could. While gasping for his life's last breath, he publicly proclaimed salvation with an explicit invitation to believe on the Lord Jesus. The key ingredients of an evangelistic sermon were present in that final act.

We've set a framework and set out evangelistic preaching from its next of kin. Let's pursue a definition of evangelistic preaching.

A Definition of Evangelistic Preaching

Such a definition certainly includes the evangelistic message and purpose, but it also includes the activity of the early church in both stance and desired response.

First of all, evangelistic preaching is *preaching*. It is not sharing, discussing, or displaying the gospel, but preaching in its technical sense—public proclamation with a view to change values, beliefs, attitudes, or conduct.

Next, it is *evangelistic.* It is not preaching to equip or edify believers, but proclaiming the person and work of the Lord Jesus Christ in reference to *unbelievers'* lack of God's salvation.

Put those two statements together and you get a simple and sound definition of evangelistic preaching:

> Evangelistic preaching is the public proclamation of the Good News of eternal salvation found in the person and work of the Lord Jesus Christ so that any unbeliever may embrace him as the only God who saves sinners.

This definition is rather simple, but its scope is large and intense. Let's unpack it to gain a working understanding of evangelistic preaching.

Public

Like all preaching, evangelistic preaching will engage an audience in a public situation. The group, however, will be composed of individuals who do not know the Lord Jesus Christ in personal salvation.

Proclamation

The word *proclamation* is rich in both biblical and homiletical history. Check its meaning and the meaning of its synonym, *preaching,* in an English dictionary, thesaurus, Bible dictionary, or lexicon, and you'll read a broad range of nuances. You'll know the meaning of proclamation and preaching, though you may be hard-pressed to characterize it succinctly. Just after I wrote the last sentence, I found the following pertinent comment in one of my frequently consulted sources:

> To preach is to proclaim, to announce, to declare a word from God, to present publicly the good news, to deliver a religious discourse related directly or indirectly to a text of Scripture. Apart from a specific context, preaching is difficult to define. Even though preaching has long been significantly linked to the life and activity of both Jewish and Christian communities, it is so varied in content, mode, audience, and purpose that it resists the constraints of a dictionary, even a Bible dictionary.[3]

Those constraints provide comfort. It's easier to define *expository* preaching, *topical* preaching, or *evangelistic* preaching than preaching per se! The adjectives generate the definition. So neither you nor I are the only ones hard-pressed to state the obvious: to preach is to proclaim, and to proclaim is to preach. Now you know why I didn't define the word *proclamation*. It is core content, then, that distinguishes evangelistic preaching, whether textually based or topically developed, from other kinds of preaching.

The Good News of Eternal Salvation

The evangelistic news is good in itself and good for those who believe that eternal salvation is immediately available to those who receive the Lord Jesus as their Savior from sin's lasting condemnation.

Found in the Person and Work of the Lord Jesus Christ

We've already discussed the critical biblical conviction and theological framework necessary for evangelistic proclamation. While the amount of time spent on the death and resurrection of Jesus doesn't make a sermon more or less evangelistic, the content of the gospel must undergird the evangelistic sermon. The person of the Lord Jesus Christ is wider and deeper than his work in human salvation, but evangelistic preaching centers on his *person* as the chosen God-Man and on his substitutionary *work* in his death, burial, and resurrection for human salvation. Those two aspects cover the content of the gospel in technical (1 Cor. 15:3–4), canonical (Rom. 1:1–4), and theological definition: "The Gospel of Jesus Christ is news, good news: the best and most important news that any human being ever hears. This Gospel declares the only way to know God in peace, love, and joy is through *the reconciling death of Jesus Christ the risen Lord*" (italics added).[4] This gospel is the only message you can preach that carries God's power to accomplish the salvation of sinners (Rom. 1:16).

I recommend including the functional and full title of the *Lord* Jesus, or even God Jesus, in salvation presentations for many reasons. While professing the lordship of Jesus does not assure a person of salvation (cf. Matt. 7:21–22), and truly confessing his total lordship requires practiced perfection, the title reveals Jesus as the God who saves. The Lord Jesus is no one else but the very God who saves! It emphasizes his unique self-resurrection in the history and theology of religions. Further, that full title is used by Paul when the jailer explicitly asks a question in reference to personal salvation: "What must I do to be saved?" (Acts 16:30–31; cf. John Harper's story above). Finally, I would like to give at least the same reverence to the Lord Jesus that people in my audiences give to their deities—for example, Lord Krishna, Lord Buddha—just as I show deep respect to the Bible in the presence of Muslim and Jewish audiences who hold their scriptures in high regard.

So That

Evangelistic preaching carries a particular purpose and anticipated result along with its unique content. Your call to nonbelievers in the sermon continues God's call in their hearts to come to the Lord Jesus. In atmosphere, an evangelistic sermon facilitates the hearers' saving response to Christ. In spirit and words, it invites unbelievers to transfer their trust to the Lord Jesus Christ as their only God and Savior.

We can add a postscript, an evangelistic appendix, to almost any sermon, but that doesn't make the sermon evangelistic. Such a sermon includes an evangelistic ending—and I encourage pastors to seek creative and customary ways to conclude sermons with an evangelistic twist—but evangelistic preaching carries a mood of entreaty, implements a rhetorical strategy of appeal and persuasion, weaves the sermon around an evangelistic purpose, and expects an evangelistic result throughout the whole sermon *so that* people come to the Lord Jesus.

Any Unbeliever

If there are no unbelievers present, preaching an evangelistic sermon will be like performing a wedding for those who are already married. The event may carry some memory and meaning, but it doesn't effect great change. Believers will go home remembering their salvation with wonder and gratitude, but evangelistic preaching will not have occurred. We are not resaving lapsed believers! An evangelistic sermon would have edified believers instead. Since there is no evangelistic preaching without unbelievers, we may need to consider a change in mind-set and execute a strategy to have unbelievers present at these occasions. Yet the success ratio of human response doesn't make a sermon evangelistic, for it is possible that no one responds to your proclamation. Instead, the spotlight of the evangelistic sermon will, discernibly but not embarrassingly, focus on the unbeliever.

Notice also that I have used the singular *unbeliever* in our definition. While you are preaching in public, and many unbelievers may be present, you are preaching Christ to *one* unbeliever. Both the biblical precedent—the shepherd going after one lost sheep and angels rejoicing over one who repents (Luke 15)—and good communication skills focus on the one in an audience of many. You speak to the many as if you are speaking to the one who needs to hear you. He will indeed hear you as though he were the only one to whom you were speaking. The one sharpens your focus during preparation of heart and sermon and in delivery technique. You too can be satisfied with joy even if one responds to Jesus's invitation through you.

The phrasing of the definition also refers to *any* unbeliever. The focus is on the individual, but there is no limitation that we can humanly discern. "Whosoever will may come," and of course, "whoever the Father draws will come." There is no arbitrary exclusion of anyone in the audience from receiving Jesus's salvation. "Any unbeliever" echoes an old hymn: "Though millions have come, there is still room for one; there's room at the cross for you." No language, ethnicity, caste, class, color, creed, or religion is barred from the evangelistic focus.

I say *any* unbeliever, because unbelievers fall on a scale of movement toward or against Jesus. We don't know where or who they are. Indeed, they themselves may not know where they fall in the gamut, but they are welcome to avoid our sociological or psychological stereotypes on their journey toward salvation.

The day after I wrote the previous paragraph, I did an evangelistic luncheon at a large company in Dallas whose vision is to become the number one replacement battery in America. Perhaps that vision statement spills over and connects to my evangelistic endeavor: to proclaim Jesus as the number one replacement Savior in the world. Twenty-five staff workers were picked to bring twenty-five nonbelievers to the event. Anticipation ran high on this afternoon, more than they or I had experienced before at such situations. After the talk, I gave the invitation, and the Lord tested me with the content of my definition, motivation, and satisfaction in evangelistic preaching. One, just one, did respond in personal decision, and I rejoiced with the angels of heaven over the one who repented.

May

Even with unbelievers present at the event, we cannot guarantee a single person's transfer from death to life. We can certainly anticipate their conversion in our purposeful preaching. We can carefully prepare evangelistic content for clarity. We can think about how to overcome communication blocks and personal objections in putting together our rhetorical strategy. Much as a midwife understands her important but limited help at the delivery of a baby, we too must realize that we are not the ones giving or causing the birth. We facilitate spiritual birth, but there is no guarantee of a spiritual baby delivered alive and healthy every time to its mother. Many times we will rejoice in a beautiful baby being born, but sometimes our help will be too early, unnecessary, or rejected. There is the petition that accompanies the evangelistic invitation, but there exists no guarantee of spiritual conversions every time.

Embrace Him

I prefer *embrace* as my catchall term to explain the faith response that clinches salvation. *Embrace* clarifies biblical concepts like believing and receiving and goes beyond the intellectual component of belief to elucidate volitional acceptance. It comprises a whole-person reliance on Jesus's offer of salvation. It does not easily permit substitutes or additions to Jesus. Personal embrace keeps people from welcoming the wrong object or hugging multiple objects in mind and heart. Too, *embrace* carries implications for the new life embraced in Jesus. But best of all, it personalizes one's relationship with God.

As the Only God

Jesus is not just the *very* God, but the *only* God who saves. That means the unbeliever cannot rely on any other way or interpretation of salvation. Alternate gods, substitute ways, and additional hedges for salvation made up of idols, concepts, or practices that provide any form of salvation meaning must yield to Jesus as the only God who saves.

And it is *God* who saves. Salvation is the work of God, orchestrated, engineered, sequenced, and implemented by God. Unbelievers cannot work their way up, out, or toward God's salvation. They call on Jesus as the only God who can save them.

Who Saves

Evangelistic preaching communicates Jesus as *Savior*. The saving provision of Christ dominates the evangelistic sermon, in substitutionary content, focus, offer, and invitation. He is the Savior of humanity from their present spiritual deprivation and their eternally disastrous future. He is much more than Savior, but the specific purpose and central proposition of the evangelistic sermon preaches Jesus as Savior.

An airline pilot is husband to his wife, father to his children, elder at his church, and friend to many. However, none of those other relational descriptions help if any of us wants to fly to New York. At that point, there is no advantage to his being husband, father, church member, or friend. We will have to trust him as "Captain So and So" and fly on *his* plane to our mutually desirable destination. Similarly, Jesus is much more than the God who saves human beings, but if we are to be saved, he must be embraced, trusted, and welcomed as the captain of our human salvation, the only One who saves from sin. The Lord Jesus Christ is the only One who possesses the eternal solution for the fundamental human problem of sin and provides the ongoing resources to please God as he pilots us from earth to heaven.

Sinners

As unpopular as the word *sinner* may be, humanity's fundamental problem within a theistic framework is moral rebellion against God. We have fallen into sin. Adam's sin is imputed to us as members of humanity (Rom. 5:12). We are born with a sin nature inherited through our parents (Ps. 51:5). We live under the ruling kingdom of sin (Rom. 3:9) and commit personal acts of sin (Rom. 3:23). Biblically, we can't get away from our status as sinners, even if we badly want to avoid being called sinners. I have actually had people tell me, "I've done wrong, but don't call me a sinner." We may need to use synonyms to communicate sinfulness, but we can't get away from our basic standing with God as sinners.

Portraying sinfulness, sin, and sinners allows the preacher to focus on the saving, substitutionary meaning and function of the Lord Jesus. We must distinguish the content of the gospel (justification before God) without concealing the scope of the gospel (living as a Christian) in evangelistic preaching. That distinction keeps us from seducing anyone into the Christian faith, promising too much, or adding to the grace means of salvation.

Further, we use the plural *sinners* in our definition to reinforce biblical truth. While we proclaim that God can save the individual unbeliever, we know that he does save sinners. The fact that he can save the unbeliever motivates us to genuinely invite any unbeliever to embrace him. The fact that he saves sinners allows us to genuinely offer his salvation to all unbelievers. So our offer is to all sinners (and that includes individuals), and our invitation is to the one who would embrace Jesus (and that does not include all sinners). Jesus came to save sinners (1 Tim. 1:15), but the individual must admit that he is a sinner needing God's salvation. Paul recognized that he was "chief of *sinners*," and the publican cried for God's mercy on him, *the* sinner (Luke 18:13 NASB).

The crux of the gospel, the center of evangelistic preaching, and the core of the final invitation to the unbeliever revolve around one declaration—"Believe on the Lord Jesus Christ as the only God who saves"—framed by the theological atmosphere of God, humanity, Jesus, and faith.[5] *Evangelistic preaching is the public proclamation of the Good News of eternal salvation found in the person and work of the Lord Jesus Christ so that any unbeliever may embrace him as the only God who saves sinners.* When the unbeliever transfers his trust to Jesus, he receives eternal salvation.

I read this interesting story in the newspaper. "Coffee evangelists" is what they have been called, or really what they call themselves. Now belonging to an elite group, the Specialty Coffee Association of America, they own exotic and expensive, steam-taming equipment. The association hopes to turn these articulate amateurs into missionaries so that "early true believers will have a catalytic viral effect." The mark of this micromovement turned missionary movement is its clarity about the basic product—coffee—and primary purpose—to "reach espresso nirvana."[6]

The coffee evangelists in that interesting news item sound not too unlike the early church, Jesus evangelists. The Jesus evangelists knew their basic product—or better, their message—the person and work of Jesus. Their purpose was the same as Jesus's evangelistic purpose—"to seek and to save what was lost" (Luke 19:10)—as is our purpose—one unbeliever embracing him. An author observes, "The truth that Jesus is the Christ . . . [is] the central affirmation of the New Testament, the core of the early church's proclamation, the theme of Peter's Pentecost sermon. For preaching Jesus as the Christ, the early apostles were jailed, and on being beaten, and released, did it again."[7] It is no wonder that the Christian micromovement turned into a missionary movement. Their clear message and purpose unleashed a catalytic viral effect across the world. In their train and legacy, we publicly proclaim the person and work of the Lord Jesus Christ so that any unbeliever may embrace him as the only God who saves sinners.

Part 3

Method

5

TEXTUAL EVANGELISTIC PREACHING

Integration with the Scripture Sculpture Process

Vagueness has ruined a lot of good speeches,
perhaps you have already sensed it.
You must know without doubt what your speech is about,
and whether you're for or against it.[1]

—Charles Osgood

Agricultural technology, a complex farming discipline, yields (unintended pun!) a metaphor for method in evangelistic preaching. Only recently have I become aware of *seed farming*. Type that phrase into your search engine to find thousands of entries regarding the agricultural industry. It's called the "seed industry," or better, the "certified seed industry." Crop experts advise planting certified seed instead of saving grain from the harvest for the next year's crop because "in the long run growers are going to build up things they don't want in their fields, and it costs a lot of money to remove them once they are there." Certified seed is "seed grown and conditioned by specialists for the sole use of planting a crop."[2]

This book on evangelistic preaching provides for both varietal purity and germination, building on the harvest and soil metaphors the Savior uses for evangelistic ministry (Matt. 9:35–38; Mark 4:3–20). The process into which you are about to enter furnishes a method for using certified seed to plant evangelistic seeds without growing things you don't want, thus avoiding the expensive challenges in removing what you unintentionally grow. You will go from seed production to seed planting in evangelistic preaching as you anticipate a spiritual harvest.

In this section, we move from personal foundations and theological framework to sermon fulfillment in evangelistic preaching. As intimated earlier, evangelistic preaching is a subset of evangelism, with further subsets of pre-evangelistic, evangelistic, and post-evangelistic preaching. Using the marriage metaphor, pre-evangelistic preaching uncovers suitable candidates, evangelistic preaching courts them toward the wedding, and post-evangelistic preaching cultivates the marriage after the wedding embrace has taken place. For further distinctions and exploration of these three subsets of evangelism, please consult appendix 3, "Shades of Evangelistic Presentation."

Evangelistic preaching, like expository preaching, may be textual or topical in nature. Textual preaching lets a single text control the central proposition and the development of the sermon. In topical preaching, the preacher controls the central proposition and the development of the sermon. This chapter deals with *textual* evangelistic preaching.

At this point, I must invite you to familiarize yourself with my companion textbook on preaching, *Preparing Expository Sermons: A Seven-Step Method for Biblical Preaching*. I have had the joy of seeing the Scripture Sculpture method used by Bible schools and seminaries in many countries and languages, and I have taught it to thousands of pastors across the world. They benefit from a straightforward method that can be applied weekly and used at any educational level and with any genre of biblical literature. That Scripture Sculpture method forms the basis of textual evangelistic preaching as well.

The Scripture Sculpture process is built on an eyeglass model, with one eye to the unchangeable text and the other to the ministry context. The left lens in the diagram below represents the Bible, and the right lens represents the audience. The left lens is ground to Scripture's prescription; the right lens is oriented to the audience's needs. The nose bridge, which we call the *purpose bridge*, keeps both lenses connected, in place, and metaphorically, on the face of the preacher. This model attempts to keep the preacher faithful to the text and relevant to his audience.

The Seven Step Process of Scripture Sculpture

Step 1: Study the Text
   Step 2: Structure the Text
      Step 3: Central Proposition of the Text
         Step 4: The Purpose Bridge
            Step 5: Central Proposition of the Sermon
               Step 6: Structure the Sermon
                  Step 7: Preach the Sermon

Or to show it in another way:

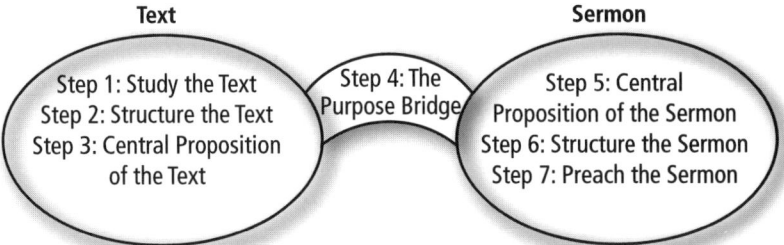

I recommend you become very familiar with the Scripture Sculpture method to enhance your textual preaching. In fact, I shall count on your understanding of that material, on which I build this chapter, so you can really enter into the textual evangelistic preaching to be described below. A laminated bookmark briefly describing these seven steps has been given to great numbers of preachers and evangelists who consult it for weekly preparation of expository sermons. Here I share the bookmark version, and the longer outline of the process is later included in appendix 2, "A Synopsis of the Scripture Sculpture Process."

1. Study the Text
    - Observe words
    - Observe relationships between words
    - Ask and answer questions
    - Analyze and apply answers
2. Structure the Text
    - Distinguish major points from minor points
    - Summarize main points
3. Central Proposition of the Text
    Write out in *one* sentence
    - what the author is talking about (theme of the text)
    - what the author is saying about what he is talking about (thrust of the text)
4. Purpose of the Sermon
    Answer this question: On the basis of the central proposition of the text, what does God want my audience to hear, understand, and do?
5. Central Proposition of the Sermon
    Write out in *one* sentence
    - what you are talking about (theme of the sermon)
    - what you are saying about what you are talking about (thrust of the sermon)
6. Structure the Sermon
    - Introduction
    - Body of the sermon (reflects step 2)
    - Conclusion

7. Preach the Sermon
   - Thoughtfully develop your sermon to accomplish your purpose (step 4)
   - Write it out, with powerful illustrations and word choice, around the central proposition (step 5)
   - Deliver your sermon effectively, with gestures and voice

If you memorize the seven steps, let me know at proclamation@rreach.org, and I'll send you a bookmark too! It will prompt your preparation process every week, whether in evangelistic or post-evangelistic expository preaching. These steps represent the *mechanics* of sermon preparation. Again, the *dynamics* almost wholly relate to your prayer coverage of these steps from the first moment of sermon preparation to the moment after the sermon has been delivered.

I need for you to be familiar with the Scripture Sculpture process. It will be really helpful for you to spend some time with the rather extensive appendices on the method at the back of this book before you work through this next section.

Integrating the Scripture Sculpture Process with Textual Evangelistic Sermons

The text side of the sermon preparation process (steps 1–3) remains the same any time we do textual exposition, evangelistic or not. An expository sermon will be grounded in and arise from the text.

- Step 1: Study the Text
- Step 2: Structure the Text
- Step 3: Central Proposition of the Text

Step 4 is the critical move, the crucial transition, the decisive and vital step in all textual preaching. I present it in the form of a question to make it easy to grasp and apply: On the basis of the central proposition of the text, what does God want my audience to know, feel, and do (or hear, understand, and obey)?

This key question in textual evangelistic sermon preparation articulates the purpose of the sermon *evangelistically*:

> On the basis of the central proposition of this text, what does God want unbelievers to know, feel, and do about his offer of eternal salvation through the Lord Jesus Christ?

This purpose bridge move is limited and liberated by the central proposition of the text. That is, a text may have as many sermons as its central proposition will allow. In constructing the purpose of the sermon, sometimes you emphasize the theme of the text and at other times the thrust of the text—or even parts of the text's theme or thrust—to then move to your sermon's evangelistic theme and thrust.

The focus of the evangelistic sermon, of course, is unbelievers in the audience. We want for them what God wants for them in eternal salvation. We certainly want them to know the truth of the gospel; feel their need for it, as well as an appreciation for God's immense work; and then do something—embrace God's offer of eternal salvation in saving faith.

Here are some spiritual, intellectual, and verbal resources needed for steps 4–7 of the Scripture Sculpture process:

Resources Needed for Sermon Steps

Sermon Step	Needed Resource for Effective Preaching
4. The Purpose Bridge	*People insights* from prayer and exegesis of your audience
5. Central Proposition of the Sermon	*Preacher's originality* from gifts, skills, temperament, experience, etc.
6. Structure the Sermon	*Rhetorical strategy* for good form and argument
7. Preach the Sermon	*Presentation and persuasion elements* (illustration, communication technique, application, invitation) to preach a textually faithful, winsome sermon

The purpose bridge, turning the central proposition of the text toward the audience, will require you to apply insights gained by prayer for and exegesis of your audience (see chapter 8, "Audience-Driven Topical Evangelistic Preaching").

Allow me to summarize the features of the purpose bridge (step 4), directing the purpose bridge toward the evangelistic sermon. The evangelistic *purpose of the sermon*

- focuses the introduction on the evangelistic subject and spiritual need the sermon will raise and address
- determines what textual content and explanation one should include and/or exclude in the body of the sermon to accomplish its evangelistic purpose
- influences the sermon's evangelistic conclusion
- launches the content and stance of the evangelistic invitation
- helps in choosing appropriate illustrations that must be used to accomplish the evangelistic purpose of the sermon
- provides a more objective way to measure the content of the sermon against its evangelistic purpose *before* it is preached

Most importantly, the purpose of the sermon

- directly contributes to the form of theme of the central proposition of the evangelistic sermon (step 5)

The importance of the purpose of the sermon as the key link from text to the sermon, evangelistic or otherwise, cannot be exaggerated. In the next chapter, I provide comment on and samples of this purpose move with sources for three kinds of textual evangelistic sermons.

6

Sources and Samples of Textual Evangelistic Preaching

> Then he said to them, "So thick-headed! So slow-hearted! Why can't you simply believe all that the prophets said? Don't you see that these things had to happen, that the Messiah had to suffer and only then enter into his glory?" Then he started at the beginning, with the Books of Moses, and went on through all the Prophets, pointing out everything in the Scriptures that referred to him.
>
> Luke 24:25–27 Message

A textual evangelistic sermon arises from one of three sources, with the last option being the weakest. You may preach from a salvation-*concentrated* text, from a salvation-*connected* text, or from a salvation-*compliant* text.

Textual Evangelistic Sermon Sources
1. Salvation-concentrated texts
2. Salvation-connected texts
3. Salvation-compliant texts

Here are the key factors in determining the pursuit of one of these three options. You may preach from (1) a salvation-concentrated text for which you can establish the evangelistic *intent* of the author, (2) from a salvation-connected text in which evangelistic *content* is evident, or (3) a salvation-compliant text from which a sermon can be extended (extrapolated extent from original audience trait) to accomplish an evangelistic purpose, as our last hermeneutical option.

Sources and Factors

Textual Source	Hermeneutical Factors
Salvation-concentrated texts: textual intent	Author's purpose; explicit gospel framework; mixed audience
Salvation-connected texts: textual content	Implicit gospel framework; mixed audience
Salvation-compliant texts: textual extent	Extrapolated connections; mixed audience

Since these three form long and intense sections of this chapter, I suggest you process this material more deliberately, even possibly applying each strategy in the pulpit before studying the next one.

A Salvation-Concentrated Text

Many texts straightforwardly relate to the proclamation of the gospel. Three critical factors clearly identify a salvation-concentrated text: *the author's purpose, the explicit framework of the gospel,* and *an original audience that included unbelievers.* Our strongest clue in discerning a salvation-concentrated text—the author's intent in writing his text—includes his own proclamation of the gospel.

Here are some examples:

Sources and Samples of Textual Evangelistic Preaching 95

- The Gospels easily fall into this category. They were expressly written to specific audiences to present Jesus as Son of God, Messiah, and Savior, "that you may believe that Jesus is the Christ, the Son of God, and that by believing you may have life in his name" (John 20:31).
- Some apostolic messages in Acts fit into the salvation text category (e.g., Peter's sermon in Acts 2; Paul in Acts 14 and 17).
- The first part of Romans (chapters 1–8, especially 1–3) sets up the need for a Savior—the explicit framework for the gospel.
- All the Epistles were written to audiences in the early church with unbelievers in them and contain pertinent encouragements, prescriptions, and warnings, parts of which are oriented toward evangelistic purposes or can be included with an evangelistic bent (e.g., Eph. 2:1–10).

I express a limitation here: most textual evangelistic preaching needs to arise from the New Testament simply because the connection to the person and work of Jesus needs to be obvious.

However, let me digress on preaching evangelistically from the Old Testament with canonical and hermeneutical limitations. If an Old Testament passage can be discernibly related to (1) the need of a Savior from sin, judgment, present futility, and eternal lostness, (2) a New Testament passage in comment or assumptions about Jesus, or (3) anticipation of the coming of the Messiah, the Lord Jesus, then by all means preach expository evangelistic messages from the Old Testament (cf. Luke 24:25–27, 44–49).[1]

For instance, I am in the book of Exodus at present for my devotional feedings. This powerful narrative gets ready for the Jesus-as-the-New-Moses theme obvious to the later Gospel writers. This morning I read about the elaborate detail of the tabernacle, and especially of the inner curtain of the Most Holy Place (Exod. 26:31–33). You could preach the passage evangelistically, for this tabernacle veil sets up for the temple veil (2 Chron. 3:14), which was torn at Jesus's crucifixion (Matt. 27:51; Heb. 9:2–3) in order to open access between God and humanity (Heb. 4:14–16; 10:19–22). You would definitely want to point out that the ripped curtain at the crucifixion was torn from top to bottom as a reminder that man could not tear it. Therefore, access to God became available to all people without exclusion.

If these canonical conditions or hermeneutical limitations on evangelistically preaching the Old Testament cannot be authentically and easily met, I ask you to be very careful in doing a *textual* evangelistic sermon from an Old Testament text.

Although meeting any of the three discerning criteria qualifies an Old Testament passage for evangelistic preaching, Genesis 1–11 meets all three conditions explicitly.[2] The entire section addresses the need for the Savior in terms of sin and divine judgment (chapters 3, 7, 11), it anticipates the coming of the Messiah in statement (3:15) and symbol (3:21), and the New Testament looks back to primeval history to establish Jesus as Savior (e.g., Rom. 5:1–12).

Let's look at a New Testament sample.

Luke 18:9–14: A Sample of the Purpose Bridge

I will take you through a sample of the purpose bridge from a salvation-concentrated text. The next few pages will be far more beneficial to you if you read Luke 18:9–14 with pen in hand and do steps 1–3 quickly before following my sample below.

Step 3: The Central Proposition of the Text (CPT)

The central proposition of the text carries a theme and thrust.

> Theme: The manner in which God must be approached for justification from sin
> Thrust: should be not like the self-recommending Pharisee, but like the publican who pleaded for God's mercy.
> Full Statement: Instead of pleading for God's justification from sin like the self-recommending Pharisee, we must ask for God's mercy like the publican.

Step 4: The Evangelistic Purpose Bridge

The evangelistic purpose bridge answers the question, On the basis of the CPT, what does God want the unbeliever to know, feel, and do about his offer of eternal salvation through the Lord Jesus Christ?

Several evangelistic purposes could flow from the CPT of Luke 18:9–14:

1. To dissuade the unbeliever from approaching God in self-righteousness and self-recommendation (emphasizing the Pharisaic section)
2. To persuade the unbeliever to throw himself on the mercy of God for salvation (emphasizing the publican section)
3. To invite the unbeliever to approach God for acquittal in the right way (preaching the entire story, especially the preamble)

If you check the chart entitled "Resources Needed for Sermon Steps" in chapter 5 (see p. 90), you will notice that step 4 states the need for *people insights* from prayer for and exegesis of your audience. My prayer and exegesis prompted the choice of purpose 3 as better representing my audience's needs.

A hint here: Your purpose statement will almost always, in raw form, provide the theme of the central proposition of the sermon. Turn your stated purpose into a question, and you will have your raw preaching theme. Your theme will be underdone (you still have to fashion and design it), but you will understand it. The purpose bridge question will save you from being unclear and uncertain about your theme—a liberating discovery and sense of internal release!

This laser-focused recasting of the CPT (step 3) of an evangelistic (or non-evangelistic) text with an evangelistic purpose (step 4) unleashes the rest of your sermon process with awareness and expectancy.

The process of steps 5–7 for evangelistic preaching develops much in the same way as in preaching to Christians, except you keep the wording, structure, and rhetorical strategy of the sermon focused on unbelievers. Instead of sharing my sermon at this point, I'll show you how I developed this text into a sermon.

Step 5: The Central Proposition of the Sermon
Theme: What am I talking about?
Thrust: What am I saying about what I am talking about?

I gave you a major mechanical hint earlier: your purpose statement will almost always, in raw form, provide the theme of the central proposition of the sermon. So let's apply the process to Luke 18:9–14.

    Step 3   The Central Proposition of the Text (CPT): Instead of pleading for God's justification from sin like the self-recommending Pharisee, we must ask for God's mercy like the publican.

    Step 4   The Purpose of the Sermon: To invite the unbeliever to approach God for his acquittal from sin in the right way

Now on to step 5, the central proposition of the sermon (CPS).

In raw expositional form, we can turn the purpose into the theme of the CPS: "How to approach God for acquittal from sin in the right way?" I will contemporize this raw form into a more memorable, homiletical style eventually, but the basic truth that I will be speaking about is rightly approaching God for acquittal from sin.

Note here that the thrust of CPS may take a number of forms:

- The theme may have to be *proved* addressing these questions: Do all my good works really not count with God? Does approaching God in the publican's way really result in God's salvation? *Proof* would certainly be the main emphasis of the sermon if one were only emphasizing the Pharisee's or the publican's approach.
- The theme may have to be *explained*. Why is self-recommendation wrong? Why is God's mercy the only way? The points in the sermon will *explain* this theme or even the whole proposition.
- The theme may have a *multiple thrust*. That's how I preached this sermon. I chose this latter format, since the text nicely divided into two parts, as discerned by the structure of the text (step 2).

> The theme: How to approach God for a not-guilty verdict
> The thrust: not by proudfully trusting your achievements ... but by humbly trusting God's accomplishments

Notice that I have tried to contemporize the statement with some catchy phrases for slightly better communication—"approach God," "not guilty verdict."

I have also tried to match some of the thrust by syllable length, conceptual parallel, rhythmic step, and alliteration of important words so people can remember the main points: "prideful" and "humble," "trusting" and "trusting," "yours" versus "God's," "achievements" and "accomplishments."

This contemporizing strategy takes some resourcefulness (see "Resources Needed for Sermon Steps" in chapter 5). God-inspired originality, creativity, and vision come from mixing the dynamics and mechanics of sermon preparation with your preaching gifts, verbal skills, personality and temperament, awareness of people, and pulpit experience.

Contemporization and alliteration are not absolutely necessary. But they help make the central proposition and main points less abstract and more memorable. They are highly stylized tools used by more experienced preachers.

> My full statement of the CPS: Approach God for a not-guilty verdict not by pridefully trusting in your achievements but by humbly trusting his accomplishments.

Step 6: The Structure of the Sermon

The body of the sermon is already grounded in step 2 (the structure of the text) and is evident in my step 5 (CPS).

In the structure of the sermon, we are dealing with the essential and identical movements of all sermons: (1) introduction, (2) body, and (3) conclusion. We will then need the resource of thoughtful rhetorical strategy for good form.

The structure of the sermon must exhibit unity, order, proportion, progress, and solid argument, building a case for the listeners' comprehension and response.

When I build a case for an impact-filled presentation, I write out what I must say *and* do in each part of the sermon (introduction, body, and conclusion) to accomplish my purpose for an audience (I analyzed the audience when I constructed the purpose bridge, step 4). For example, I don't think my religiously inclined non-Christian audiences think of themselves as needing anything (i.e., helpless [cf. Luke 18:9]) in any way at all. So I have to keep establishing the uselessness of their efforts, their helplessness before God, throughout this sermon in a variety of ways. I have to present a case for their best works having no merit before God. At this stage, I plan where these matters must be brought in, discussed, or illustrated—in the introduction, point 1 or 2 of the body, or the conclusion.

I structured this sermon on Luke 18 as follows:

Introduction (See "Introduction" in appendix 2.) My introduction will revolve around my purpose—to invite the unbeliever to approach God for his acquittal in the right way—and the theme—how to approach God for a not-guilty verdict.

I must work on the issue of acquittal, especially the need for personal acquittal before God. Most of my audience acquits themselves all the time, and I must address the need for access to God by the right approach.

Body (See "How to 'SAVE a Point' " in appendix 2.) In terms of this sermon, the main points of my body will be as follows:

> I. You can approach God for a not-guilty verdict, not by prideful trust in *your* achievements.

I must undercut pride and prideful trust in religious attempts to reach God and communicate the utter impossibility of self-commendation before God resulting in God's acquittal.

> II. You can approach God for a not-guilty verdict by humble trust in *his* accomplishments.

I must show how it takes God and his accomplishments to give me access to his acquittal.

Conclusion Review the central proposition of the sermon.

Apply the purpose and invite them to respond (see chapter on "evangelistic invitations").

I need to culminate this sermon with a summary that brings in the ingredients of its theme and thrust and moves into the invitation segment.

Step 7: Write, Practice, and Deliver

In step 7 you strive to write, practice, and preach the sermon with all the elements of your preparation for textual faithfulness and all the elements of a sound presentation (excellent communication techniques, illustration, application, and invitation) for a winsome preaching event that may result in salvation. I strongly suggest that you preach without notes, especially in an evangelistic sermon, for if sermons are public conversations, an evangelistic sermon is even more so. Just like you would prefer a musician or actor to remain free of notes, an evangelistic sermon is best preached without notes. And by the time you go through the Scripture Sculpture process, you will be quite able to deliver your message without notes and without fear of forgetting your sermon.[3]

We proceed from preaching salvation-concentrated texts to the second kind of textual evangelistic exposition—salvation-connected texts.

A Salvation-Connected Text

While salvation-concentrated texts can be identified rather easily and preached evangelistically, there are also salvation-*connected* texts in the Bible. Though not evangelistic in intent, these texts contain evangelistic content. In that content, you'll find some or all of the theological framework of the gospel assumed, hinted at, highlighted, or clarified.

Bryan Chapell's theological insight for expository preaching to Christians carries special relevance for evangelistic preaching from salvation-connected texts:

> *Since God designed the Bible to complete us, its contents necessarily indicate that in some sense we are incomplete. Our lack of wholeness is a consequence of the fallen condition in which we live.* Aspects of this fallenness that are reflected in our own sinfulness and in our world's brokenness prompt Scripture's instruction and construction. Paul writes, "Everything that was written in the past was written to teach us, so that through endurance and the encouragement of the Scriptures, we might have hope" (Rom. 15:4). *The corrupted state of our world and our being cry for God's aid.* He responds with his Word, focusing on some facet of our need in every portion. *Our hope resides in the assurance that all Scripture has a Fallen Condition Focus (FCF).* God refuses to leave his frail and sinful children without guide or defense in a world antagonistic to their spiritual wellbeing. No text was written merely for those long ago; God intends for each Scripture to give us the "endurance and encouragement" that we need today. The FCF is the mutual human condition that contemporary believers share with those to or for whom the text was written that requires the grace of the passage [italics added].[4]

As seen in the previous two chapters, the gospel is built and presented within a theological framework. Any biblical text controlled by the theological framework of the gospel—God's nature in relation to sin, or the human situation without Christ, or the provision of Jesus as Savior, or the salvation condition of faith—can be skillfully spun into an evangelistic sermon without naively or deceitfully twisting it into a *textual* evangelistic sermon. The content and the contours of the gospel are evident in such texts.

For example, Romans 1–3 clearly comments on the unbeliever—all are under sin and come short of the glory of God. That is a great section to preach directly to the *condemned*. However, from Romans 4 on, Paul's emphases relate to the *justified* but are controlled by the gospel's theological framework—What does it take to be justified before God? How is God's righteousness applied to the unbeliever who has become a believer? How does a believer continue to please God when sin is still present in the believer?

Whenever Paul reflects on our former state in what we were before and without Christ's salvation or how we are being transformed from sin, you'll find texts controlled by that theological framework of the gospel: God—Humanity/Jesus—Faith.

As a case in point and for your homework with this manual (I must fulfill my professorial obligations with homework), let's introduce Romans 5:6–8. Paul is writing to Christians in the context of justification by faith (vv. 1–4) and powerfully presents what Christ has done for the ungodly—"While we were still sinners, Christ died for us" (v. 8). It's very difficult to demonstrate the evangelistic intent of this text, for he is primarily speaking to Christians, only possibly in the hearing of non-Christians. I am quite certain that a non-Christian in Paul's mixed audience would be attracted to what Christ had done for him in spite of his presently being "ungodly" (v. 6). The passage pulsates with evangelistic content that can be seized for but not squeezed into a textual evangelistic mold.

Here's the criterion for utilizing a salvation-connected text in textual evangelistic preaching: *Does the central proposition of the text highlight or connect with any part of the theological framework of the gospel (God—Humanity/Jesus—Faith)?* (See also appendix 1 for the content of the *gospel*.)

Question: How can one be certain that a biblical text is controlled by the theological framework of the gospel so it can be seized for textual evangelistic preaching?

Answer: The CPT (step 3) will disclose whether any part of the theological framework of the gospel can be seized from any part of that CPT for textual evangelistic preaching. If any part of the theme or the thrust of the CPT reflects any dimension of the theological framework of the gospel—(1) God's expectation, (2) humanity's situation, (3) Jesus's provision, or (4) the faith condition—you can construct an evangelistic purpose (step 4) from the CPT and preach it evangelistically with textual integrity and authority.

Romans 5:6–8: A Sample of the Scripture Sculpture Process

I illustrated the key purpose bridge (step 3 to step 5) from the more difficult Synoptic Gospels genre (Luke 18:9–14) earlier. I'd like to take you through steps 1–6 (only the sermon writing and preaching itself will be yours!) on a salvation-connected text from the Epistles. The better you follow (but not mindlessly or slavishly imitate) this fuller sample, the better you'll comprehend and practice the expository method proposed in the Scripture Sculpture process.

Use one page per verse. Write or type out each verse in full. If you can translate from the original, by all means, do so.

> Verse 6: "For while we were still helpless, at the right time, Christ died for the ungodly" (NASB).
>
> Verse 7: "For one will hardly die for a righteous man; though perhaps for the good man someone would dare to die" (NASB).
>
> Verse 8: "But God demonstrates His own love toward us, in that while we were yet sinners, Christ died for us" (NASB).

Step 1: Study the Text

Observe Words. Study their meanings in dictionaries, Bible dictionaries, or encyclopedias, and study their usage in concordances and marginal references. Write your findings on the page for each verse.

In Romans 5:6–8 you will observe long, unusual, repeated words, such as *helpless, time, died, ungodly, righteous, demonstrates, dare, His own love, sinners*.

Observe Relationships. Observe relationships between the words you have picked out to study. Here you will observe relationships such as *while, still, right time, hardly die, righteous man, though perhaps, own love*; the parallels between *helpless, ungodly, sinners*; and the parallel between "Christ died for the ungodly" (v. 6 NASB) and "Christ died for us" (v. 8 NASB). You will also notice the repetition of the little word *for* at the beginning of verses 6 and 7 as well as in the middle of phrases.

Ask and Answer Questions. Write out the questions you bring to this text. What are some questions your audience could bring to this text? For example, you could probe questions concerning our utterly helpless condition in ungodliness and sin. Write out answers on the page. Don't worry about going too long or being wrong at this juncture. You can throw out the bad observations and shorten the long answers later. Here is a beginning list of questions and suggested answers.

Verse 6: "For while we were still helpless, at the right time Christ died for the ungodly" (NASB).

Some Questions. Why does Paul pick this description of the human race—ungodly? What does "at the right time" mean? What is God's view of time? What about those who lived before Christ? Did Christ die for all the ungodly or only for those who will be saved, as in "us"?

Some Answers. Check the immediate context (Rom. 5:1–21), even the entire book of Romans or Pauline theology, on this description of the human race who are now believers.

"Ungodly" means *against God* and *as far from God as possible* in nature, preference, attitude, and action.

"At the right time"—God decides the critical center of historical time. He is not one minute too soon or a minute too late. Christ's death provides for all the ungodly at the precise time.

"Those who lived before Christ" are addressed in Romans 3:25–26.

The "ungodly" and "us" can't be the same group, for there are ungodly people who will never ever be part of "us." There is much theological blood spilled on this question. But ask hard questions like these. You can actually make such statements in your sermon.

Verse 7: "For one will hardly die for a righteous man; though perhaps for the good man someone would dare even to die (NASB)."

Some Questions. What is the force of the meaning of *for*? Why is it repeated in its different and particular locations? Is Paul speaking of dying *for* another man's benefit or dying in his place, as a substitute? Do we have any examples of v. 7b today, of those who dared to die for other good men?

Can you come up with some more questions on verse 7?

Some Answers. Use of the word *for* carries a substitutionary (dying instead of the ungodly), not just a beneficial (dying for the sake of a good or righteous person) force. Salvation benefits come to us because of Christ's substitution.

For illustration, men in the military die for the benefit and in the place of the rest of us.

I would make a note here that a strong parable or illustration is needed and set about looking for one in the news or my other reading.

Verse 8: "But God demonstrates His own love towards us, in that while we were yet sinners, Christ died for us" (NASB).

Some Questions. Why does Paul use the strong word about God's *demonstration* of his love? Though Paul didn't *see* the crucifixion, he saw the cross as God demonstrating his love. How can something you have not personally seen carry that kind of demonstrative weight? How does God keep on showing his love? And what about the phrase "His own love"? Why the redundant, *his* and *own*? What does the emphasis mean in terms of God's love?

It is time now for you to come up with more questions on verse 8 and answers to my questions above as well as to your own. You may be aware of my view of the advantage of being well-versed in the original languages of Scripture: you can ask better, more intensive questions of the text at step 1 and discern the structure of the text more clearly at step 2. Of course, the better the questions, the more the material and the stronger the exegesis and the less the time wondering about unnecessary questions.

I hope you have started preparing this sermon on Romans 5:6–8. Are you finding some early, good content emerging for your sermon? I am sure you are if you are practicing on this test passage.

Analyze and Apply Answers.

Some Analysis. Using the tests of interpretation detailed in appendix 2, analyze your answers. Also, check Bible commentaries and study Bibles to see what other people of God have to say on the text. You can also check other study sources on the concepts embedded in this text. For instance, you can look up *atonement* or *the death of Christ* or *substitution* in Bible dictionaries or type "Christ's substitution" on your Internet search engine for reams of material.

For instance, one commentator writes, "Jesus' death is totally different. Its force as a sustaining demonstration of God's love stems from its having occurred at just such a time as conventional religion would least expect it of God, on behalf of those who in no way deserve it."[5] You could either quote or refer to this comment in your sermon.

Some Early Application—Personal and Sermonic. Do I really understand how desperate and powerless we are before God? Think through ways in which your audience can begin to appreciate the timely character and extent of God's love—for ungodly "me" and for helpless "we." You may also start looking for illustrations that fit your discoveries. Start a new file (paper or electronic) for this sermon. Place your observations and illustrations in it.

Step 2: Structure the Text

Distinguish Major Points from Minor Points. Underline or circle "little words" that carry major meaning. These are usually words that are grammatically influential, so discern connections with surrounding text or within the text. These little grammatical words also mark a change in subject or content from one point to the next.

Verse 6: *For* relates the text back to verses 1–5 to show how our justification provides us confidence and access to God by faith (vv. 1–2) as well as endurance and hope in the middle of affliction (vv. 3–5).

While reveals the time of Christ's death, and that timely provision is reinforced by the phrase "at the right time."

Verse 7: *For* connects verse 7 to verse 6, simply contrasting the death of Jesus with the deaths of those who may die on behalf of others, and thus does not begin a major point. Verses 6–7 stay together to form the first major point of this three-verse text.

Perhaps separates two subpoints under verse 7—"one will hardly die for a righteous man" and "for the good man someone would dare even to die."

Verse 8: *But* marks a major contrast between verse 8 and verse 7 and sets off a separate point. Hence the text divides into a two-point structure:

I. Verses 6–7
II. Verse 8

The twofold division reveals the structure of the passage. Attempt to simplify and group "smaller bones" under "larger bones" as much as possible, or your structure can get quite unwieldy.

Summarize Main Points in Full Sentences. Let's go with my structure for now. Always use full sentences to summarize your main points. Unless you write out your main points in full sentences, you'll never know how unclear your statements are! They do not have to be highly polished, but they have to be correct, clear, comprehensive, and concise.

Correct—reflecting the observations and choices in the text
Clear—in the least ambiguous way possible
Comprehensive—reflecting the whole section
Concise—not too much longer than the text itself

Reflecting our grammatical analysis above, Romans 5:6–8 may be summarized in a two-point full sentence structure like this:

I. Christ died for *ungodly* people at the right time, though we rarely find anyone dying for good people (vv. 6–7).
II. The demonstration of God's own love for us is found in Christ's death for us while we were yet sinners (v. 8).

A grammatical laying out of the structure of the text is a sturdy and reliable way of understanding the author's argument and intention. Often you have to take grammar *and* content factors into consideration as you make decisions between major and minor points. How can you decide priorities in displaying structure?

Usually, grammatical cues take priority over content cues, because the former always influence the latter, while the latter can occur without grammatical indicators. However, grammatical cues *plus* content cues take priority over grammatical cues or content cues by themselves.

Look at verse 8. Here is a grammatical-plus-content (literary) understanding of this text's structure. I noticed that the last part of verse 8—"While we were yet sinners, Christ died for us" nearly identically, and significantly, parallels verse 6—"While we were still helpless, at the right time, Christ died for the ungodly." In my understanding of literary structure, the author seeks to emphasize the timeliness of Christ's death (at the right time) but also the time of Christ's death (while we were *still* helpless, *yet* sinners). So both the time and timeliness of Christ's death demonstrate God's love for us, over and against the occasional martyrdom of courageous men for good men. That parallel accents God's demonstration of love for us in Christ's death as *the emphasis of the author*. Christ's death demonstrates God's love in spite of our helplessness and wickedness (the repetition of the phrases in vv. 6 and 8) when he died instead of us (the substitutionary meaning of *for*, deeper but including the benefit meaning of *for* discovered in step 1).

Step 3: Central Proposition of the Text

Write out in *one* sentence

- what the author is talking about (theme of the text)
- what the author is saying about what he is talking about (thrust of the text)

Since the death of Christ is noted, repeated, and explored as proof of God's love for us, we have decided that the author's theme and thrust in Romans 5:6–8 are as follows:

> Theme: The unmistakable demonstration of God's own love for us
> Thrust (complements or completes the theme): . . . is found in Christ's timely, substitutionary death when we were still helpless, ungodly, and sinners.
>
> Full statement (putting the theme and thrust together in one complete sentence): The unmistakable demonstration of God's own love for us is found in Christ's timely, substitutionary death when we were still helpless, ungodly sinners.

Step 4: Purpose of the Sermon

Answer the evangelistic purpose question of this text:

> On the basis of the central proposition of the text, what does God want unbelievers to know, feel, and do about his offer of eternal salvation through the Lord Jesus Christ?

At this point I establish the crucial "compatibility" issues of my purpose statement:

The exegetical and theological compatibility question: Can I make an exegetical or theological case that my purpose statement is within the purpose of the author or the function of the text?

The psychological and sociological compatibility question: Can I make a psychological or sociological case that my purpose statement fits the audience's evangelistic needs?

Here is my evangelistic purpose bridge for Romans 5:6–8:

> To unequivocally establish God's incredible love in Christ's timely and substitutionary death for helpless sinners.

Exegetical and theological compatibility: My purpose closely reflects Paul's purpose in the text so that no one will wonder if my purpose reflects the text.

Psychological and sociological compatibility: I need to make a winsome, powerful case at every level (spiritual, intellectual, emotional) for my unbelieving audience to embrace Jesus's remarkable death for them. Therefore, the words *unequivocal* and *incredible* are found in my purpose statement. I will attempt to make the audience aware of the awesomeness of Jesus's death.

Step 5: Central Proposition of the Sermon

Write out in *one* sentence

- what you are talking about (theme of the sermon)
- what you are saying about what you are talking about (thrust of the sermon)

Do you remember the mechanical hint for moving from step 4 to step 5? To find the raw form of the theme of the CPS, turn the evangelistic purpose into the question you'll address in order to accomplish that purpose in your sermon. Creativity and experience will show themselves strongly at this point. You will introduce many layers of information about your audience at this stage. The basic audience factor, of course, is that they are unbelievers. The raw form of the theme will help you understand what you are talking about, for if you can't establish what you are talking about, your listeners will be at a major loss.

The raw form of my sermon's theme came out this way:

> Theme: What could it take for God to unequivocally establish his incredible love to undesirable sinners like us?

The thrust in this text and sermon rather easily flows as an answer to the theme question:

> Thrust: Christ's timely and substitutionary death

Put your theme and thrust into a full statement, and you get your sermon's central proposition:

> Full statement: The unequivocal proof of God's incredible love for us arrives in Christ's timely and substitutionary death for sinners.

This raw form can now be homileticized—stylized into an evangelistic focus. I will take out terms unfamiliar to audiences (*substitutionary death*) and add more unusual terms to pique interest (*deathly love*). I may also use some alliteration and rhythm (in this case, by suffixes—*miserable* and *desirable*).

> For God to turn miserable sinners into desirable people took Christ's deathly love.

I wouldn't leave my sermon's central proposition even in that form. I'd continue to polish it and shape it and put it in a form that would be very clear in formal expression as well as meaningful for personal appropriation. I don't want anyone to leave with questions about my theme, and definitely not with a lack of understanding of the whole central proposition.

Step 6: Structure the Sermon

Covered by persistent prayer and sustained thought (this means I need to study and pray in private with as little distraction as possible), I will seek to structure the sermon in its three essential movements: introduction, body, and conclusion. I will strategize for its maximum impact given my study of the audience—their educational background, awareness of the gospel, even levels of antagonism to Christ. As I think through this structure in an atmosphere of prayer, I will "sequence" the sermon. Simply speaking, an effective sermon strategy is made up and accomplished by structure, sequence, and speech.

Effective Strategy
1. Structure
2. Sequence
3. Speech

I continue with my illustration from Romans 5:6–8.

Introduction. I develop an attention-getting introduction that raises the *need* from my purpose (to unequivocally establish God's incredible love in Christ's timely and substitutionary death for helpless sinners) and *orients* the audience to my theme (what it takes to turn *Les Miserables*, or *Les Indesirables*, into *Les Desirables*).

You'll notice that I got my audience's attention by borrowing from the world's most popular musical.

I raise need with the question, "Who's the most despicable, most undesirable and miserable person you know?"

I then orient them to the theme: "Who do you think are the most undesirable, *Les Indesirables*, that God knows?" (To keep their attention, I use the French true cognate so there will be sustained interest and anchor words for the whole sermon.)

Finally, I state my purpose: "I'd like to show you how God shows his love to *Les Indesirables* and turns them into *Les Desirables*."

Body of the Sermon (reflects step 2). I would repeat the theme (how God turns us from *Les Indesirables* to *Les Desirables*) or restate the theme (how God moves humanity from a "deep foe" status—an enemy metaphor and phrase used during war—to a "deep friend" status).

With certain literary observations, I protect the twofold structure (step 2) in this way:

I. God demonstrates his love by Christ's deathly love *in spite of* us *Les Indesirables*—who we were (vv. 6–7)!
   A. We were helpless—without competency for self-salvation.
   B. We were godless—without capacity to relate to God's person.
   C. We were sinners—without conformity to God's standards (also see v. 10).

II. God demonstrates his love by Christ's deathly love *instead of* us to make us *Les Desirables*—what he has done (v. 8)!
   A. His death was "just in time" (to emphasize timeliness).
   B. His death was "just in place" (to emphasize its substitutionary nature).
   C. His death was "just because of love" (to emphasize the "only antecedent necessity" of salvation, God's incredible love, which resonates through the passage).

I'll review and repeat the phrases "just in time," "just in place," "just because of love" several times as my sermonic thrust, along with the sermon's theme in the conclusion so they grasp the full statement.

Conclusion. Here I must include a powerful illustration that will capture the time, substitution, and love theme as clearly as possible and lead me to the invitation.

Step 7: Preach the Sermon

- Thoughtfully and prayerfully write out your sermon.
- Develop your sermon to accomplish your purpose (step 4).
- Incorporate the sermon strategy (structure and sequence) you have worked through (step 6).
- Find impact-filled illustrations and connect them to your commentary on the text woven around the central proposition (step 5).

- Deliver your sermon effectively (using the speech elements of sermon strategy), if necessary with some practice, using appropriate gestures and voice.
- Invite people to embrace the Lord Jesus Christ as the only God who saves sinners.

Moving on from salvation-concentrated texts and salvation-connected texts, we shall now consider the third form of textual evangelistic sermons.

A Salvation-Compliant Text

In addition to salvation-concentrated texts with evangelistic intent and salvation-connected texts with evangelistic content, there are salvation-*compliant* texts we can *extend* to serve evangelistic purposes. I have some difficulty in calling this strategy evangelistic preaching per se, but such extension acknowledges a theological truth and an audience reality (and, in reality, acknowledges an often erroneous, well-practiced format of trying to find an evangelistic ending for any sermon).

The *theological truth* is simple: the features and blessings of the believer's life are available to the unbeliever should he embrace the Lord Jesus as his Savior.

The *audience reality* is plain: the readers of the New Testament were believers not only at different stages of Christian growth but also at varying points in their journey to salvation. There were people who possessed salvation, those who professed salvation, and those who were not yet saved. Apparently, in the biblical texts written *to believers*, there were truths that could penetrate unbelievers. Salvation-compliant texts take into account the description of evangelistic preaching as "the kind of preaching which is primarily addressed to those who already trust the gospel but which, at the same time, says to those who overhear it, 'This is for you, too. The household of God is not complete until you know that you also are a son . . . a daughter. You belong here.'"[6]

Salvation-compliant texts are texts that are only one step away from an unbeliever's experience of Christian faith and blessings. If preachers have to jump through several theological hoops and perform mental gymnastics to link a text to the possibility of salvation, they will compromise textual authority as well as inner authenticity. Such interpretive maneuvering is also likely to result in fogginess in the unbeliever's mind and attendant doubt about the use of the text evangelistically.

With hermeneutical precaution and theological boundaries around these one-step-removed texts, they can be utilized for authoritative and effective evangelistic *endings*—not as afterthoughts but as postscripts. In fact, you'll preach a mini-evangelistic sermon at the end of a regular sermon.

These texts do *not* exhibit the theological framework for the gospel—those would be salvation-connected texts. Yet they may be made to serve an evangelistic sermonic postscript, because they are merely one step away—the faith response—for the CPT to become true for the unbeliever. An unbeliever can't know, feel, or do anything that the Christian hears, understands, and obeys for one reason: he does not know Jesus. Thus an evangelistic appendage is the way to introduce the unbeliever to Jesus even by way of what he does not yet have. We don't have to twist the text, but we do need to add to the sermon's ending, an extrapolation based on an exegetically sound central proposition toward an evangelistic focus. Remember the old dictum "one meaning, many applications" in basic Bible study methods courses? In this final textual evangelistic preaching scheme (and quite a scheme it is!), a text doesn't carry evangelistic meaning but can carry extrapolated evangelistic application.

I alert you to three cautions in this additional evangelistic use of the central proposition of the text:

1. *Hermeneutical Precaution.* Be sure that the features and blessings of salvation are only *one step* away from the unbeliever's grasp. That is, there is no way for the unbeliever to receive the benefits, but he is only one step away from appropriating the provisions of Christianity if he embraces Jesus.

Let's say you are preaching from the forgiveness parable of Jesus in Matthew 18:21–35—something like "vertical forgiveness is the basis for horizontal forgiveness" (cf. my *Preparing Expository Sermons*, pp. 117–19). The parable is not evangelistic by intent or content, only by extent. At the evangelistic close, you can introduce the benefit of receiving Christ (vertical forgiveness) to provide the resource for healing in the unbeliever's broken relationships (horizontal forgiveness).

To reiterate: if you are more than one step away from this hermeneutical maneuver or are being dishonest with the text, you'll struggle in your preparation. You'll have to ask yourself if the inner struggle indicates a forcing of the evangelistic turn with a text that doesn't lend itself to the clean, clear offer of salvation. Since you and I can prove pretty much anything from any part of Scripture, we need to be honest with ourselves. If God's promises and prescriptions are more than one step away from saving faith, then you can't use this form of textual evangelistic preaching

2. *Spiritual Deficit.* Using a non-salvation-related text for evangelistic endings through this one-step-away procedure is built on the assumption that there is no spiritual reality or capacity in the unbeliever to meet the expectations of God and prescriptions of the central proposition of the text without Jesus. For example, God expects payment for sin, and the unbeliever can't meet that condition; or God demands holiness in life, and the unbeliever can't please God; or God wants us to treat our spouses right, but without Jesus there are no resources to meet that obligation.

Again, make sure that the blessings of salvation (hermeneutical precaution) and prescriptions for Christians (spiritual deficit) are only one step away from being received or met by unbelievers—through a faith embrace of Jesus. If they are more than one step away, then do not use a non-salvation-related text for evangelistic endings. In non-salvation-related texts, you emphasize unbelievers' failure, their fallen condition, their sin that needs a Savior.

Let's say you are preaching on the role of husbands in 1 Peter 3:7. Peter wants men to treat their wives right "so that [their] prayers will not be hindered" (NASB). Unhindered prayers are a benefit to Christians indeed, but in this verse, the means to unhindered prayers is not by becoming saved. That result is distinctly Christian for those who treat their wives rightly. Yet the unbeliever cannot begin to treat his wife rightly without the resources of Jesus in his life. So he has to (1) trust Jesus and (2) treat his wife rightly so that his prayers are answered. The unbeliever is two steps away from this text. Your outline could read this way:

   I. Trust Jesus and you'll treat your wife rightly.
  II. Trust Jesus and you'll treat your wife rightly so your prayers will be unhindered.

If you could preach only the first point, then your non-evangelistic passage could be turned into an evangelistic ending; but since you can't separate the first point from the second point for textual integrity, this text cannot be used in an integrated evangelistic way. At this point, the "PS" principle, the evangelistic appendage, takes over with a one-step move to faith response. The passage points to the unbeliever's failure in a bad marriage that can be addressed by Jesus. You do not promise him any answered prayers, just the way of salvation in his failure.

Here's the separate mini-evangelistic sermon that you may incorporate into your conclusion:

   a. *Transition to evangelistic introductory need*: "Don't worry about getting your prayers answered without treating your wife rightly, because you can't treat your wife rightly unless you have the resources of the Lord Jesus Christ."
   b. *The evangelistic framework of God—Humanity*: "You know you haven't treated your wife rightly and thus have confirmed your sinful rebellion against God."
   c. *The evangelistic framework of Jesus—Faith*: "God has done something about your rebellion. . . ." (Go into a gospel explanation.)
   d. *Evangelistic ending*: "Embrace him as the only God who saves you to be cleansed from all your sins, including the sin of not treating your wife rightly. Tell Jesus that you repent of these wrongdoings, that you trust him as the One who took your penalty for these sins, that you believe him because he raised

himself from the dead to prove his ability to save you. Invite him to be your only God and Savior."

You use the unbeliever's spiritual deficit, his fallen condition, to point him to his need for a Savior—that's all.

3. *Theological Boundary*. Only promise a non-Christian what you can biblically and *unconditionally* guarantee upon his coming to Christ. Let's say you decide to preach from Psalm 16. The psalmist speaks of God's earthly care with deep confidence in the afterlife for believers. This Old Testament passage meets the criteria laid out for preaching Old Testament passages evangelistically. Since it anticipates the coming of the Messiah, and Peter references Jesus from this psalm in the New Testament, we stand on firm ground in choosing it for an evangelistic sermon. However, we can't easily discern the author's *evangelistic* intent or a plain path from its content to a New Testament *evangelistic* theological framework.

So you seize the one-step-away, evangelistic *extent* of the text for unbelievers' consideration. You slide into an evangelistic stance and glide into the evangelistic invitation without glitches, because these promises of God are not given to those who don't know Jesus as their Savior. They are just one faith step away from salvation if they would not harden their hearts and instead hear God's voice. At the point of conversion, these powerful promises (cf. Psalm 16) could become true for them as well. Further, it is highly likely that the original hearers of this personal psalm included those who did not relate to YHWH by faith. Now, whatever happens, I will *not* promise that all a person's earthly problems will be solved, though that was the psalmist's eager anticipation. Even the psalmist's earthly problems were not all solved. All we can unconditionally guarantee is the immediate possession and assurance of eternal life if the unbeliever relates to Jesus as his Savior from sin, bringing in the features and benefits of the gospel.[7]

Again, the PS tactic does not technically make an evangelistic sermon, since the sermon focuses on the believer rather than the unbeliever. But the theme and thrust of the passage could lend themselves to an *unbeliever's* need of Christ in order to experience the text's features, privileges, and benefits to believers. That is, you explore the sermon's implications for the *non*-Christian embrace of Jesus, based on the reality of mixed audiences hearing the original text, along with how a nonbeliever may experience the Christian realities of the sermon. To move on to the evangelistic appendage, I often use a transition like this: "If you have not embraced the Lord Jesus as your Savior, nothing that I have said relates to you. The only way all I have spoken about can benefit you is for you to make a decision to welcome Jesus as your only God and Savior. If that is your desire, please listen carefully." I then go on to present the framework for salvation—God's nature/humanity's situation; Jesus's provision/the saving-faith response.

Ephesians 6:10–12

Let's consider this passage, because we have used it to help understand the Scripture Sculpture process in my previous book *Preparing Expository Sermons*. If you consult that book, you will see that I have already done much of the homework on this text for you. Here I append an evangelistic conclusion to a sermon given to believers (originally and today), turning that salvation-compliant text into an evangelistic sermon.

> Step 3—CPT: Putting on the whole armor of the Lord's strength enables us to stand against the schemes of the devil and to struggle against the system of the devil.
> Step 4—The Purpose Bridge: to motivate people to put on the armor of God's strength in their struggle against the devil
> Step 5—CPS (In raw expositional form, we can turn the purpose into the theme of the CPS—usually in the form of a question to begin with before we stylize and polish it further):
>
> Theme: Why Christians should put on the whole armor of God's strength
> Thrust: to stand against the devil's schemes
>   and
>   to struggle against the devil's system

I want to make the evangelistic turn. It will go something like this:

a. *Transition to evangelistic introductory need*: "God's strength against Satan is available only for those who know his Son. Satan plays a major role in your life (whether you realize it or not) if you don't personally know the Lord Jesus. If your conscience does not bother you when you do wrong, Satan is working in you. When you suppress your guilt, when you are afraid, when you rationalize your wrongs, it comes from Satan. If you would like the protection of God's strength in your life, you'll have to rightly relate to God."
b. *The evangelistic framework of God—Humanity*: "But you can't rightly relate to God because of the great spiritual distance between you and God." (Explain the moral distance.)
c. *The evangelistic framework of Jesus—Faith*: "God has bridged the distance, opened up the block between you and him, through the Lord Jesus." (Explain what Christ has done.)
d. *Evangelistic ending*: "Embrace him as the only God who saves you, for only he can give you his sovereign strength to stand up to Satan, to defeat Satan's designs on you for eternal death. Tell Jesus that you would like his salvation to steel you against Satan and that you are sorry for giving Satan a stronghold in your life by your sins. Invite the Lord Jesus to become your sovereign Savior, for he can become your sovereign strength. Trust the Lord Jesus to have paid the price of your sins, to have bridged the distance, and to have opened the way between you and God. Thank him for raising himself from the dead to prove that he can save you from your sins and from the schemes and systems Satan has built around you. Call on the Lord Jesus to be your only God and Savior."

The fact that the offer of victory against Satan is one step away from an unbeliever's realization permits us to make a winsome, bold, and urgent evangelistic connection to Jesus's salvation. Again and always, be careful that Jesus's adequacy for the non-Christian is only one step away from the theme or thrust of the text and sermon, or you'll be farther away from your text's authority than hermeneutically authorized or theologically sanctioned. Your sermonic authenticity will ring hollow because textual authority has been compromised for situational, pragmatic reasons.

Conclusion

Let's conclude these chapters on the method of preaching textual evangelistic sermons. May I suggest that you read them slowly and in sections, perhaps several times? Study the three samples of textual evangelistic preaching with dimensions and angles that may be new to you or peculiar to the texts themselves. Your stronger authority for a *textual* evangelistic sermon comes from passages for which you can establish an exegetical case for evangelistic intent or theological case for evangelistic content. The third but weaker evangelistic possibility—salvation-compliant texts—allows the original mixed group of hearers to share an audience trait with our audience today. Finally, some scriptural passages may be appended with evangelistic endings. However, a sacred compulsion to preach evangelistically cannot downplay the internal authenticity needed to confirm and affirm that you are faithful to the text of Scripture. Sacred compulsion can give you competence before unbelievers, but spiritual confidence in the text comes from using a text as intended. If the author could have attracted unbelievers in his audience to Jesus, you too can preach a non-evangelistic text in the hearing of unbelievers to attract them to Jesus's salvation. However, be very careful that you are not circumventing the author with interpretive gymnastics buttressed by raised volume, ardent fervor, and entertaining delivery when the textual, theological, or audience foundations are weak.

Action Step

Over your next evangelistic preaching opportunities, I'd like you to try your hand at the various kinds of textual evangelistic preaching outlined above. Below I'll suggest a text for you, and you come up with a message. If you preach that message and send the outline to proclamation@rreach.org, I'll send you a text version of my manuscript for mutual enhancement of preaching ministries. Send me some good illustrations too. I'm always looking for them, and upon reading this chapter, I realize it could have used some!

Textual Source	Critical Hermeneutical Factors	Suggested Homework Passage
Salvation-concentrated texts: textual intent	Author's purpose; explicit gospel framework; mixed audience	Luke 15:4–7
Salvation-connected texts: textual content	Implicit gospel framework; mixed audience	1 Timothy 2:4–6
Salvation-compliant texts: textual extent	Extrapolated connections; mixed audience	Matthew 7:24–27

7

TEXT-DRIVEN TOPICAL EVANGELISTIC PREACHING

> Any list of the ten sermons which have most decisively influenced world culture and society consists mostly if not entirely of topical sermons.
>
> —David Larsen, *The Anatomy of Preaching*

I was ushered into the U.S. consul's office in Monrovia, Liberia. The consul was a Sikh citizen of the U.S. importing general goods out of India to a war-ravaged "Christian" country. His staff were all Sikhs and Hindus who did not want anything to do with Christians, for they killed each other in tribal and ritual killings. Worshiping Jesus as his "heart God," he wanted a fellow Indian to make a case to his senior staff and relatives to also consider Jesus.

He brought them into his living room after office hours and publicly opened the meeting up to me, saying, "Tell us about Jesus." He wanted his colleagues and subordinates to hear about *Jesus*. Not about Christians, but about Jesus. For the next two hours, I preached Jesus, opened the floor for questions, guided the discussion, answered their questions, and eventually invited them to embrace the Lord Jesus as their only God and Savior. I liberally quoted our Lord's words but did not develop the sermon from one text. Neither did I cite the book, chapter, and verse to them. I pursued a topical evangelistic sermon.

Topical Preaching

Textual or topical? That choice is not as theologically significant as Calvinism vs. Arminianism! Yet it is a strategic and practical choice you have to constantly consider, whether you are preaching evangelistically or post-evangelistically.[1] The normal guideline is to use textual preaching for the steady feeding of your believing audiences and to use topical preaching more sparingly for sowing and reaping events. Of course, he who sows sparingly will reap sparingly! Earlier I noted that in textual preaching, a single text controls the central proposition and the development of the sermon. In topical preaching, the preacher controls the central proposition and the development of the sermon.

Another factor guides the textual versus topical choice as well. You can liberally utilize *textual* evangelistic preaching to reach people from Christian backgrounds, those with some exposure to the Bible who recognize its authority for the human situation. Usually done in churches, where the atmosphere is quite Christian, with singing, prayers, and offerings, textual evangelistic preaching expounds salvation from one text. Most often these settings assume a Christian worldview and especially some acknowledgment of the authority of the Bible in personal life.

Those who are not acquainted with the Bible or do not feel positive emotion toward it need exposure to the gospel through *topical* evangelistic preaching. Non-Christian audiences will feature both ignorance of Christian assumptions and apathy toward biblical truth. The farther away your audience is from a Christian worldview, the more topical preaching you pursue (even if you use various parts of the Bible for your sermon content and development). Once people come to salvation, nurture them with solid textual exposition.

Topical Evangelistic Preaching

A topical evangelistic sermon could pick a text-driven topic or an audience-driven topic.

Text-Driven Topic	Audience-Driven Topic
Single-text-driven topic	Existential or spiritual topic
Multi-text-driven topic	Intellectual or philosophical topic

Of course, it's one topic per sermon!

I suggest the following method in pursuing topical sermons. (Please consult appendix 13 in *Preparing Expository Sermons*.) I will explain and illustrate the single-text- and multi-text-driven topical sermons below.

Topical Exposition
1. Choose your topic.
2. Limit your topic.
3. Build your topic.
4. Preach your topic.

Allow me to apply the Scripture Sculpture process to the preparation of the topical evangelistic sermon.

Step 3: The Central Proposition of the Topic

In topical evangelistic preaching, you start with step 3 of the Scripture Sculpture process—a full statement of a theme and thrust of *your* choosing. The advantage of topical preaching is that you can pick a single word or concept theologically rampant in the Bible and turn it into a full sentence, a theme and thrust, the central proposition of the topic, before you expand it.

A topic is more than a title, a subject, or a theme. It's a full-sentence concept, a proposition, whether articulated or not. You don't want one word or one concept like "grace" unless you can state and develop that single word or concept in a full sentence. What exactly about grace are you going to talk about (theme), and then what are you going to say about it (thrust)? If you don't have a clear grasp of the concept, you won't be able to articulate it into a full sentence or proposition.

Further, a full-sentence statement of the concept will help you distinguish one topical sermon from another sermon you preach on the same subject (or theme). For example, take these two full sentences: (1) "The difference between Christianity and the religions of the world is grace." (2) "The difference between Christianity and other grace claims in the world is the cross." Though these two sentences both speak about the subject of grace, they feature two different topics that require two different sermons. Grace is a topic, but when you limit it by writing out a full sentence of theme and thrust, you have a central proposition to develop and preach. I will illustrate from the second proposition above.

Step 4: The Purpose Bridge

Take this full-sentence proposition of the topic to step 4, your purpose bridge: "to show the difference between Christianity and other *grace* claims in the world." Your purpose helps you limit the topic too. As was shown before in the move from the CPT (step 3) to the purpose bridge (step 4) and then to the CPS (step 5), turn your purpose into a question to get a theme for your sermon's central proposition.

Step 5: The Central Proposition of the Sermon

Step 5 will reveal what you are talking about, your theme (What is the difference between Christianity and other grace claims in the world?), and what you are going to say about it, your thrust (Christian grace is grounded in the cross). I would stylize, fashion, and design the question to "Is it really grace when God simply overlooks sin without paying its full penalty?" as the theme.

Step 6: Structure the Sermon

Build your topic around Scripture's answers (in text-driven sermons) or people's issues (in audience-driven sermons). A topical sermon *always* follows a multiple-complement thrust form. You will have two, three, four, or more points as needed for you to accomplish the purpose of your sermon—hopefully within the time allotted.

You can pursue one of two options in structuring multi-text topical sermons:

1. Choose Scriptures to develop your CPS—your sermon's topic (found in the theme and thrust sentence).
2. Outline the topic according to the Scriptures you pick.

OR

1. Outline the topic (developing the theme and thrust sentence).
2. Find Scriptures for each major part of the outline.

I must—yes, must—make a critical observation that will safeguard your topical sermon's textual authority and integrity. Please read this next sentence carefully. *In multi-text topical sermons (and therefore multi-point sermons), let each major point you find or develop be based on the central proposition of the text you chose to substantiate your theme.* In this way, you can preach a message that is intended in the texts even as you pick them for topical use. "It is important that the sermon expresses the *intended* message of [or in, not by or through[2]] the biblical text....The sermon must be authorized and shaped by the message of the text."[3]

So you'll have to come up with a CPT for the passage you'd like to use in your point for topical purposes (the process from steps 1–3 will become quicker with practice) and then compare it with the point you want to make out of the passage for your topical development. If the text's central proposition is sustained by your point, then you are safest. If your point is sustained by any part of the central proposition of your text, you are still safe. However, don't pick one word or pull one verse out of a text to arrive at your point. Topical preaching is often seen as easier (and less authoritative) than textual preaching, but it can be more difficult if you want to be careful with God's Word and not treat it like play clay. You can turn God's Word to an evangelistic purpose in a salvation-connected text if it doesn't carry an evangelistic purpose. And yes, you can twine its purpose evangelistically in a salvation-compliant text. But don't twist a text and choke it with your impulsive, time-bound need to preach something immediately or entertainingly that cannot be sustained by the central proposition of the text you choose. I will illustrate this guideline below on my sample topic.

Step 7: Preach the Sermon

A topical evangelistic sermon will feature all the good aspects of sermon creation, construction, and communication. (See chapter 6 in *Preparing Expository Sermons* for more on this.)

>Introduction
>>Attention
>>Need
>>Orientation to topic or theme
>>Purpose
>
>Subintroduction
>>Preview structure if deductive in form, or first point in an inductive development of your sermon
>>Introduce entire CPS in deductive sermon, or the full theme (not just your topic) in inductive development
>
>Transition to first point
>
>Body (Let your structure be uncomplicated and easy to remember. Use pedagogical devices—simple organization, creative rhythm, word choice, or alliteration—to help listeners remember your structure.)
>>I. First point. Again, in text-driven structure, use the SAVE (a) Point acronym.
>>>*State* the point.
>>>*Anchor* the point in your text.
>>>*Validate* your point from that text.
>>>*Explain* your point—textually and illustratively keeping your evangelistic purpose (step 3) in mind.

(a)pply the point evangelistically. In evangelistic sermons, there's no question that you must apply each major point right after you preach it.

Show how Jesus or the gospel addresses your point. Highlight any pertinent part of the theological framework of the gospel (God—Humanity distance/the Jesus—Faith bridge).

Cast or issue point-sensitive invitations.

II. Second point. The second point must be separately justified as equal in weight to the first point. You will have at least two points in topical sermons, for they always follow a multiple-complement sermon structure. Develop this point and more major points in the same way as point I above.

Conclusion

Review for the final time your CPS, your purpose, and how the purpose has been accomplished by Jesus in the points of the gospel.

Explain any part of the framework of the gospel (God—Humanity/Jesus—Faith) that has not been stressed (God's expectation, humanity's failure, Jesus's provision, faith's condition).

Bring sermon to a close with how the Lord Jesus or the gospel speaks to the theme and invite listeners to embrace Jesus as their only God and Savior.

Transition to invitation.

Invite listeners to trust the Lord Jesus as their only God and Savior (see chapter 10, "The Evangelistic Invitation").

Action Step

How about developing the topic I have introduced in the previous section—the difference between Christianity and other grace-claiming religions? You will need persistent prayer, awareness of your audience, theological astuteness, and intellectual engagement, especially if you just found out that there were other grace religions in the world. I've actually given you some answers in my stylized theme already.

Text-Driven Topical Evangelistic Preaching: Samples and Distinctions

Single-Text-Driven Topic

Usually in single-text-driven sermons—textual exposition—the preacher discovers the central proposition of the text, processes it through the purpose bridge to arrive at the central proposition of the sermon, and develops a sermonic structure that is compatible with the textual structure. However, in a topical sermon based on a single text, the preacher chooses his own theme and structure to develop the sermon. If the theme and structure of the sermon reflect the theme and structure of the text, then it is a textual exposition. If the preacher reads the text through his own theme and develops it according to his thoughts, then it is a topical exposition of a single text. Sometimes called "thematic exposition," this tactic is really topical exposition in the guise of textual exposition. The topic is biblically sound and theologically found, but the sermon is not an exposition of the central proposition of the text nor governed by the structure of the text. The preacher brings his own theme to the text, reads the text through his theme, and develops it regardless of the *grammatical* structure of the text. Let me illustrate the single-text-driven topical strategy from the all-time favorite verse of evangelists, John 3:16.

In the Scripture Sculpture process for textual exposition, step 2 (the structure of text) will yield a twofold grammatically determined structure:[4]

    I. The extent (or manner) of God's love for the world is seen in the sacrificial gift of his one and only Son (v. 16a).
    II. The motive of God's sacrificial love gift of his Son is to provide eternal life for all those who believe in him (v. 16b).

The text's theme is rather straightforward:

God's amazing love for the world

The text's thrust is twofold:

1. is found in the gift of his one and only Son
2. so people who believe on him may not perish but immediately possess eternal life

Instead of preaching the twofold structure of the text in textual exposition, I introduced my own theme based on the central proposition of the text. I explored the contours of God's great love from the angle of getting a jury to convict God of inadequately loving the world. It is a topical exposition of a theme embedded in the text, but it is developed topically from the text regardless of grammatical structure. I built a five-point case for the jury to consider from each major turn but not from the grammatical structure of the text.

I. God himself is the ultimate definition of love—"God."
II. God loved the world to the utmost degree[5]—"so loved the world."
III. God gave an unparalleled demonstration of his love—"that he gave his one and only Son."
IV. God's love makes a universal demand—"whoever believes on him."
V. God's love provides a unique destiny for all people—"shall not perish but have eternal life."

The freedom that *I* have claimed in order to develop this text according to how *I* perceive that it must be delivered must still meet the hermeneutical precaution and theological boundaries (mentioned in the previous chapter concerning salvation-compliant texts). Yet *I* selected the theme and developed the sermon according to how *I* decided it should be—a thematic sermon in topical evangelistic exposition.

Action Step

How about choosing a salvation-concentrated text or a salvation-connected text from which to develop *your own* (rather than the text's) sermonic theme and structure? Send me your work (proclamation@rreach.org), for I am constantly looking for new material.

Multi-Text-Driven Topic

Topical sermons usually follow the multi-text form.[6] (I present topical sermon preparation in a sizable appendix with appropriate safeguards in *Preparing Expository Sermons*, appendix 13.) In text-driven topical evangelistic preaching, you choose a topic applicable to unbelievers and find texts to develop your theme. As I said earlier, let each main point be sustained by the central proposition of the text from which it is drawn, in order to protect your text from your interpretive manipulations and textual machinations.

I expanded the biblical theme of Jesus as Shepherd to apply it to unbelievers so that they would come to him for salvation.

> I. God owns you like a shepherd owns his sheep—you are accountable to him (1 Pet. 2:25).
> II. God knows you like a shepherd knows his sheep—you are exposed to him (John 10:14).
> III. God cares for you like a shepherd cares for his sheep—you are valuable to him (Matt. 9:36).
> IV. God pursues you like a shepherd pursues his sheep—will you be found by him (Luke 15:4–7)?

Notice that I applied the topical metaphor only as I honestly could apply it directly to unbelievers. I could develop another entire topical sermon on Jesus as Shepherd of the believer (guides, guards, etc.), and I could expound on how the unbeliever is one step away from those privileges and benefits in a salvation-compliant way.

Notice also that each point is sustained by the central proposition of the text from which it is drawn. For example, point IV is based on the central proposition of Luke 15:4–7: "Like a good shepherd, Jesus pursues one lost sheep to rescue and return home with joy." I have chosen a part of the CPT that most suits my development of my topic, but that choice is obviously traceable to the central proposition of the text.

This Shepherd sermon is mine, not yours, so I can develop it from my awareness of biblical texts on this topic as well as my awareness of the audience's situation. Here were some audience factors I took into account:

- Some in my audience need to be accountable to God as the owner of their lives—hence "Jesus owns you."
- Some think they can hoodwink God, like they do their spouses—hence "Jesus *knows* you."
- Some hold that they are too lost—hence "Jesus *cares* for you."
- Some believe they need to be rescued—hence "Jesus *pursues* you."

I could add points to or subtract points from this talk as needed based on practical considerations, such as the length of the time available (one of the great advantages and weaknesses of topical sermons). As you gain experience, you'll learn how to control the theme of your topics as well as points within the topics. In fact, strong topical preachers are known by the quality of their topics and how they frame the theme and develop the thrust of the topical sermon.

Action Step

How about choosing a biblical topic appropriate to unbelievers and developing a quick outline? Send it to me (proclamation@rreach.org), and I'll enjoy learning from you.

Or find and evaluate a written topical evangelistic sermon. Study the preacher's sermon process, introduction, structure, and conclusion according to the principles proposed above. What can you learn from him? What could he have done better?

8

Audience-Driven Topical Evangelistic Preaching

"PEW RIGHTS? How do you spell it?"
"Just like it sounds: Pew rights."
"Do you mean, Rites? R-i-t-e-s?"
"No, I'm thinking about pew rights, as in civil rights."
"Never heard of them. Are you sure there are any?" [1]

—Roger E. Van Harn

The twenty-first century did not begin well, nor did it bode well, for the human race. Terrorism, wars, viruses, and tsunamis dominated news headlines worldwide. The entire world of opinion leaders, my audience, was troubled by thoughts on the problem of evil. However, God was opening up an annual global audience for me on prime-time secular television. What would I say to them? How could I link their experience and questions to a presentation, and possibly a proclamation, of the Lord Jesus Christ? Would I pursue a textual or topical message? That last issue was not a real question at all, for most of my audience did not hold to the Bible in personal authority or to Jesus as a plausible Savior. Would I be text-driven or audience-driven in my choice of topic? I chose the latter option, since most of my audience would not share my Christian worldview. I would have to incorporate pre-evangelistic subject matter and assume a pre-evangelistic style of delivery. Let me first address audience-driven topics and then take you to pre-evangelistic preaching as a finer shade of evangelistic preaching.

Audience-driven choices of topics arise from the needs of your audience—contemporary people who need Jesus's salvation. These are audience-driven needs, but the only preaching solution, of course, is text-based—the Lord Jesus Christ!

Text-Driven or Audience-Driven Topics

Factors	Text-Driven	Audience-Driven
Need	Shared worldview between preacher and audience	Worldview distance and dissonance between preacher and audience
Sources	The text as source: Bible-driven topics that apply to nonbelievers by way of embracing Jesus	The audience as source: some audience-driven topics addressed and anticipated in the Bible but only resolved by embracing Jesus
Sermon development—multiple thrusts to a single theme	Determined and/or developed by biblical texts available on a particular topic	Shaped to meet *their* issues—developed in view of audience's needs, values, beliefs, experiences, and behavior

Here's the distinguishing feature of audience-driven topical preaching: your choice of the topic *and* the development of the sermon (your structure) are not text-driven.

Why? Your sermon topic and structure are not text-based for a simple reason: some audiences don't hold the Bible in authority. When an audience shares the same worldview as the preacher, he may use phrases like "the Bible says" for points to take root, to make waves, and to incite response from the audience. You can definitely do that with multi-text topical sermons.

However, if preacher and audience do not share the same worldview, the preacher is left to find audience-driven topics and develop them in terms of audience categories and experiences via non-text-based presentation. You would use biblical concepts. You would normally not repeat, "The Bible says" to state or prove your point. That would be like a Muslim evangelist preaching, "The Koran, Sura 10, says" to prove his point to a Hindu or Christian audience, with no great advantage to his presentation.

Worldview matters much more than you might acknowledge. We operate not out of vacuums but from worldviews. A worldview is the comprehensive console that controls everything about a person—his virtues and values, his beliefs and behavior. One's worldview answers questions of origin (where did I come from?), identity (who am I?), meaning (why am I here?), destiny (where am I going?), and morality (what should I do?). While "not straightforwardly verifiable or falsifiable,"[2] a worldview functions to explain, evaluate, justify, integrate, and adapt to life.[3]

In contemporary cultures, the majority worldview can change within a generation. For instance, much was made of postmodernism both in the academy and among the intellectual elite in the last two decades of the twentieth century. Then came September 11, 2001, when Western postmoderns began to debate calling anything *universally* evil. Some defected back to the shredded and discarded philosophical underpinnings of undeconstructed modernism.

You can't even assume homogeneity of worldview at *church* anymore. Though churchgoers are likely to share a Judeo-Christian worldview, or they most likely won't be at church, you still can't take worldview affinity for granted. People who have rejected the Judeo-Christian worldview can still make sense of the preacher, for normally they know what they have rejected (it was formally proposed that a person who rejected the Christian worldview be called a "bright").[4] But when speaking to people outside the dominant Judeo-Christian worldview, you have to present the gospel in terms of their concepts and categories for understanding and assimilation. Worldview distance and dissonance between preacher and audience causes a misunderstanding of the message, not to mention a mistrust of the preacher. In topical evangelistic preaching, you can better address the misunderstanding problem.

How? By choosing audience-driven topics and developing your sermon in view of the audience's needs, values, beliefs, experiences, and behavior. Missionaries have long practiced communication principles and techniques across worldview, culture, and religion, often in one-on-one situations. Preachers also use these cross-cultural missions principles to overcome worldview distance in public and formal environments.

Topical sermons driven by audience needs can either be evangelistic or pre-evangelistic in form, stance, and nature (you can derive textual sermons from audience needs too).

Where? Where does one find audience-driven topics, topics that are also addressed and anticipated in the Bible but only resolved by embracing Jesus? One finds them in the breadth of human experience—whether needs, values, beliefs, experiences, or behavior. Actually, there is no limit to these starting points for launching a topical evangelistic sermon. God has built into every life and culture issues and needs that only Jesus can resolve. If you look, you'll find. Further, the nature of the Bible as adequate for issues that have not yet arisen, questions that have not yet been asked, and experiences that have not yet happened allows us to find sermonic correlation in the final movement of the topical sermon that results in Jesus as the God who saves sinners.

I know all this may sound complex, and I too wish we could merely quote the Bible for people's quick recognition of the truth. Yet it is not as complex as it seems, nor is it as simple as quoting the Bible to those of another worldview. Just like you must do hard work for any preaching, you must take additional audience factors into thoughtful and prayerful consideration as you prepare for unbelieving audiences. Remember, you are not alone in the process of preparing and delivering sermons. There is One who has gone ahead of you into the audience, and not only in the inspiration of Scripture. He is anxious to get his salvation message to those who do not share your worldview through you. So depend on him, exegete your audience,[5] prepare your sermon, keeping the "rights of the pew" for a clear and winsome presentation of the gospel to the audience in mind.

Pre-evangelistic Preaching

Pre-evangelistic preaching will always be topical in nature for the reasons just given. Since pre-evangelistic preaching is not just Christian moralism, it will name and point to Jesus. Christian moralism, the covert and surreptitious verbalization of Christian principles for the challenges of life, assumes that Christian virtues and values will assist people whether they turn to Christ or not. I place that stealth operation in the category of pre-evangelistic *presentation* but not in pre-evangelistic *preaching*. There we are helping people with a Christian way of doing life, and we hope that it will take. Our motive allows us to use the word *evangelism* in that pre-evangelistic witness. We give people some right words to live by in life, leadership, or love. We may point to Jesus as teacher without necessarily mentioning Christ as Savior. For example, while speaking to business leaders or athletes, we talk about the value of teamwork (a solid Christian value) or the need for integrity (a core Christian virtue).

No more is pre-evangelism an exotic exercise undertaken outside the church and meant only for sophisticated, antagonistic audiences. It is very likely that people in your own audience, invited by friends, perhaps, to a special evangelistic event, hail from diverse worldviews imbibed via academia, media, or relationships.

Now, what is the difference between pre-evangelistic and evangelistic preaching? They fall in a continuum of evangelism and were actually practiced by Paul where he did not quote Scripture at all when speaking to audiences that did not share his worldview (Acts 14, 17). To the Greek, he really became as a Greek, while he prolifically peppered his talks to Jewish audiences with Scripture. The fact of the matter is that people fall into varying spiritual *and* intellectual categories—pre-faith, pre-Christ, or even pre-God.[6] To pre-faith people, you preach evangelistically. To pre-Christ (and pre-God) people, you communicate pre-evangelistically.

Charts usually aid in grasping nuances, so I present one in appendix 3, which portrays types of evangelistic ministry, shades of evangelistic approaches, especially distinguishing pre-evangelistic, evangelistic, and post-evangelistic preaching. It would be very helpful for you to consult the chart now. You may read the full appendix later.

In pre-evangelistic preaching, we always pick audience-driven, salvation-compliant topics. Salvation-compliant topics, like salvation compliant texts, are one step away from an unbeliever's experience of Christian faith and blessings. We attach them to textual bases or theological reasons to make them serve an evangelistic purpose. Pre-evangelistic sermons often begin with *existential* entry points and problems to which Jesus is the solution if the root problem of sin is resolved. These problems are addressed in the Bible either by plain text or theological implication. They are issues that simply don't go away from the human situation.

Some audience-driven subjects belong to academic apologetics, but I prefer existential apologetics simply because most audiences are not asking theoretical questions (e.g., Does God exist? Did Jesus rise from the dead?) as their *first* questions. People ask existential questions (e.g., How do I fill the spiritual hole in my heart?[7]) to find order and meaning and resolution. I can always move from existential to philosophical levels of engagement.

Here I list some universal spiritual *needs* that lend themselves to audience-driven development and conclude with the Lord Jesus as the salvation (re)solution, because all these needs are rooted in sin and separation from God:

forgiveness
peace
stability
hope
afterlife
love
survival
wisdom

purpose
spiritual quest
demonic oppression (supernatural evil forces)

Below is a short list of widespread intellectual *questions* that can be seized for a salvation ending. These questions have been relatively stable over history, and you can find more subjects in theoretical apologetics books written by Christian philosophers and apologists.

Some Philosophical Questions
- What is the nature and existence of truth?
- Does God exist?
- What is the nature of God?
- What about the problem of evil?
- Is religion efficacious?

Some Scientific Questions
- Are miracles possible?
- How do you reconcile the religion versus science debates?

Some Jesus-Related Questions
- Why is Jesus God?
- Why is Jesus unique?
- Why is Jesus exclusive?
- Did Jesus rise from the dead?
- What destiny awaits those who have not heard about Jesus?

Some Bible-Related Questions
- Is the Bible reliable?
- Do the Bible and science conflict?

Here's a list of common existential *issues* that can be seized for a salvation ending in the final movement of your sermon:

- anxiety
- fear
- inner conflict
- happiness
- freedom
- satisfaction
- significance
- broken relationships
- loneliness
- restlessness
- sense of loss
- self-concept
- victimization
- inability to change
- adventure
- sense of limitations
- direction in life

In these ideas, questions, and issues, you are looking for the audience's underlying spiritual needs and the ways they attempt to resolve or address them without Christ. Their needs and attempts furnish topics and illustrations for preaching evangelists (see the upcoming chapter on support material). The comprehensive nature of the Bible allows a thousand entrées into the nonbeliever's issues and needs for which Christ is the only answer. If Jesus Christ is placed in human hearing, he enters the human heart in a hundred different ways. Ask a few people what drew them to salvation, and you'll find various creative ways in which God showed them their need for Christ. He uses the entire spectrum—broken hearts over sin all the way to broken hearts over relationships—in order to bring people to a realization of their ultimate spiritual need, with salvation clinched by our presentation of the gospel.

You'll find entry points for topical choices and illustrations in contemporary beliefs and events. These beliefs and events are what your audience is thinking and talking about. Therefore, they become fodder for audience-driven, text-based, or theologically reasoned, topical pre-evangelistic sermons.

A cursory look at my newspaper headlines today evokes the following topics:

> "Doctors Overlook Depression, Even in Themselves"
> "Search for Life Out There Gains Respect, Bit by Bit"
> "Practicing Patience, A Virtue of Some Urgency"[8]

If I were preaching on these subjects, I would see if I could attach these audience-driven topics to textual bases or theological reasons in order to achieve evangelistic finales. With evangelistic experience and an observant eye, you'll catch topics that possess evangelistic potential. For instance, "depression" as a topic attaches to a *textual base*: Jesus's claim to give people a joyful rather than depressing existence (John 10:10). And the news item can work as an opening or concluding illustration, or it could conceivably help in developing the points of the sermon.

The topic of "the search for life out there" attaches to a *theological reason*: the yearning to make contact with extraterrestrial intelligence as part of our search to find God or to displace him. Then we can proceed to how Jesus brought God from "out there" to "in here," perhaps attaching the theological reason to John 1:1–18, or even John 1:18. Again, the news item can work as an opening or concluding illustration or help in developing the points of the sermon.

Ensure that the topic from the text you are attaching to the audience-driven need is founded and derived from its central proposition. In this way, you will not be taking some obscure part of the text to make your point with your audience. Always remember, the central proposition of the text (step 3) is derived from the text's structure (step 2) as the safeguard from your penchant to make the text say whatever you want it to mean.

Pre-evangelistic preaching points to the Lord Jesus, mentions his name, and offers his salvation for the human situation. The PS principle of *textual* preaching, a salvation-appended text and sermon, places the evangelistic twist at the end of the sermon's *conclusion*.

In a pre-evangelistic sermon, the evangelistic twist always arrives as the last movement of the *body* of the sermon: Jesus is the answer to the human dilemma the audience faces as a result of human sin.

I introduced the concept of a theologically reasoned attachment a moment ago. You may not find a proof text to address an audience need, but you could find a theologically reasoned attachment to the need. Of course, theological reasons are built on textual grounds, from a variety and repetition of texts that permit more certain theological conclusions by sound hermeneutical and theological method.[9] While many theological matters are deeply debated, the substitutionary work of Christ and his resurrection for the sake of human salvation through faith alone is not a divisive issue among the wide spectrum of evangelical Christians. So if you can find issues that people face or needs that people have that can be attached to the salvation sequence via theological reasons, your evangelistic underpinnings are firm and your evangelistic offerings will be uncomplicated.

For example, I developed a series of evangelistic radio talks on the audience-driven need of freedom. Freedom is viewed as both a human right and a personal preference, with spiritual freedom resonating in the human soul, along with other kinds of freedom—political, economic, or religious. Of course, this human need of freedom can be attached to many textual bases and theological arguments.

Here's a sample of topics on life as a prison. (Visit our evangelistic website, www.rameshrichard.com, for sample talks to discern themes and thrusts.) I point to the Son who makes people free. As in apologetics-slanted pre-evangelistic sermons, I identify their heart yearnings or faulty premises or I remove their objections and clarify Jesus's claims to provide specific answers. Look below to find an outline for a short sermon series, with text-based, theological arguments in pointed brackets. The numbered items are individual talks.

1. Life Is a Prison—Introduction

<<Miniseries: Human Existence Itself as Captivity>>

2. Body Prison

3. Soul Prison
4. Spirit Prison
5. Mind Prison
6. Will Prison
7. Heart Prison
8. Conclusion to Series

<<Miniseries: Human Sinfulness as Imprisonment>>
9. Sin Prison—Introduction
10. Inherited Sin
11. Personal Sin
12. Imputed Sin
13. Kingdom of Sin

<< Miniseries: Satan as Jail Warden>>
14. Satan Prison

<< Miniseries: Law and Good Works as a Spiritual Locker>>
15. Law Prison 1
16. Law Prison 2
17. Law Prison 3
18. Good Works Prison

<< Miniseries: Death as a Life Sentence>>
19. Death Prison 1
20. Death Prison 2
21. Death Prison 3
22. Death Prison 4

<< Miniseries: Superstition as Incarceration>>
23. Superstition Prison 1
24. Superstition Prison 2
25. Superstition Prison 3

<< Miniseries: Fear as Captivity>>
26. Fear Prison 1
27. Fear Prison 2

<< Miniseries: Anxiety as a Labor Camp>>
28. Anxiety Prison 1
29. Anxiety Prison 2
30. Anxiety Prison 3
31. Anxiety Prison 4

<< Miniseries: **Meaninglessness as a Penitentiary**>>

32. Meaninglessness Prison 1
33. Meaninglessness Prison 2
34. Meaninglessness Prison 3
35. Meaninglessness Prison 4
36. Meaninglessness Prison 5

<< Miniseries: Specific Shackles>>
37. Despair Prison
38. Doubt Prison
39. Bad Habits Prison
40. Wealth Prison
41. Boredom Prison
42. Success Prison
43. Bitterness Prison
44. Superficiality Prison

<< Miniseries: Guilt as Imprisonment>>
45. Guilt Prison 1
46. Guilt Prison 2

<< Miniseries: Review and Finale>>
47. Freedom Concepts
48. Freedom—Grand Finale

Back to my opening comments in this chapter about a global audience of leaders frustrated by evil personally, intellectually, or vicariously. I developed a sermon entitled "Unmasked: Facing the Mystery of Evil." In audience-driven topical sermons, the text you study (roughly akin to steps 1–3 of the Scripture Sculpture process) is the human situation itself. That is, while pursuing an audience-driven topical sermon, you begin with contemporary existence as your text and context. You exegete culture by observing, interpreting, and applying culture for evangelistic purposes. Instead of beginning with the biblical text (you always begin with a biblical worldview), you begin with a human "text," which provides the questions people are asking, the issues people are facing, the premises people are assuming, and the consciences people are ignoring, to provide the topic you will turn into a theme and thrust (the central proposition of the topic). The audience-driven topic (step 3) started in audience-driven terms (steps 1 and 2) resulted in an audience-driven proposition (step 5) and was structured with audience-driven movements (step 6), but it ended with the Lord Jesus—the (re)solution that is not audience driven.

I had to have a clear purpose (step 4) for my sermon: to show Jesus as the God who experienced comprehensive human pain so that humans can experience the hope of an eternity without pain. And of course, I had to have a theme and thrust based on what I observed, interpreted, and applied in the human context of extreme pain worldwide. Here is mine.

Step 5: Central Proposition of the Sermon

> Theme: How can we experience hope in an earthly life filled with all kinds of pain?
> Thrust: By embracing Jesus as the God who gained victory over the roots of pain for our eternity

Then comes my outline (step 6)

> Introduction
> Body
>> First Sermonic Movement
>>> I. Evil unmasks who we are as humans.
>>>> A. We are not animals—we experience intellectual pain.
>>>> B. We are not machines—we experience moral pain.
>>>> C. We are not demons—we experience emotional pain.
>>>> D. We are not angels—we experience physical pain.
>>>> E. We are not God—who doesn't experience any pain!
>>> Second Movement (I said earlier that the last movement of the body of the pre-evangelistic sermon always ends up with Jesus as the (re)solution. Jesus continues to dominate your conclusion and invitation. In this talk, I actually moved into a miniature multi-text-driven topi-

cal sermon. You can focus on one aspect of Jesus that relates to the gospel and make the most of it for your presentation. Here is how I pursued my second and final movement.)

II. Evil unmasks who God is—the Lord Jesus.
   A. Jesus experienced intellectual pain (scripturally supported but not cited or quoted).
   B. Jesus experienced moral pain (scripturally supported but not cited or quoted).
   C. Jesus experienced emotional pain (scripturally supported but not cited or quoted).
   D. Jesus experienced physical pain (scripturally supported but not cited or quoted).
   E. But he overcame pain and gave us an assured hope of a pain-free environment for eternity (scripturally supported but not cited or quoted).

Conclusion

Offer or Invitation (The salvation ending of this audience-driven sermon will differ according to audience. If a pre-evangelistic close is needed, I would *offer* them Jesus. If an evangelistic mode is appropriate, I'd *invite* them to embrace the Lord Jesus.)

Action Step

1. I didn't develop the patience concept from the third newspaper headline listed on page 143 in this chapter. How would you use the concept of patience to attach an audience-driven need to either a textual or a theological base? And then how would you move on to an evangelistic finale?
2. Find ten topics from this week's news (via newspaper, Internet, television), record them in some way (I usually tear them out of newspapers), write out a topic heading under which they can be filed and explored, and jot down your immediate thoughts on how to attach the topic to evangelism. For example, yesterday I read about a con man who died at age thirty-nine having conned the elite of New York into thinking he belonged to them. I wrote a note on the paper cutting, "Death—the only thing he couldn't con!"
3. If you don't have one, start an "Evangelistic Topics" file in which to keep your findings. You will consult this file every time you need to prepare a topical evangelistic sermon or write a book like this one.

Part 4

Special Issues

9

SUPPORT MATERIALS

Illustrating the Evangelistic Sermon

> There is no such thing on earth as an uninteresting subject; the only thing that can exist is an uninterested person.
>
> —G.K. Chesterton

Have you ever been caught in a poorly lit and crowded space, wanting to get out? Public speaking, especially evangelistic preaching, without adequate support material and appropriate illustrations causes that anxious feeling for audiences. They need some relief, a revolving door, so they can go out and come in as needed. Caught on the inside, they can see the light outside, but the revolving door seems to be stuck. Or there's activity inside that invites participation, but the door panels can't be budged. But when the revolving door operates smoothly, they get in and out as needed. When there's freedom of access and flow of activity, they don't even notice the door.

Effective illustrations are like well-oiled and easily operated revolving doors. You know when they are not working, because your information doesn't flow through to your audience. They wear quizzical looks. You can feel the disconnect. They give you every possible nonverbal cue that you are on a different, even an opposing, side of the presentation. You can't wait to finish. They can't wait to leave. You have indulged in the abstract idea, the novel truth, a rival Savior, without enough good support material for them to access the light, to breathe the fresh air, to join the action. Your points are stuck either going in or coming out. You need support material strong in nature and number for good communication, especially for effective evangelistic preaching. Your illustrations are going to carry your point into their hearts and draw them to a serious consideration of the gospel.[1] Illustrations connect the mind, the emotion, and the spirit, but more so, they influence the hearer's heart toward decision—the goal of evangelistic preaching.[2]

Illustrations Needed!

An evangelistic sermon desperately needs illustrations—and in greater number and of higher quality than post-evangelistic sermons. Our Lord and his Word profusely employ profound illustrations—story, narrative, humor, questions, even one-liners—to communicate truth. Illustrations help the audience avoid misunderstanding content, distraction in thought, tedium in active listening, and a quick disposal of truth.[3]

Unbelievers (and believers) better remember and greatly benefit from a speaker who salts and peppers his talks with illustrations. Clear understanding of content forms the basis for acceptance or rejection of the gospel. It is better for the listeners to understand and reject your point than accept it without understanding it.

Your illustrations provide staying power for serious subjects such as the holiness of God, personal sin, the uniqueness of Jesus, and the exclusive condition of faith. They also provide relief for the audience (and you) during the intensity of the proclamation. Illustrations, especially from personal life, authenticate your humanness. A vulnerable preacher is a believable preacher.

Generously sprinkle your evangelistic sermons with a variety of illustrations to enable understanding, retention, and appropriation of truth for all your listeners. People who learn verbally differ from those who learn graphically, and some exhibit multiple learning styles.[4] So go about finding, storing, and retrieving illustrations that enhance your evangelistic preaching.

There are many kinds of illustrations. Most books on preaching, rhetoric, and communication will list them for you. I borrow a summary list from an older source that is rather complete:

Kinds of Illustrations
figures of speech
analogy
allegory
fable
parable
historical allusion
biographical incident
personal experience
anecdote[5]

While many kinds of illustrations add variety to your sermons, all illustrations should exhibit the following two characteristics.

Clear and often concise. Illustrations should be clear. They should not need additional explanation when they *are* the additional explanation for your sermon. You need to know your audience well enough to use illustrations that will not confuse them. You shouldn't need to force your point. Clarity also means concreteness, so you don't illustrate ideas with ideas, abstraction with abstraction, concepts with concepts. Indeed, illustrations make the ideas and concepts concrete. Appeal to the listeners' senses and imaginations, and let them vicariously live the illustration.

Illustrations should also be concise. Make them as short as possible to explain your point, to make yourself clear, and to accomplish your purpose.

Correct and usually current. Illustrations must be correct, both theologically and historically. Since illustrations can take your audience down their own trails, you have to prevent theological misinterpretation by making sure your point sticks.

You want your illustrations to be theologically correct but also historically correct. In one illustration, I mixed up the two Roosevelts (American presidents) because I had not done enough homework. Find the right information and keep from embellishment and forced connections when you are working on a true story. Tell the story as is, and make the distinctions and connections as necessary.

In evangelistic sermons, you want to use as many *current* illustrations as possible—current issues, current stories, current problems, current language, current values. Remember, non-Christian audiences do not normally possess the theistic, biblical framework to rightly process your illustrations. Contemporary events will help break the communication distance between you and them and show them examples from the real world as they presently know it, giving your sermon an immediacy and relevance.

So your illustrations should always be clear and correct, often concise, and usually current.

Action Step

Since I am a believer (and user) of big dictionaries, and since you may not have access to the old book just cited, look up the words in the kinds of illustrations listed above (p. 153) in your dictionary and write out their definitions. You'll even find illustrations in the exercise, but you'll learn the art of *illustrating* in studying the science of illustration.

Illustrations Explained!

Illustrations illustrate. How redundant is that? At the risk of mundane repetition (which illustrations help evade), I emphasize again that illustrations are not added as padding to elongate a sermon or as diversion to keep the audience amused. Illustrations illuminate, enlighten, or throw light on a truth so people can distinguish it, comprehend it, and in preaching, receive it. Or better, illustrations

Support Materials

help you accomplish the evangelistic purpose of your sermon (step 4) in impact-filled ways. If they don't help accomplish that purpose, you are using illustrations for some other reason—probably to entertain or to fill time.

Illustration is only one type of support material, though it is the most recommended and used type of support material for contemporary audiences. Other support materials include fact citation (54.613 percent of all statistics are made up on the spot) and personal testimony (lends credibility but not certainty to your point as having been confirmed in life's laboratory). While we focus on contemporary audiences, audiences across culture and history share a human trait of learning through events and experiences, directly or vicariously.[6] Too, witness the cross-cultural need for news items and the presence of parables and proverbs across histories. Present-day audiences are oriented toward story in sight and sound in addition to verbal instruction. Today's listeners multitask and multiengage with the speaker. Illustrations engage the audience (whether they entertain or not).[7] Illustrations and other support material in evangelistic sermons include humor and use visual support as needed.

Humor disarms the audience and can turn the brick wall into a revolving door to let you and your thoughts into their hearts and minds. Humor increases audience connectedness and helps people remember your points.[8] Also, there are different kinds of humor, and there is even a subtle logic to humor (for an interesting exercise, look up "humor" on your search engine or consult sources on the serious study of humor). While working on a sermon addressing death and the afterlife, I came across the story of the man who hoped and prayed that there wasn't an afterlife. Then he realized there was a contradiction involved there and merely hoped that there wasn't an afterlife.

Visual support that enhances oral communication could be as natural as appropriate gesturing or could involve more sophisticated graphics like clips from movies. I remember illustrating the ontological status of evil as a parasite by tearing a hole right in the middle of a good piece of paper. Many people commented that that visual helped them understand how evil does not have an independent status on its own and could not be called a thing in itself. Therefore,

God need not be the cause of evil, since he created only all things that exist in and by themselves.

Or in visually illustrating the afterlife, I make the point more dramatic. I bring in an urn that looks like it could contain the ashes of the dead. I talk about how the Japanese are getting away from the custom of placing the ashes of deceased loved ones under gravestones or scattering them in remote areas and oceans. Bereaved families now increasingly look for alternatives.

> On Dec. 20, 1999, the ashes of people, 10 of them Japanese, were launched on board a three-stage rocket known as Taurus. Seven grams of ashes were placed in lipstick-sized capsules and installed in the tip of the rocket.
>
> The satellite entered orbit at 250 kilometers above the earth and would stay there for between one and slightly more than 10 years. Eventually, the satellite will re-enter the Earth's atmosphere, burning up, and looking like a shooting star for the rest of us.
>
> Nine people attended the launch, including friends and families of the deceased.
>
> One capsule of ash was that of a 28-year-old Hokkaido policeman who died after being hit by a car while on traffic control duty. His family said by burying him in space, they liked to think of him riding around in the heavens on his beloved white motorbike, then turning into a shining star.
>
> Another man sent his wife's ashes into space because after visiting 41 countries, the couple had hoped to go on a space trip together.[9]

The sad humor of these attempts to cope with the afterlife is balanced in the sermon by the seriousness of bringing in an urn that could actually contain ashes.

Action Step

Look for humorous sources (maybe the Internet or *Reader's Digest*—but go back about a year, for some of your listeners likely subscribe to the magazine as well). For your next evangelistic sermon, come up with one creative idea for visual presentation. It could be as simple as a single theme graphic for your outline using presentation software, a graphic for your central proposition on a bulletin page with an outline your audience can fill out, or a physical prop to add visual support to oral communication.

In *Preparing Expository Sermons*, I have suggested three questions to help you see the need for illustrations.[10] As you write out and absorb your sermon for the preaching event, ask these questions:

- *The correlation question* (to help them understand): What illustration will meet the need for additional explanation of a particular point?
- *The credibility question* (to help them believe): What illustration (or part of it) will help the audience seek, believe, and accept the truth of my point?
- *The claim question* (to help them proceed): What illustration will help the audience explore the implication and application of the point to their lives?

Let's say you are in the final movement of your sermon. You have presented your conclusion and are about to head into the invitation. I think the following rather popular evangelistic illustration meets the criteria of the three questions introduced above.

A wealthy man and his son loved to collect works of art. They had in their collection works ranging from Picasso to Raphael and Rembrandt. When the Vietnam war broke out, the son was drafted and sent to fight in 'Nam. He was very courageous and died in battle. The father was notified and grieved deeply for his only son.

About a month later, a young lad appeared at the door to his house and said, "Sir, you don't know me, but I am the soldier for whom your son gave his life that fateful day. He was carrying me to safety when a bullet struck him in the heart. He died instantly. He used to often talk about you and your love for art. Here's something for you," he added, holding out a package. "It is something that I drew. I know I am not much of an artist, but I wanted you to have this from me as a small measure of memory and thanks."

It was a portrait of his son, painted by the young man. It captured the personality of his son. The father's eyes welled up with tears as he thanked the young man for the painting. He offered to pay for the picture, but the man replied, "Oh! No, sir. I could never repay what your son did for me. It is my gift to you."

The father hung the portrait over his mantel and showed it proudly to all his visitors along with all of the great works of art he possessed. Some time later, the old man died. As decreed in his will, his paintings were all to be auctioned. Many influential and rich people gathered together, excited over the prospect of owning one of the masterpieces.

On a platform nearby also sat the painting of his son.

The auctioneer pounded his gavel. "Let us start the bidding with the picture of his son. Who will bid for this picture?" There was silence.

A voice shouted from the back, "Let us skip this one. We want the famous masters."

But the auctioneer persisted. "Ten dollars, twenty dollars, what do I hear?"

Another voice came back angrily, "We didn't come here for this. Let's have the Picassos, the Matisses, the van Goghs."

Still the auctioneer persisted. "The son. Anyone for the son? Who'll take the son?"

Finally a quivering voice came from the back. It was the longtime gardener of the house. "I'll take the son for ten dollars. I am sorry, but that's all I have."

"Ten dollars once, ten dollars twice, anybody for twenty dollars? Sold for ten dollars."

"Now let's get on with the auction," said a wealthy art aficionado sitting in the front row.

The auctioneer laid down his gavel and spoke. "I am sorry, but the auction is over."

"But what about the other paintings? The masters?"

"The auction is over," said the auctioneer. "I was asked to conduct the auction with a stipulation, a secret stipulation that said that only the painting of the son would be auctioned. Whoever bought that painting would inherit the entire estate, paintings and all. The one who took the son gets everything."

The correlation question helps the audience understand—You must receive the Son, though he may not seem to be the most attractive alternative for your salvation. *The credibility question* helps them believe—*I* haven't set the exclusive condition. God has set the condition of embracing his Son. *The claim question* helps them proceed with response—"Will you take the Son?" The gardener had to pay ten dollars to buy the portrait. At this point, clarify the claim. The gardener in the story bought the son's picture for ten dollars. We can't buy salvation at all. We don't even have the ten dollars. God's Son has made the provision for whatever we needed for salvation if we would only receive him. It would be like the auctioneer offering the picture for free and no one wanting it, though people were willing to pay the price for the masters. In your case, you don't have anything with which to buy the Son. The Son comes to you free if you are willing to receive him. He who takes the Son gets everything.

Illustrations Sighted!

One of the evidences of God's involvement in your preaching comes from his provision of illustrations for your sermonic needs. Since he is more anxious to communicate his Good News than you are, and he knows how limited you are in effectively delivering his truth, he provides illustrations along the way as you pray and look for them. In fact, I wrote in my prayer journal this morning that he will furnish the illustrations I need for this chapter to show his support of my writing endeavors! After all, what good is a chapter on illustrations without illustrations? As you prepare sermons, you'll find a heightened sensitivity to the themes, thrusts, and topics that need illustrative reinforcement. Rest assured, for God *will* place illustrations in your path for you to find and use.

Interested persons, as our chapter's opening quote implies for preaching, find and use interesting subjects and make them interesting. You can sight illustrations everywhere, literally everywhere, *if you look for them.* I was in a wreck recently, and I had to leave my car at the shop for nearly three weeks. The rental car agency put me in a Nissan Maxima SE. I suddenly saw many Nissans, Nissan

Maximas, and Nissan Maxima SEs all over the place. Your need and desire to sight illustrations, and illustrations of a particular kind, will increase your chances of finding them. You can find illustrations if you look for them in circumstances, conversations, media (news, entertainment, other events)— wherever. For instance (that's a good transition phrase for illustrations), knowing that I would need a new, clear, and powerful illustration on substitution, God provided me one in a magazine last night. I ripped out the page, wrote initial thoughts on it, brought it to my study, filed it in my evangelistic illustrations folder, and hope to use it later in this chapter.

> **Action Step**
>
> Sources of illustrations include *personal* life, *someone else's* life, *everyone's* life or *no one's* life. I'd like you to look at your last sermon, evangelistic or not, and classify the illustrations you used. From what sources did you derive those illustrations? Was there enough variety, or did personal life dominate the talk? Did you use too much cultural or racial history (someone else's life) to support your points to an audience of a different history who couldn't connect with those accounts? In your next evangelistic sermon, intentionally salt your talk using all four sources of illustrations.
>
> If you have access, discipline, and time, peruse the Internet to garner one or many illustrations. If you type in just the main words or phrases of your central proposition or main points, your search will yield huge amounts of information.

Illustrations Saved!

Perhaps you thought *saved* was an evangelistic term. Recording and retrieving illustrations takes effort and discipline. "The strongest memory is weaker than the faintest ink," goes a Chinese proverb. I have lost hundreds of illustrations for not having recorded them in the middle of the night, or during a shower, or while driving. Consequently, I have had to develop both the inclination and the mechanism to see and store them.

Developing the desire to find illustrations has been easier than implementing a system for retrieving them once recorded. Yet I attempt to use every recording device I have to save illustrative material—

Support Materials

writing in a journal, scribbling on napkins, tearing out newspapers, slowly entering information by thumb or stylus into my PDA. I place evangelistic illustrations and prompters (illustrations prompt additional illustrations by associative thoughts) alphabetically into burgeoning files entitled "evangelistic illustrations" in front of my evangelistic sermon files. Good stewardship of your calling, your gifting, *and* your job depends on illustrations. So don't miss out on them.

Action Step

Think through a system for recording and retrieving illustrations. I suggest starting a file—a hardcopy folder or a folder in your word processing program (documents/sermons/illustrations/evangelistic)—and storing them there. Consider further subheadings, and start your first entries today. You may never use an illustration you found and saved, but you never know when you'll need it or get to use it. If you have developed a creative way of storing and salvaging illustrations, let me know. Not only will I benefit from it, but I might also share it in a future edition of this book and give you credit! Better yet, I will pass it on to thousands of pastoral leaders worldwide through our networks. Recording and retrieving illustrations may even be classified as a spiritual discipline, since sermon preparation is a spiritual discipline for preachers.

Illustrations Exploited!

An evangelistic sermon *exploits* illustrations to their highest advantage. People in general and unbelievers especially need the power of the story to introduce, clarify, and reinforce your preaching at every point. You enter the doors of their hearts with illustration, lodge there for a while in conversation, and come back out as you reinforce truth. Illustrations generally follow this sequence:

Sequencing Illustrations

State the point that needs illustration.
    (Forward transition—enter revolving door—to the illustration.)
Illustrate.
    (Return transition—reenter revolving door—to the point that needs illustration.)
State (reinforce or repeat) the point.

There are few variations from this sequence, although an opening illustration may begin with the illustration rather than the point. Let's say you are working on John 4 (a salvation-concentrated text), where Jesus refers to himself as the source of living water (v. 10), in the third movement of the body of the sermon:

> III. Jesus offers himself as living water for your thirst. (You would illustrate how we need water for spiritual thirst, just like we need water for physical thirst.)
>   A. Jesus's water of life is *plentiful*. (You would illustrate this point, and could do so by describing the lack of drinking water in weaker economies—the two billion who are dying for water.)
>   B. Jesus's water of life is *pure*. (You would illustrate this point too. I do it this way):

The point: If water is not pure, it's not good for you even if it is available in plenty.

Forward transition to illustration: I have seen plentiful water but not potable water in weaker economies.

Illustration: Dipankar Chakraborti sends holiday greeting cards to fellow scientists with photographs of arsenic-poisoned villagers, their skin covered with ghastly lesions and patches of decay, reading, "Hey, scientist, Don't you have some duty to these people?" The problem is that tests of the water supply indicate that more than twenty million villagers in Bangladesh and the Indian state of West Bengal have been drinking from tube wells sunk into an aquifer that is naturally tainted with harmful levels of arsenic. All four millions wells were part of a safe-water program financed by the government of Bangladesh and charitable groups, principally UNICEF. No one had tested the water for arsenic before sinking the cylinder wells into the ground. And while the project saved many people from deaths caused by bacteria present in the surface water, it was poisoning others.[11]

Return transition to the point: What good is water that is available in plenty but poisons you?

The point: Jesus's water is available in plenty for you, but it doesn't poison you. It gives you life, pure life—*pura vida*, as the Costa Ricans would say it—with a supply of pure water that will never run dry.

Actually, it is possible that in a *topical* evangelistic sermon, the illustrations influence the development of the sermon into the major points. The truth the illustration points to plays the final role, makes the last point.

> The point of the already-chosen illustration
>   (Forward transition to the illustration)
> Illustrate
>   (Return transition to the point of the illustration)
> Reinforce the point

I once developed a topical pre-evangelistic talk called "The Maze of Life." I divided it into three points before introducing and offering Jesus in the fourth.

> I. Life is an enigma—you can't understand it.
> II. Life is a mystery—you can't explain it.
> III. Life is a puzzle—you can't solve it.
> IV. There is One who can help you understand the enigma of life, explain the mystery of life, and solve the puzzle of life forever.

However, I chose and developed these points from the illustrations I had already selected to create the *need* for each point, justify its distinct validity, and confirm the point along the way. For example (by the way, "for example," is a good transition phrase, but the phrase "by the way" may not be so good), this is how I worked our illustration:

> I. Life is an enigma—you can't understand it.

The point of the already chosen illustration: Life can be an enigma to us.

Forward transition to the illustration: I found the archetypal enigmatic life when my family and I waited in long lines, ambled up cobblestone walkways, and climbed steep, narrow staircases in a castle in southern Germany.

Illustration: King Ludwig II of Bavaria was a reclusive romantic. He is a still beloved "mad king" born about 150 years ago (August 25, 1845). Over five thousand books have been written about him, as well as plays, films, poems, and dances. Neuschwanstein is the castle he built "to embody his extravagant visions." Indeed, this castle is so much like a fairy tale that it was adopted by Walt Disney as the model for the castle of the Magic Kingdom in Disneyland. Ten thousand visitors visit the Neuschwanstein castle every day. The castle is a mass of pinnacles and towers, with only fifteen rooms completed out of the planned eighty rooms.

The news reporter who wrote about Ludwig's 150th birthday presents the king's entire life as an enigma. Synonyms for this enigmatic life are *royal enigma, tragic mystery, tragic beauty*, and *melancholic solitude*. While young people admire him for his independent spirit, "older people are fascinated with the whole tragic mystery of his life and death." Ludwig considered this world "a crude world." As the years passed, Ludwig withdrew into melancholic solitude, sleeping during the day and spending his nights listening to private recitations of poetry or racing through the moonlit countryside in a sleigh. He said he detested "the applause of the masses" and said, "No! No! I can't come out of my shell—not ever again." The Bavarian parliament declared him insane. The forty-one-year-old king was indignant and went to a retreat near Munich. Three days later his body was pulled from a nearby lake. Most likely, he committed suicide. There are some who argue that he was murdered, a victim of palace intrigues.

One thing is true about King Ludwig II of Bavaria, says the reporter. He is an enigma, because Ludwig wrote, "I want to remain an eternal enigma to myself and the world."[12]

Return transition to the point: Like King Ludwig II, we can be enigmas not only to ourselves but also to others.

Reinforce the point: The problem of life as a maze crops up when we are enigmas to ourselves (remember, "life is a maze" is my overall theme). Why do we consider life an enigma, a perplexity? Why do we feel baffled? How can we find a way to understand life? Hang on for a bit, and I'll give you some direction.

The transition to the second major point: We find that life is not only an enigma, it is also a mystery—an unsolvable mystery.

> II. Life is a mystery—you can't solve it (I had another illustration of life's a mystery to develop this second point . . . and so on to the third point).

Action Step

I'd like you to practice the sequence of exploiting illustrations to their maximum potential for your sermon purpose. Develop your points and transitions, keeping the audience in mind so they will get the most out of your illustrations. In fact, look over one of your illustrations from your last preaching event to see if you have followed the revolving door analogy for effective illustrations.

Illustrations Positioned!

In any sermon, but especially in an evangelistic sermon, you need illustrations at the following turns of the sermon.

Introduction: Do not begin a sermon, especially an evangelistic sermon, without an introduction. Think about that comment for a moment. Is it possible to begin without an introduction? No, but I know some preachers who come close to doing that! They begin the sermon, mimicking not a plane's takeoff but a firecracker that suddenly shows up—and blows up. Your illustration launches your sermon. A good opening illustration will explicitly or implicitly contain many ingredients of a good introduction: getting attention, raising need, orienting theme, and indicating purpose.

Conclusion: Your conclusion lands the plane. You'll need a powerful landing (not a crash) to summarize, clarify, and climax your sermon. Often in an evangelistic sermon, the final illustration will easily lend itself to the upcoming invitation.

Major points: I require students to find a strong illustration for each major point—to review the point and finish the point—before transitioning to the next point. If you preach an illustration-based topical sermon, you'll constantly refer to the point of the illustration throughout its exposition.

You may check appendix 4, "A Sample Pre-evangelistic Sermon," to see how I use opening and closing illustrations as well as embed a variety of them throughout the sermon's development. In addition to these normal locations of illustrations, evangelistic illustrations positioned across the sermon address solid, specific, and standard evangelistic subjects.

Standard, but not stock, illustrations around three specific subjects—sin, substitution, and saving faith—are included in any evangelistic sermon. You need illustrations to highlight

> *sin* so unbelievers can see their need for Jesus,
> *substitution* to show God's provision of salvation, and
> *saving faith* to explain the *means* of salvation.

Sin: Illustrations on sin reveal the personal nature of sin. Such illustrations will elicit question, response, understanding, implication, or connection. The audience will react in some way, mostly internally. They must know that they themselves have *personally* fallen short of God's expectations. Here's an illustration on sin.

The remotest part of the earth that I have visited is the Andaman Islands in the center of the Bay of Bengal. You can still view the world as it was when time began. England started colonizing the islands and created the first jail in 1858 for political prisoners in the main city of Port Blair. Thousands of mutineers were sentenced to life imprisonment where fellow countrymen were incapable of hearing their heartrending voices.

The tour book to the archipelago describes one of the most feared jail superintendents of the Cellular Jail. An Englishman named Barry was "a sadist and a racist, a bulldog, 1.60 meters tall . . . a creature especially created by Providence to keep prisoners under absolute control." Barry bellowed his reasons for cruelty to Indian freedom fighters. He boasted of his absolute power: "In the Universe, there is one God and He lives in the Heaven above. But in Port Blair there are two: one the God in Heaven, and another the God of the earth. Indeed, the God of Earth in Port Blair—that is myself. . . . My name is D. Barry. . . . If you disobey me, may God help you. At least I will not, that is certain. Remember also that God does not come within three miles of Port Blair."

Having talked about sin, I'd connect the illustration to the audience to establish personal sin. I would say something like, "You may not be as blatant as Captain Barry in defying God and keeping him at a distance, but you've experienced the same sentiment. You too have kept God at a distance, for you think you can run your life better than he does. You have flouted what you know to be God's expectations of you. You've marked off the territory in your life into which God cannot enter. God calls that cosmic treason, moral failure, sin."

Substitution: In many ways, substitution is the heart of the gospel. You'll have to find plentiful illustrations to try to explain what God has done for the human situation. Nothing on the earth can fully grasp or convey substitution: God became man to die instead of the human race, to pay the penalty for sin. But you can *try* to find the parallel, a pointer to Jesus's work on the cross: the vital organ donor who died to provide a way for someone else to live, the firefighter who lost his life while saving another, the soldier who died to keep a nation free, the man who took the capital punishment for another's liberation. These kinds of illustrations approximate Christ's substitution and abound around us.

I told you that God placed an illustration before me in answer to my prayer for this chapter, and here it is: I often seek to affirm moral people for their good works without giving them hope for salvation in those good works. These religious people are not as good as they can be, but neither are they as bad as they can be. What good are their good works, which are good in themselves but merit nothing before God? Just like people carry "bad" baggage past their conversion that Satan may seize for his purposes, is there "good" baggage that can be seized by the Holy Spirit for his purposes? Good works are good in themselves, but they cannot save. How else can they be useful? My point: good works can't save you, but they can be harnessed for faster and greater growth once you are saved. The subtly nuanced point can be seen in the containing of dangerous and damaging forest fires.

In order to contain forest fires from consuming fury, in 1934 the U.S. Forest Service set up Blacks Mountain Experimental Forest, a ten-thousand-acre area within the Lassen National Forest, for ecological study. In September 2002, a massive fire burned two thousand acres of the National Forest, sixteen hundred of which were in the Blacks Mountain Experimental Forest. When the Cone Fire (named for the hill where it was first thought to have begun) "swept through these woods, it came to a patch of forest that was different from the rest, and stopped dead, like a mime at an invisible wall." What stopped the fire at this experimental plot? This area had been "treated" before the fire, selectively logged to thin it, and had been previously burned in a controlled fashion.[13]

Selective thinning helped the forest recover, but the prescribed burning was necessary for the fire to stop. Once the fire stopped, the selective thinning allowed for plant growth, tree growth, and wildlife survival. Plants and trees could not grow if the fire had not already been stopped. And if the trees had not been thinned, the underbrush would have exacerbated the fire.

Another fire, a judgment fire, will one day blaze across the human race. For centuries we have tried selective thinning with human efforts at reaching God, with philosophies to help us live, with religions to absolve us from wrongdoing. But our thinning efforts were thin! Our best efforts, thoughts, and ideas were not adequate or diverse enough to keep out God's fire. These good works may have kept us from growing tall in our sinning, but the underbrush, what we have hidden on the floor of our lives, remains to become fuel for the future fire. As someone once said, "You're not as bad as you can be, but you are as bad off as you can be." Neither are we as good as God expects, though we may be better than our neighbors. The fires of God will come.

Your good works will not prevent the fire from consuming you. I don't know, but maybe you'll have less of a punishment in hell than all those neighbors, friends, and colleagues of yours. You may have the advantage of having been good and done good, but those virtues will only help in the recovery *after* the fire has blazed through, if it didn't touch you. You can carry your good works into the future but only after having stopped the oncoming fire.

Is there a way to stop the coming fire? Both the Forest Service and God hold the same view of stopping a fire. You stop a fire by giving it nothing to burn. The Forest Service calls it prescribed burning. Once a fire has been set to an area, there's nothing there to burn. In the same way, the Lord Jesus was God's prescribed burn for the human race. He got burned ahead of time, so those who accept his death as their prescribed burn will be kept safe. If we do not accept it, God's judgment fire will ravage us. But if you are willing to receive his provision for you and instead of you as God's prescribed protection from his judgment fire, fire will not burn the same place twice. Once you receive his provision by faith in his work on the cross for you, you will be safe. Once you know for sure that his fire will not touch you, you can carry out all the good you wanted to do before you were rescued. You can continue doing good with selfless, new motivation and enhanced energy given by God himself. In fact, doing good after you are saved will grow you into a living tree of good for God and neighbor. Don't depend on your selective thinning of having done good, because the underbrush will burn. Depend on God's Son, who already burned instead of you, paying the penalty for your sin, taking your punishment upon himself, and then you'll be safe from God's fire. You can then take your good works to God, and he will use you in greater ways than you ever imagined.

Saving faith: Your sermon's finale must clarify the single condition of salvation, close the presentation effectively, and possibly clinch the response in the invitation. An illustration like the following may help.

Nationally (in the U.S.), more than eighty thousand people are waiting for an organ—a number that is expected to hit a hundred thousand by 2010. Two-thirds of them, more than fifty-five thousand, are waiting for a kidney. Organ donations from the living surpassed those from the dead in 2002. "The vast majority of such good Samaritans act to help a relative or a close friend, but transplant centers report an increasing number of 'altruistic donors'—that is, people who want to give of themselves, literally, to whoever doctors decide is in need."[14]

The doctor has qualified the donor, who has undergone a demanding kidney-donor selection process. After the doctor approves the gift and the match has been established, the surgery takes place. New life can then begin. The mere willingness of the donor and the exactness of the match does not benefit the ailing person unless he is willing to trust the doctor and receive the gift of new life.

Similarly, human beings are in a deathly state, away from God, facing life separated from him forever. God has identified a precise match to solve our deathly state. Recently a seventeen-year-old girl died after mistakenly being given a heart and lung transplant from the donor with the wrong blood type, "a unique tragedy in a system that has done thousands of transplants over 30 years."[15] God has qualified the donor—his perfect Son—whose blood type matches yours. He has done millions of spiritual transplants over thousands of years, and none has been mismatched. He is ready to implant life in you—if you are willing to trust the divine doctor and receive his gift of eternal life in the Lord Jesus, starting immediately. The surgical process is complex to you but not to him. Will you acknowledge your extreme helplessness and trust the divine doctor and receive the gift of life? You can receive the gift of his life by . . . (At this point, I'd go ahead with the invitation and clarify the response mechanism.)

Action Step

Start collecting illustrations in subfiles titled "Sin," "Substitution," and "Saving Faith" behind your evangelistic topics files. Set yourself a goal of ten illustrations in each of these categories in the next three months.

I received an email illustration on substitution. I'd like you to exploit and position it just right in your next evangelistic sermon. You will want to complete it for your purposes.

One Easter Sunday morning, George Thomas, a pastor in a small New England town, came to church carrying a rusty, bent, old birdcage and set it by the pulpit.

Several eyebrows were raised, and as if in response, Pastor Thomas began to speak.

"I was walking through town yesterday when I saw a young boy coming toward me swinging this birdcage. On the bottom of the cage were three little wild birds shivering with cold and fright. I stopped the lad and asked, "'What you got there son?'

"'Just some old birds,' came the reply.

"'What are you gonna do with them?' I asked.

"'Take them home and have fun with them,' he answered. 'I'm gonna tease them and pull out their feathers to make them fight. I'm gonna have a real good time.'

"'But you'll get tired of those birds sooner or later. What will you do then?'

"'Oh, I got some cats,' said the little boy. 'They like birds. I'll take them to those cats.'

"I was silent for a moment.

"'How much do you want for those birds, son?'

"'Huh? Why, you don't want them birds, mister. They're just plain old field birds. They don't sing—they ain't even pretty!'

"'How much?' I asked again.

"The boy sized me up as if I were crazy and said, 'Ten dollars?'

"I reached into my pocket and took out a ten-dollar bill. I placed it in the boy's hand. In a flash, the boy was gone.

"I picked up the cage and gently carried it to the end of the alley, where there was a tree and a grassy spot. I set the cage down and opened the door and, by softly tapping the bars, persuaded the birds out, setting them free."

Well, that explained the empty birdcage on the pulpit, and then the pastor began to tell this story. [The point of the story is not that good illustrations cost money!]

"One day Satan and Jesus were having a conversation. Satan had just come from the Garden of Eden, and he was gloating and boasting. 'Yes, sir, I just caught the world full of people down there. I set me a trap and used bait I knew they couldn't resist. Got 'em all!'

"'What are you going to do with them?' Jesus asked.

"Satan replied, 'Oh, I'm gonna have fun! I'm gonna teach them how to marry and divorce each other, how to hate and abuse each other, how to drink and smoke and curse. I'm gonna teach them how to invent guns and bombs and kill each other. I'm really gonna have fun!'

"'And what will you do when you get done with them?' Jesus asked.

"'Oh, I'll kill 'em,' Satan glared proudly.

"'How much do you want for them?' Jesus asked.

"'Oh, you don't want those people. They ain't no good. Why, you'll take them, and they'll just hate you. They'll spit on you, curse you, and kill you! You don't want those people!'

"'How much?' he asked again.

"Satan looked at Jesus and sneered, 'All your tears and all your blood.'

"Jesus said, 'Done!' Then he paid the price."

The pastor picked up the cage, opened the door, and walked from the pulpit.

10

The Evangelistic Invitation

> I want to tell of one lesson I learned that night which I have never forgotten; and that is when I preach to press Christ upon the people then and there, and try to bring them to a decision on the spot. I would rather have that right hand cut off than to give an audience a week now to decide what to do with Jesus.
>
> —Dwight L. Moody

Fiji Telecom hosted a breakfast for its upper echelon. Not adequately briefed on the spirit and purpose of the event, I didn't feel free to conclude my talk with an invitation to embrace the Lord Jesus. I was mistaken, but Pastor Pita (Peter) didn't hesitate. Instead of finishing up with the benediction as planned, he decided to turn the moment into a time of response. About a dozen people professed Christ that morning because of another's faith to seize a divine opportunity. The pastor taught me a deep lesson in evangelistic preaching: "Cast the net if you are doing evangelistic fishing. You never know when you'll catch some. It's better to cast the net and not catch any than not to cast the net and not catch any!" With permission and preparation, I include at least an implicit invitation with explicit response options to trust the Lord Christ at the end of every evangelistic sermon I give.

Soon after that learning incident, I was in Prague, Czech Republic. Invited by friends who tapped into the vice president of parliament's inclination toward Christianity, I addressed about two hundred people at this private dinner for businessmen and professionals. Of course, the new elite were more interested in shaking the vice president's hand than hearing this spiritual philosopher. The plush red-carpeted, chandeliered, double-decked hall turned into hallowed ground. When I started the talk, people were still speaking into their mobile phones, perhaps to publicly demonstrate their newly gained social status. I believe one man's phone rang while he was pretending to speak into it! In any case, they eventually settled down as I continued. While I kept the early part of my talk pre-evangelistic, I ended up implicitly inviting them to transfer their lives to Jesus. My host led them through explicit options on response cards. To my amazement, fifty-four people transferred from death to life. I wonder when they would have had another invitation to receive Jesus had we not seized that moment right away. God creates opportunities for people to trust Christ. We don't. But we can seize opportunities that God creates, knowing that it is better to err on the side of having our invitation rejected than to not have invited them at all. After all, they are rejecting Christ, not us. A good dose of humility, which all of us evangelists continuously need, can be received when inviting people to trust Christ, since it is quite possible that none will respond.

Biblical Precedent: Why Do We Do It?

Do we have any biblical precedent for the evangelistic invitation? The evangelistic invitation in the forms practiced now may be viewed as a historical and cultural development for theological and contextual reasons concerning the nature of repentance, belief, and regeneration. The forms and models of the evangelistic invitation cannot be absolutized, but their function and meaning are biblically premised—giving people the opportunity to turn from sin, to come to Jesus.

God *invited* Adam—"Where are you?" (Gen. 3:9)—and in Adam invited all mankind to return to him. God was not asking for information on Adam's physical location. It was an invitation to turn and return. And it was not a public invitation, for there was no public to verify his return. But God's question implied an invitation, and the invitation demanded a response.

Other Old Testament invitations to salvation include the Servant's call to the remotest parts of the earth to "turn" or "come" to God (e.g., Isa. 1:18; 45:22; 49:1ff.; 55:1). Nineveh repented at the preaching of Jonah (cf. Matt. 12:41). That assumes at least an implicit summons to the Ninevites by Jonah.

The Lord Jesus *invites* all who are weary and heavy with life's burdens to receive his rest (Matt. 11:28). Whether the invitation is public or personal, Jesus himself becomes the object to whom one may come. He came to "call" sinners to repent and believe the gospel (Matt. 9:13). Theologians distinguish between the general and efficacious call of God to humanity. The general call of the Holy Spirit goes out to all humanity—for he convicts the *world* of guilt in regard to sin, righteousness, and judgment. A component of his efficacious call includes a personal response to his gracious and sovereign workings (including his invitation) in the eternally elect toward that salvation through our preaching. People are called according to his predestination (Rom. 8:30), but he calls those whom he has chosen (1 Thess. 1:4–5) through the preaching of the gospel (2 Thess. 2:14). The trinitarian invitation encourages, if not exemplifies, the invitation in evangelistic preaching—a decision of response rather than choice.

When you proceed to apostolic precedents, Peter and Paul invite people to respond to their message. Acts 2:38 responds to the Jewish crowd's question with a straightforward evangelistic invitation—each one of them is to repent (change their minds concerning Jesus as Messiah), and all of them are to be baptized (to show personal change of outlook). Paul's sermons end up with Jesus each time, but he goes beyond persuasion to appeal—"Therefore, we are ambassadors for Christ, God making his appeal through us. We implore you on behalf of Christ, be reconciled to God" (2 Cor. 5:20 ESV). Think of the implications of *God appealing through us*, and us imploring people *on behalf of Christ*, to replicate the heart of God and Christ in our invitation.

Both Peter and Paul go beyond telling, declaring, and announcing Jesus to pleading with people to believe (2 Cor. 5:20), convincing them about Jesus (Acts 28:23–24), and summoning them to repentance (Acts 17:30; cf. Mark. 1:15; Acts 3:18–19), for God himself commands repentance. Paul uses strong words in relation to his agency in the salvation process. He himself saves some (Rom. 11:14; 1 Cor. 9:22). Neither preaching nor faith saves as the ground of salvation, but preaching that results in the invitation and response process *must* play a role in human salvation. Even the lack of a response is a decision against the invitation. People are already heading toward an eternal perishing, but they can receive eternal life if they believe on God's one and only Son. All that being said, the very nature of salvation from sin requires the giving of an invitation from the preacher and a response from the unbeliever. In the evangelistic invitation, you echo the Spirit and the bride, who say, "Whoever is thirsty, let him come; and whoever wishes, let him take the free gift of the water of life" (Rev. 22:17).

Once a year, between Christmas Day and New Year's Day, the entire evangelical community of churches in Ndjamena, Chad, works together to present the gospel with a well-thought-out follow-up program. Whether churches working together is the greater miracle or not, tens of thousands of people respond to their evangelistic endeavors. Early one New Year, they slotted me to speak in a non-Christian community near the capital city. The gospel had never been presented there before. The audience of twelve hundred people was comprised of 90 percent unbelievers standing in a large circle for three eventful hours. I spoke on a rickety makeshift platform through a primitive sound system run by a car battery, preaching with two simultaneous translations in the dominant languages. The process was tedious (think of tripling the length of my already long sermon) and ended with an invitation. A few people stirred. I remember one, maybe two, who walked to the front. At that point, my host asked me to step back and requested a dozen men to summarize my talk in their local tongues (imagine the tedium!). Then *he* gave an explicit invitation. About two hundred—yes, two hundred—people of another religion and various languages came forward to turn from their god to Christ. I still wonder, "What if the evangelistic invitation had not been given that day? What if we hadn't presented Jesus as their eternal option and invited them to embrace him?"

Strategic Necessity: Can We Do without It?

The discussion of whether or not an evangelistic invitation is necessary doesn't mitigate its strategic necessity, homiletically and personally.

In terms of the sermon, the evangelistic invitation functions in the following ways:

1. To state or restate the sermon's purpose (step 4 of our Scripture Sculpture process). In any case, you will have reviewed the sermon's purpose in the conclusion. The invitation seamlessly flows from your conclusion and thus summarizes the sermonic purpose. Let's say your purpose was to invite the unbeliever to approach God for his acquittal in the right way. To begin your invitation, you would simply state or restate your purpose: "I want to invite you today to approach God for his acquittal in the right way."
2. To facilitate an opportunity for the hearer to personally trust the Lord Jesus Christ in terms of your sermon's theme and thrust in a crisis[1] of decision that culminates the hearer's process of coming to Jesus.
3. To clarify the terms of the gospel in the hearer's mind so that he knows exactly what he is embracing without adding conditions for salvation or concealing the cost of trusting Jesus as the only God who saves sinners.
4. To induce the hearer to receive your personal, gentle, but direct offer. The invitation dialogue becomes intensely per-

sonal—you as a person asking the hearer as a person to accept your proposition, the Lord Jesus's proposal.
5. To readily and urgently submit to the Holy Spirit's workings toward salvation in the hearer's life. If the hearer is ready, as prepared by the Holy Spirit, your invitation gives him the opportunity to respond to Christ without delay.
6. To later confirm the birth event, by date and circumstance, as the Holy Spirit gives the hearer assurance through his Word of possessing eternal life.

Let me share a sample invitation following my talk on Luke 18:9–14, with italicized and bracketed comments on this method:

"I want to invite you today [*'today' communicates urgency*] to approach God for his acquittal in the right way." [*My purpose statement moves me from the conclusion of the sermon to the invitation. This first statement is an important transition. It shows you are transitioning from a stance of declaration to petition.*] You ask how you can approach God in this right way [*notice that I am gently direct but singular in focus and pronoun*]. You understand that you have been touting your good works before God, recommending yourself to him as better than your neighbors. Yet you've always wondered if God wouldn't say to you, 'Your good works fell short.' How many good works are needed to be declared righteous by God? Nine? Ninety-nine? Nine hundred and ninety-nine? Can you hear God saying you should have and could have done one more good work to become righteous before him? The problem with approaching God with good works in hand is that they are never enough to meet his expectation of perfection from you. You'll never be sure you have performed adequately, perfectly. [*I clarified a part of the gospel as not by works in that segment.*] Today I want you to approach God for his acquittal in the right way, depending not on your own achievements but on his accomplishments [*facilitating response with a quick review of the CPS*]. In order to facilitate your approach to God today, I'd like you to talk to God. Will you bow your head for a moment? Will all of you bow your heads for a moment? [*Pause.*]

"[*Here I introduce the decision-making, crisis moment*]. If you are ready [*validating the hearer's apparent readiness*] to pray to God honestly and humbly like the tax collector did, ask God to have mercy upon you. Just tell him that. [*Pause.*] Admit that you are a sinner. [*Pause.*] Don't worry about anybody else today. Ask God to have mercy upon you. Put your name in there: "Have mercy on me, the sinner." [*Pause.*] Tell him you want to depend on Jesus's accomplishments on your behalf [*I would have explained and illustrated how God enacts justification in the body or conclusion of the sermon*]. Quietly and honestly speak to God. Say something like this to him [*clarify the terms and conditions of the gospel*]: "God, I admit I am a sinner. [*Pause.*] I seek your mercy. I have been depending on my good works to save me. [*Pause.*] I change my view on that strategy for your acquittal. [*Pause.*] Thank you for acquitting me by sending the Lord Jesus to die instead of me and to take my place of punishment. [*Pause.*] Thanks for raising him from the dead to prove to me that his payment is effective for me. [*Pause.*] I depend on his payment for my sins. [*Pause.*] I receive your acquittal in faith. [*Pause.*] I embrace the Lord Jesus alone as the God who can save me.

"If you have spoken to God, and you believe on the Lord Jesus to have covered for your sin, you will have God's mercy. You can walk out of this room declared not guilty by God himself.

"I would like to know that you no longer depend on your own accomplishments for God's acquittal. If you would have liked to have prayed that prayer yourself but were at a loss for words, or if you haven't prayed at all for a long time but you understand God's method of acquittal, I'd like to know about it. Would you raise your head, make eye contact with me, and nod? Just raise your head, make eye contact with me, and nod as I sweep across the audience. Yes, I see you, friend. On the basis of God's Word, I am here to assure you that because you depend on Christ's work for your acquittal, he declares you not guilty. Anyone else? Yes, sir. Yes, ma'am. Yes, friend. I see you. You can remember today [*I mention the date for the later witness of the Holy Spirit, assurance of his Word, and confirmation by others*] as the day you were declared not guilty by God because Jesus paid the price for you. I want you to tell someone that you made this decision today. Tell the person who invited you about this decision." [*When the majority of the audience is Christian, I usually finish the invitation time with a prayer of affirmation or ask my local host to do that. If the majority of the audience is non-Christian, I let them know that they can now raise their heads, that the meeting is about over, and that I am very grateful that they have spent the time with me. I tell them about books and materials available for visitors and invite them to register on our website for ongoing dialogue, any questions, and a weekly spiritual insight from us. We attempt to "capture" as many names as possible of those who do not know Christ, whether they responded at that time or not, for additional follow-up initiatives.*]

Practical Considerations: How Can We Do It Well?

Let me share with you the atmosphere of invitation that pervades the whole sermon and some practical considerations in constructing your invitation.

The Atmosphere of the Evangelistic Invitation

The atmosphere of the evangelistic invitation is set quite early in the sermon. I suggest that somewhere after stating your evangelistic purpose in the introduction, you bring in the hearer's need to make a decision by the time you are finished speaking. Think of the atmosphere as both courtroom and coffee shop, as prosecutorial and relational, with the holy-loving prosecutor serving on the side of the sinful defendant. Yet the defendant is also a jury of one! You will be calling for a response, a choice, and a verdict. You are gunning toward a personal ruling, a judgment, a finding, without gunning the audience down in the process.

The verdict atmosphere pervades your presentation and defines your stance toward the listeners' response. You are providing truth to allow them to make a *conscious* rather than a nervous response. But you also call for a *conscientious* response—presenting repentance to the conscience. Listeners could experience guilt, regret, brokenness, sorrow, and conviction over pursuing avenues of sin, over giving up alternate ways and means of salvation. They may sense divine conviction about the ramifications of coming to the Lord Jesus. But hope of forgiveness and joy and promise could also pervade the atmosphere of the verdict-oriented presentation.

Though you facilitate a public forum, you will want to preserve privacy of the heart in decision making. Listeners' private response toward personal embrace will soon be publicly acknowledged.

The atmosphere and relational environment pervading the evangelistic invitation is marked by struggle, mystery, urgency, and compassion.

Struggle

You must request a heightened sensitivity to the Holy Spirit as you approach the evangelistic invitation. Bathed in prayer, having confessed known sin, you must invite him to fill you for the task, to protect you in it, to accompany your words into hearts into which he has preceded you, and to powerfully permeate the invitation time. Billy Graham wrote, "[At the moment of the invitation] I feel emotionally, physically, and spiritually drained. This is the part of the evangelistic service that often exhausts me physically. I think one of the reasons may be the terrible spiritual battle going on in the hearts of so many people."[2] When I cast the invitation, I feel fear, ambiguity, and doubt. So I need to trust the Holy Spirit's empowered sentness (remember that word from our first chapter?) into this spiritual battle.

Mystery

Part of the struggle and ambiguity in the invitation is my awareness of the theological disputes between Calvinism and Arminianism, especially in terms of the evangelistic invitation: are we prompting a salvation choice among those who are not elect? At this point, I rely on the great truths of Scripture and evangelists of both stripes. Though the "whoever wills may come" invitation goes out to everybody (thus, I can genuinely invite everyone), I am aware that none will be mistakenly saved. No one will be saved unless the Father draws him (wrong responses will not stick). I would rather risk a non-elect person responding to the invitation than not give the elect an immediate chance at salvation! John

6:37 addresses the concerns of both theological camps: "All that the Father gives me will come to me, and whoever comes to me I will never drive away." It is a decision of response, not a decision that initiates salvation.

I seek to be Arminian in personal earnestness but Calvinist in personal assurance. It is God's problem to convict and convert; ours is to convince and communicate. Presbyterian evangelist, and Baptist Billy Graham's brother-in-law, Leighton Ford tells the story of the young man at John McNeill's crusade who was deeply concerned that he might offer free grace to some who were not of the elect. "Don't worry if the wrong person gets saved; the Lord will forgive you," said McNeill. I am quite confident that I would not disrupt the correct *ordo salutis*, especially since I am ignorant of the presence and identity of the elect in my meetings.

Urgency

You must go into the evangelistic invitation with ambassadorial urgency, with an eager anticipation of signing a peace treaty between enemies. The ambassador's announcement is clear: "God's arms have again reopened at Jesus's cross. Though you look away from God, all you can and have to do is to fall into them backward, to be reconciled with the God of heaven for eternity. You can decide to do that today, even right now, beginning immediately."

Find an urgent man, and you will find a keen and sure man. If you sense this ambassadorial urgency, you will be characterized by a spiritual enthusiasm, since God is going to save some, or begin the steps to save some, at that very event. You will not manipulate a response, but like the apostles did, you will show the listeners that Jesus is the Christ they must consider. Your presentation will be persuasive but not coercive, marked by urgency *for their sake* but not intimidating. You will not lengthen the invitation to force anybody to an emotional submission. Yet the air about you is one of anticipation: God will bring some to salvation out of your feeble efforts. Your ambassadorial privilege will show throughout your sermon. If you aren't excited or confident about unbelievers receiving salvation, why should they trust you, your message, or our proposition?

Compassion

The relational atmosphere of the evangelistic invitation cannot smack of pride, ridicule, or a provoking spirit—remember the beggar analogy? You can even tell them about hell with earnest compassion. You can speak to their consciences in love. You can empathetically address their wills. At all times be courteous. Don't get angry or disappointed if there is no response. Don't be defensive at this tender time, trying to explain the apparent good or bad response to yourself or your hosts. Remember, you are sowing seeds in some lives, cultivating them in other lives, and reaping a harvest in yet others.

The Characteristics of an Effective Evangelistic Invitation

Clarity, Clarity, Clarity in Content

Basically, your evangelistic invitation comprises the elements of an evangelistic sermon in short form. The listeners must know what they are accepting and rejecting, what Christ is promising, and what he is not promising during this time. So you have to be clear about the following:

1. Clear as to their state, status, standing before God.
2. Clear as to Christ's provision for their *root* problem (sin) that only he can meet.
3. Clear as to language. A respected evangelist recalls, "[When I heard,] 'Welcome brother, you're part of the body of Christ now. Walk in the Spirit and avoid the flesh,' I thought, 'How can I be a part of the body and avoid the flesh?' It sounded ghoulish."[3]
4. Clear as to the object of trust. They are trusting the Lord Jesus Christ. Faith does not save them; the prayer of faith does not save them. It is the Lord Jesus Christ who saves them. That salvation is through faith in him.
5. Clear as to the condition and content of faith. They are trusting the Lord Jesus Christ as the only God who can save sinners. They turn through faith from alternate saviors to him alone. You explain the core and framework of the gospel: God—Humanity/Jesus—Faith.

6. Clear as to the manner of response. Whatever the form of the invitation, you must emphasize that this is a *private* response (even in group decision situations) that launches a *personal* relationship with Jesus. This personal decision is to be *publicly* acknowledged in the next few moments.

Change, Change, Change in Procedure

A pastor who preaches evangelistically will have to practice an assortment of ways to make people's decisions public. After listeners privately decide to personally embrace the Lord Jesus, you must provide a variety of methods for public acknowledgment and follow-up possibilities. You already let them know in the early part of the sermon that you'd be calling for a decision. After you present the invitation, explain the procedure. Tell them why you want them to publicly acknowledge their decision—not to become saved, but to express their salvation. You want to help them understand the decision with new materials and offer possible friendship and ongoing dialogue. Tell them what will happen. For example, "In a moment, I am going to ask you to walk down the aisles of this auditorium [or run down the stairs of the stadium] to meet me up in the front. I want to pray with you, firm up your decision, and provide some materials, and then we will break for the evening."

An itinerant evangelist can practice similar methods every time. Group conformity and anticipation allow same or similar methods to yield great public results. I remember being filled with awe and humility as half the audience at the Pretoria, South Africa, rugby stadium walked forward. I had told them early on that I would be anticipating that response and prepared the entire group for the climactic moment.

While pastoring, however, I practiced various methods of public acknowledgment. With everyone's eyes closed, I said,

> "Would you raise your head and make eye contact with me and nod your head?" (Sometimes they even smile!)
> "Give me a thumbs-up sign."
> "Wave to me."

"Walk forward during the final song or after the meeting."

"Fill out a response card." (Open card or with categories listed—see below.)

"Register on our website."

"Stay in your seat, and we'll come to you."

"Come to the front rows, and I'll meet you for additional questions and comments."

Here's a sample response card we use at our evangelistic settings that permits us to secure the quality of the response and allow for intentional follow-up:

Title of the Event:
Location:
Speaker Name:

___ I would like to learn more about a personal relationship with God.
___ I have spiritual needs I would like to discuss. Please contact me.
___ I have embraced the Lord Jesus as my personal and only Savior today.
___ I am interested in future events like this one.

Comments/Questions:

Name _____ Email _____

Address _____

City _____ State _____ Zip _____

Phone (optional): _____

I am guest of _____

Feel free to email us at info@rameshrichard.com
Or register at www.rameshrichard.com
Phone: 972-733-3402
Fax: 972-733-3495

Caution, Caution, Caution—Some Don'ts of an Evangelistic Invitation

1. Don't promise too much. Promise only what the Bible *unconditionally* promises to Christians.
2. Don't conceal the implications of coming to Jesus, but don't complicate what is already a hard issue. Believing on Jesus alone is not easy. The only condition of salvation is to trust in the Lord Jesus Christ alone as the only God who saves sinners.
3. Don't prolong the invitation unless you really sense the Holy Spirit's prompting. Be patient but don't prolong.
4. Don't get them to go through several steps—they will think the steps saved them! For example, don't say, "First close your eyes. Then raise your hand. Next, stand up. Finally, come forward." That process undermines your integrity as well. Stick with only one public form of acknowledgment.
5. Don't give a mixture of invitations—for salvation, for recommitment, for missions, for healing, for prayer, for joining the church, for baptism, for a closer look at my face!
6. Don't use incentives—like materials or books on evangelism. Incentives (a nice meal, entertainment, friendship, a grand prize) are okay to get people to come to the evangelistic event—but they are not evangelism. You may use incentives for *pre*-evangelistic drawing to the evangelistic event, but people are not saved by receiving the incentives. By all means, deliver what you promised to give them in reasonable time.
7. Don't twist anyone's arm to trust Christ. You offer salvation. You can't save them!
8. Don't abandon people after they respond. In many cases, follow-up is evangelistic but is not evangelistic *preaching*. The history of the public altar call ranges from Charles Finney's "anxious benches" to Asahel Nettleton's "anxious rooms" to D. L. Moody's use of the invitation for the sake of public response and private counsel.[4] We must remember that the manner of decision is not the faith, nor the expression of faith, but a response of faith that can be followed up in the near future, formally and informally. The response is not to

join a church or to be baptized, although those occasions could follow.

Why is it necessary for us to create an opportunity for people to show anyone in any way that they are receiving Christ? Does the invitation play a spiritual or psychological role in assurance of salvation? Or is it primarily for follow-up reasons?

I primarily practice the evangelistic invitation for reasons of evangelistic follow-up rather than for reasons of assurance of salvation. For effective follow-up of those on the journey from pre-God, to pre-Christ, to pre-faith, to faith, a public response is recommended. There is no other human way of finding out whether they are still in process or have experienced the crisis of regeneration. People can be saved without public acknowledgment, and in many parts of the world, it is not wise to call for a public confession of salvation.

So let effective follow-up be the *purpose* of your public invitation, and let spiritual assurance become the *result* of the gesture. When spiritual assurance becomes the purpose of the public invitation, then both faulty theology and practice could result. People come forward to find out if they are saved rather than to begin the journey to discipleship. Again, in evangelistic preaching, I view the purpose of public acknowledgment to be follow-up rather than personal assurance.

Follow-up is a soul-conservation process and can help distinguish between inquirers and converts, professors and confessors, nominal Christians and real Christians. I suggest that follow-up begins the moment the meeting finishes. A group of like-hearted co-workers can be identified and trained to nourish people's interest in the gospel. Have some materials for people to take home right away. Make them feel special in that the materials were meant only for them as special guests. If they filled out the names of the people who brought them, contact the hosts right away. Ask them to tell their hosts within twenty-four hours that they made this decision, perhaps even on the way back from the meeting. Arrange for the hosts to take them out within one week to discuss the matter. If they want to remain anonymous, invite them to your website, which should have clear directions for those who respond to Christ. If they are not from your city, encourage them to attend a church where the preacher speaks from the Bible. Prepare your own material for new believers. The major challenge in conserving respondents is just beginning at this point.

One of the finer moments of my evangelistic preaching with one of the better invitations I have given happened in southern India. Addressing a denomination that had wavered far from its evangelical roots, I dedicated one night to preaching an evangelistic sermon. A much-maligned bishop with evangelical convictions was able to steer his diocese back to the Bible and saw my time with them as influential in that return. I believe the tide turned toward evangelicalism (i.e., the emphasis on personal faith in Christ and evangelism) when I gave the evangelistic invitation at their annual convention. We concluded with an opportunity for public expression of faith in the Lord Jesus as the only giver of eternal life beginning right then and there. About 5,000 people had been seated that evening in deep attention. They had already been exposed to God's Word in their heritage, but nominalism had kept them from a decisive personal embrace of Jesus. I proceeded to invite them to publicly acknowledge their private decision to personally embrace Jesus by standing at the time of response. And I couldn't believe my eyes. About 250 people stood, rising from the ground. I asked those who were already standing in the overflow crowd at the back to wave, and about 50 people waved to me. Not sure that they really understood the invitation and too surprised at the response, I clearly rehearsed the meaning of the invitation. In fact, I gave them the opportunity to sit back down if indeed they had misunderstood the exclusive invitation of Christ. I waited for some to sit down. Instead, another 100 or so stood up, having embraced salvation by grace through faith as the gift of God that night. Having clarified the precise nature of the gospel—repenting from believing on anything else as God and trusting the person and work of the Lord Jesus as the One who can save them—I was able to close the meeting in good conscience and report its impact with integrity in this book.

The Evangelistic Invitation

I conclude with a well-worn illustration on the need for evangelistic invitations that summarizes what I have attempted to say in this chapter with passion:

> On Sunday night, October 8, 1871, Dwight L. Moody was preaching to a great congregation in Farwell Hall, Chicago. This was the text of his sermon: "What shall I do then with Jesus?" At the close of the sermon he said: "I wish you would take this text home with you and turn it over in your minds during the week, and next Sabbath we will come to Calvary and the cross, and we will decide what to do with Jesus of Nazareth." Then as usual, he turned to Sankey and asked him to sing a hymn. Sankey sang:
>
> Today, the Saviour calls,
> For refuge fly;
> The storm of justice falls,
> And death is nigh.
>
> But the hymn was never finished, for while Sankey was singing there was the rush and roar of fire engines on the street outside and the heavens were crimson with the reflection of the great Chicago fire. In the morning Chicago lay in ashes. To his dying day Moody was full of regret because he had told that congregation to wait until next Sabbath to decide what to do with Jesus. "I have never dared," he said, "to give an audience a week to think of their salvation since. If they were lost, they might rise up in judgment against me. I have never seen that congregation since. I will never meet those people until I meet them in another world. But I want to tell of one lesson I learned that night which I have never forgotten; and that is when I preach to press Christ upon the people then and there, and try to bring them to a decision on the spot. I would rather have that right hand cut off than to give an audience a week now to decide what to do with Jesus."[5]

A powerful stimulus indeed. Applied to the evangelistic invitation, Richard Baxter's definition of preaching as a "dying man to dying men" infuses our hearts. This may be the last time people hear the message, but this may also be the last time you preach, so preach as a dying man to dying men.[6]

Action Step

Like other parts of the evangelistic sermon, you ought to prepare your evangelistic invitation. Pray over, think of, and write out an evangelistic invitation with the following ingredients in mind:

1. Write out the transition from the sermon's conclusion to the evangelistic invitation. See the sample on pages 178–80. You could also cite Scripture at this point.
2. In writing, clarify your sermonic purpose (step 4) and theme (step 5) in terms of the theological substance of the invitation—the object of trust and content of the listeners' faith, the scriptural motivation in considering their "trustful turn" toward Jesus, and a whole-person focus (their cognition, conscience, and choice). You could use quick illustrations at this point and really at any point of this segment. One-sentence similes would really help: "Faith in the Lord Jesus is like exclusively trusting a surgeon with your destiny because he too has undergone your surgery, possesses expertise, and exhibits a track record that is unmatched anywhere else."
3. Write out the form of the procedure and the words you are going to use in confirming the listeners' call to the Lord Jesus *and* your upcoming follow-up strategy by taking into account the cautions listed on page 186.

Appendix 1

Relevant Terms in Evangelistic Preaching

One of the early requirements in my course on evangelistic preaching has to do with defining biblical and theological words. If the preacher is confused as to his understanding, the evangelistic sermon will be empty at best and heretical at worst. The biblical and theological concepts have to be clear in your mind before you formulate and deliver your sermon. These words have generated major discussion in theological and missiological circles, and you have to arrive at your own conclusions. The basic concepts are agreed upon by most evangelicals. The word *evangelical* too is debated[1] but may be simplified to denote those who believe in a personal saving relationship with Jesus and seek to personally share his salvation with others.

The *gospel* is the Good News that in Jesus's death, burial, and resurrection, eternal salvation is made available to anyone who believes on him alone as God's only Savior from his sin.

Evangelism is engagement in effectively presenting the gospel, in personal response to the commission of Jesus and one's experience of salvation, to those who do not yet believe on Jesus and eventually inviting them to embrace the Lord Jesus Christ as the only God who saves sinners. Evangelistic preaching is a subset of evangelism (cf. chapter 4, "A Definition of Evangelistic Preaching").

Saving faith is the instrumental condition through which an unbeliever receives God's eternal salvation. Acknowledging lack of personal merit and repenting of trust in the wrong objects of salvation, he instead transfers his complete trust to the person and work of the Lord Jesus Christ.

Conversion is the regenerating work of the Holy Spirit simultaneous to the exercise of the unbeliever's faith response, which confirms his election, endows all God's unconditional promises, and launches him into a journey of life in Jesus. The content of the gospel is distinguished from the scope of the gospel—the fruit and implication of conversion in a converted person's life.

Appendix 2

A Synopsis of the Scripture Sculpture Process

Following is an outline of the Scripture Sculpture process that I discuss in detail in the book *Preparing Expository Sermons*.

Introduction

    I. Definition
        Expository preaching is the contemporization of the central proposition of a biblical text that is derived from proper methods of interpretation and declared through effective means of communication to inform minds, instruct hearts, and influence behavior toward godliness.
    II. Explanation
        A. The "What" of Expository Preaching

1. Contemporization
   2. Central proposition of a biblical text
  B. The "How" of Expository Preaching
   1. Interpretation
   2. Communication
  C. The "Why" of Expository Preaching
   1. Inform the mind
   2. Instruct the heart
   3. Influence behavior
 III. Overview: The Seven Step Process of Scripture Sculpture

Fill out these blanks by referring to their delineation earlier (p. 87). In our preaching seminars, we rehearse these steps so many times that pastors can repeat them while sleeping . . . through my preaching at the seminars.

Step 1: _____

Step 2: _____

Step 3: _____

Step 4: _____

Step 5: _____

Step 6: _____

Step 7: _____

Step 1: Study the Text

  I. Seeing
   A. Observe Words
    1. Long words
    2. Unusual words

    3. Repeated words
  B. Observe Relationships
    1. Grammatical relationships
    2. Logical relationships
    3. Chronological and/or geographical relationships
    4. Psychological relationships
    5. Contextual relationships
      a. The context of the Bible
      b. The context of the book
      c. The context of the text
    6. Generic relationships
      a. Teaching: didactic or discourse material like Jesus's sermons or the form of the epistles
      b. Narratives: narration of historical events
      c. Poetry: Psalms, Proverbs
      d. Parables: primarily in the parables of Christ
      e. Miracles: primarily found in three periods
      f. Prophecy: Daniel, Ezekiel, Revelation
II. Seeking
  A. Asking Questions
    1. Questions for words
      a. What do these words mean now?
      b. What did these words mean at the time they were written?
      c. How have the Bible, the Author, and authors used these words elsewhere?
    2. Questions for relationships
      a. Grammatical relationships
        (1) Tense
        (2) Number
        (3) Gender
      b. Logical relationships
        (1) Cause and effect
        (2) Reason
        (3) Result
        (4) Contrast
        (5) Comparisons

(6) Conditions
(7) Purpose
c. Chronological and/or geographical relationships
d. Psychological relationships
e. Contextual relationships
    (1) The context of the Bible
        (a) The historical context
        (b) The biblical context
        (c) The cultural context
        (d) The theological context
    (2) The context of the book
    (3) The context of the text
f. Generic relationships
3. Summary: kinds of questions
    a. Background questions
    b. Fact questions
    c. Meaning questions
    d. Application questions
B. Answering Questions: Interpretation
C. Analyzing Answers: Five Tests
    1. The test of *authenticity*: Can I make a good case for this interpretation as that which *the authors* authentically meant in penning these words?
    2. The test of *unity*: Is there unity of meaning of terms, affirmations, and interpretation of the text?
    3. The test of *consistency*: Is the interpretation consistent with the rest of the chapter, the book, and the Bible? Can I explain a seeming difficulty?
    4. The test of *simplicity*: Is my interpretation simple or contrived? Plain or mystical?
    5. The test of *honesty*: Have I been careful not to read my own or others' (e.g., my Bible teacher's, denomination's, seminary's) prejudgments and preconceptions into the text?
D. Applying Answers
    1. What kind of application should I draw from the text: content, conduct, or conduct based on content?

2. What is the application from the text?
3. Is the application really based on this text?
4. How can I leave the people absolutely sure that this is the application from the text?

Step 2: Structure the Text

I. Structuring the Sections of the Text
   Grammatical and content keys will help separate the major points from the minor points of the text, the big bones from the small bones.
   A. Grammatical Keys

   Grammatical Keys Indicating Structure

Meaning	Little words serving as structure indicators
Cause	for, because, since, as,
Reason	for, because, since, as, that
Result	that, so that, so, which
Purpose	in order that, which, to, unto, until, toward
Means	by, from, through, out of, in
Time	until, till, to, when, whenever, from, through, of, in, by, according to, against, with, concerning, to, out of
Place	where, wherever, from, in, through, into, upon, with, concerning, till
Manner	just as, just, as, with, to

   B. Content/Subject Keys
      1. Content changes
      2. Introduction of a new subject
      3. Repetition
      4. Change in the form of statement
   C. Steps to Structure
      1. Identify all structure markers
      2. Distinguish major structure markers from minor structure markers for outline sequence and importance

    I.
       A.
          1.
             a.
                (1)
                   (a)
    II.
       A.
          1. etc.

To put it another way, the structure markers discerned from grammatical and content keys show the *relative* importance of the words they influence. The less important will move toward the right side of the page.

Major markers: Roman numerals—I, II, III, etc.
   Next level: capital letters—A, B, C
      Next level: Arabic numerals—1, 2, 3
         Next level: lowercase letters—a, b, c
            Next level: numbers with two brackets—(1), (2), (3)
               Next level: letters with two brackets—(a), (b), (c)
etc.

    3. Decide the meaning or the force of the more major markers

    4. Construct an outline of the text according to the emphasis of major and minor structure markers

  II. Summarize the Main Sections of the Text: Summarize the thought contained at the major levels of the outline by putting it into a complete sentence.

You now have a rather full outline of the text you desire to preach. This is a very interesting, helpful, and faithful means by which you can preach your text, any text.

Step 3: The Central Proposition of the Text

   I. What is the central proposition of a text (CPT)?
   The CPT is the single unit of thought that binds together and gives meaning to all the particulars of a text.
   II. What does the CPT look like?
   It is *always* in the form of a full grammatical sentence. If it is less than a sentence, it is not a proposition, by definition.
   III. What does the CPT contain? It contains two parts:
   A. The *theme* of the paragraph: The theme of the paragraph answers the question, What is the author talking about?
   B. The *thrust* of the paragraph: The thrust of the text answers the question, What is the author saying about what he is talking about?
   IV. From where do you get the CPT?
   You get it from the structure of the text. At each grammatical/content cue, you make a division for a section. The subsections deal with minor grammatical/content cues. For each major section you discern the theme following the way the author relates these sections to ascertain and propose the CPT.

Let us dissect this statement with a sample text, Ephesians 6:10–12. Those who have read *Preparing Expository Sermons* will recognize this passage as my key Action Step passage. I illustrate the reorientation toward evangelistic preaching of a passage normally preached to Christians in chapter 6 of this work.

> The *theme* of the text: The reason for putting on the whole, strong armor of God's strength
> The *thrust* of the text: to enable us to stand against the schemes of the devil and to struggle against the system of the devil

At this point in the process, it will be well worthwhile to do the following (see sample form below):

1. Give a working title to the text: For Ephesians 6:10–12, it would be "Reasons to Put on God's Whole Armor" (this sounds like your theme, and your theme could be a good working title).
2. Write out the central proposition of the text (theme and thrust in full-sentence form): Putting on the whole armor of God's strength enables us to stand against the schemes of the devil and to struggle against the system of the devil.
3. Write out the outline (in full sentence form). You already constructed the outline in step 2. See above.

You are now culminating the sermon preparation process as far as the text is concerned.

A Sample Form

Title
Scripture

Verse-by-Verse Translation or Paraphrase
v. 1:

v. 2:

v. 3:

Central Proposition of Text
Theme:

Thrust:

Full-Sentence Statement:

Outline
    I.
        A.
            1.
            2.
        B.
            1.
    II.
        A.

A Synopsis of the Scripture Sculpture Process   201

    B.
        1.
        2
        3.
    C.
III.

Step 4: The Purpose Bridge

    I. The key question that helps you articulate the purpose of the sermon:
On the basis of the central proposition of this text, what does God want my people to hear, understand, and obey from this sermon?
   II. The Purpose of the Sermon
      A. Focuses the introduction of the sermon on the need one has to raise in the sermon
      B. Determines what one should include and/or exclude in the body of the sermon
      C. Influences the sermon's conclusion and any application
      D. Helps in choosing the illustrations that need to be used to accomplish the purpose of the sermon
      E. Provides an objective way to measure the success of the sermon
      F. Directly contributes to the form of theme of the central proposition of the sermon
   III. Writing the Sermon's Purpose
A purpose statement always begins with *to* plus a verb to state what you are going to do in the sermon. For example, to challenge . . . , to encourage . . . , to present . . .
   IV. Compatibility Questions
      A. Can I make an exegetical or theological case that my sermon's purpose is compatible with the *purpose* of the text?
      B. Can I make a sociological or psychological case that my sermon's purpose is compatible with the *needs* of my audience?

A hint here: Your purpose statement will almost always, in raw form, provide the theme of the central proposition of the sermon (step 5).

Step 5: The Central Proposition of the Sermon

    I. The Central Proposition of the Sermon (see step 3 above and replace the word *author* with *preacher*)
        A. Theme: What am I, the preacher, talking about?
        B. Thrust: What am I saying about what I am talking about?
   II. Illustration from the CPT of Ephesians 6:10–12 to the CPS

Step 3   CPT: Putting on the whole armor of the Lord's strength enables us to stand against the schemes of the devil and to struggle against the system of the devil

Step 4   The Purpose Bridge: To motivate people to put on the armor of God's strength in their struggle against the devil

Step 5   CPS (In raw expositional form, we can turn the purpose into the theme of the CPS—usually in the form of a question to begin with before we polish it further):

    Theme: Why Christians should put on the whole armor of God's strength
    Thrust: to stand against the devil's schemes and to struggle against the devil's system

At this point, it may well be worth it to convert the theme to more memorable phrasing for better preaching. You could reword the theme as follows:

    Theme: Why sovereign strength is sufficient for your strategy against Satan
    Thrust: It enables you to stand against Satan's schemes.
          It enables you to struggle against Satan's system.

I will contemporize this raw form into a catchier, homiletical style later. The basic truth I will be speaking about is God's sovereign strength as sufficient for our strategy against Satan.

Note here that the thrust of CPS may take a number of forms:

1. The theme may have to be proved addressing this question: "Is God's sovereign strength really sufficient to strategize against Satan? Will he really enable us against Satan?"
2. The theme may have to be explained: "the nature of God's sufficiency as it strengthens us against Satan's schemes and system" or "how God's enablement becomes real to us."
3. The CPS may have a multiple thrust to the theme: For example,

> Theme: The sufficiency of God's sovereign strength
> Thrust: To enable you to
>   stand against Satan's schemes
>   and
>   struggle against Satan's system

I chose the latter form for the text nicely divided into two—as discerned by the structure of the text (step 2).

Contemporization and alliteration are not absolutely necessary. But they help make the central proposition and main points less abstract and more memorable.

Step 6: Structure the Sermon

    I. Structuring the Sermon
       A. Features of a Reliable Structure
          1. Unity
          2. Order
          3. Proportion
          4. Progress
       B. Forms of Sermon Development
          1. Deductive form
          2. Inductive form

A written sermon usually reflects this structure:

> Title
> Text

Introduction
Ingredients of an effective introduction
1. Gets attention
2. Raises need
3. Orients to theme (step 5)
4. States purpose (cf. step 4)

(CPS is placed here if preaching a deductive sermon. In an inductive sermon, only your theme will be introduced here.)

Sub-introduction: background, context, transition, etc.

Body of the Sermon
Development of the points in a sermon: How to "SAVE (a) Point"
1. *State* the point
2. *Anchor* it in the text
3. *Validate* its election
4. *Explain* it by illustration, analogy
5. (*a*)*pply* the point if it accomplishes your purpose

Your structure of major and minor points will look like this:

I. First main section (if the sermon carries multiple thrusts, the first thrust will complete the theme here)
   A. First subsection
      1.
      2.
   B. Second subsection
II. Second main section (if the sermon carries multiple thrusts, the second thrust will complete the theme here)
   A. First subsection
   B. Second subsection

III. Third main section (if the sermon carries multiple thrusts, the third thrust will complete the theme here)
   A.
      1.
      2.
   B.
      1.
      2.
      3.
   C.
      1.
         a.
         b.
      2.
(The entire CPS is stated here if inductive sermon)

Conclusion
   1. Review CPS
   2. Apply the purpose
   3. Invite response

Let me show you my structure of Ephesians 6:10–12:

Beating Satan at His Own Game, on His Home Field
Ephesians 6:10–12

I. The Lord's strength is sufficient for you (vv. 10–11a)
   A. The Lord's strength is sufficient if you find your strength in him (v. 10)
      1. You must be strong in the Lord (v. 10a)
      2. You must be strong in the strength of his might (v. 10b)
   B. The Lord's strength is sufficient if you put on the whole armor of God (v. 11a)
II. God's strength is sufficient for your strategy against Satan (vv. 11b–12)
   A. Putting on God's armor of strength enables you to stand against Satan's schemes (v. 11b)

B. Putting on God's armor of strength enables you to struggle against Satan's system (v. 12)
   1. Satan's system is not made up of mere flesh and blood (v. 12a)
   2. Satan's system comprises a supernatural hierarchy (v. 12b)
      a. There are rulers
      b. There are powers
      c. There are wicked forces
      d. There are spiritual forces

Step 7: Preach the Sermon

I. Preaching the Sermon
   A. Pen the Sermon
   B. Practice the Sermon
   C. Preach the Sermon
II. Pen the Sermon
   A. Manuscript Writing
   If you write out what you intend to preach, you will benefit from the following:
   1. You can actually see the development of the sermon. You have an objective record of the sermon, which enhances your evaluation of it.
   2. You can practice and internalize the sermon before you preach it.
   3. You will have a permanent record of the sermon for later use.
   4. You can improve the sermon as new or better information needs to be included.
   5. You can repeat the sermon later without leaving out much.
   6. Your sermon manuscript will reveal areas that need to be touched up: illustrations, transitions, nonuseful material, irrelevant language—even after you preach it.

7. Your manuscript will tell you what illustrations you have already used so that you can keep from repeating too many of them.
   8. You may eventually be able to publish your sermons in a booklet form.
   9. You can get an idea as to how much time the sermon will take.
   10. Your manuscript will provide memory clues when you are in the pulpit.

Note: You will not need to take your manuscript to the pulpit. Actually, you should not take any notes at all. Once you have gone through the process I am advocating, you will know your material so well that the text will provide memory clues to the manuscript. Do not be afraid of forgetting parts of your sermon. Only you and the Holy Spirit will know that you have left out portions of your manuscript. He is good at making up for what you have left out as long as you have worked hard in preparation for preaching and teaching.

 B. Sources for Illustrations
  1. Your life
  2. Someone else's life
  3. Everyone's life
  4. No one's life
 C. Levels of Application
  1. What?
  2. So what?
  3. Now what?
 D. Voice and Delivery Issues

Sorry, but I am not writing out my sermon on Ephesians 6:10–12 for you!

Appendix 3

Shades of Evangelistic Presentation

Below you'll find a chart (followed by an illustration) comparing several shades of evangelistic presentation. In it we especially set preaching apart from mere presentations. We distinguish pre-evangelistic *preaching*, evangelistic *preaching*, and post-evangelistic *preaching*, with parallel presentations preceding and succeeding the preaching columns. Standing in a continuum from early nonverbal witness to post-evangelistic nurture, the shades of presentation are separated by dotted rather than rigid lines. There is considerable overlap, and one streams into another. A couple of comments will help you process this chart:

- Evangelists, preachers, and personal evangelists jump around between boxes in each row often without awareness or constraint.
- Unbelievers move around the boxes without awareness and constraint as well.

- I distinguish mere presentation from preaching to emphasize the public and formal nature of the latter. Whenever the word *evangelism* is in the category, somehow Jesus must appear in the verbal presentation, because Jesus is the center of evangelism, the Good News.

I think the chart is self-explanatory, but feel free to let me know of ways to enhance it (proclamation@rreach.org).

Pre-evangelistic ⟶ Evangelistic ⟶ Post-evangelistic

Category	Pre-evangelistic Presentation	Pre-evangelistic Preaching	Evangelistic Presentation	Evangelistic Preaching	Post-evangelistic Presentation	Post-evangelistic Preaching
Audience	Pre-Jesus in knowledge—needs to know the name of Jesus	Pre-Jesus in knowledge—needs to know the name of Jesus	Pre-Jesus in belief—needs to believe on the person and work of Jesus	Pre-Jesus in belief—needs to believe on the person and work of Jesus	Pre-Jesus in discipleship—needs to grow in the life of Jesus	Pre-Jesus in discipleship—needs to grow in the life of Jesus
Purpose	Attract people to the Christian; points to Christ as motive and reason for our lifestyle	Public call to consider Jesus; introduces the name of Jesus; offers Jesus; no evangelistic invitation	Introduces them to the person of Jesus; personal offer of salvation and personal invitation	Public call to embrace Jesus; public offer and public invitation	Intensify relationship with Jesus; personal discipleship	Public call to grow in Jesus, learn from him, and return to Jesus; public edification
Christological Content	Show Jesus as the model and motive for good works and right words; Jesus is at least a teacher of humanity	Introduce Jesus as serious alternative to present means to life and salvation	Share Jesus as the only God who saves—against alternatives and additives	Communicate Jesus as the only God who saves—against alternatives and additives	Position Jesus as means to grow in salvation	Expound Jesus as means to grow in discipleship
Spirit's Role	Creates a thirst, an expectation toward salvation through their observation	Creates a thirst, an expectation toward salvation through pre-evangelistic preaching	Convicts and regenerates the unbeliever through personal conversation	Convicts and regenerates through evangelistic preaching	Initiates and transforms the believer through discipleship	Initiates and transforms through post-evangelistic preaching
Format	Personal or public good works and right words	Public and formal proclamation	Usually personal and informal	Public and formal proclamation	Usually personal and informal	Public and formal proclamation
Strategy and Approach	Attraction: by personal and public lifestyle. A soft witness may address worldviews and lifeviews.	Proclamation: with reason always addressing worldview and lifeview issues	Presentation: in word at worldview, life-view, and Christological levels	Proclamation: Christological level	Nurture: in personal word and Christological meaning	Proclamation: preaching the Word and giving Christological meaning

Stance and Demeanor	Candidating: relationship oriented, no offer of Jesus's salvation	Declaration oriented: implicit offer	Courting: relationship oriented, explicit offer and implicit invitation	Declaration oriented: explicit offer and explicit invitation	Cultivating: relationship oriented, growing salvation	Declaration oriented: growing disciples
Relationship Metaphors	Candidating: uncovers suitable candidates to marry	Continued candidate identification in public setting	Courting with a view to getting married; begin marriage	Continued courting or beginning marriage in public setting	Cultivating new marriage	Continued cultivation in public settings

Pre-evangelistic Proclamation

Toward a Three-Phased Philosophy and Strategy

As I shared in the text, evangelistic preaching is distinguished from pre-evangelistic presentations of the gospel. Evangelism introduces Jesus to people—the focus is on Jesus. Pre-evangelism introduces people to Jesus—the focus is on the people. Pre-evangelistic preaching opens the gap between God and humanity, while evangelistic preaching closes that gap.

Here is an illustration and application of my preaching process from pre-evangelistic to evangelistic preaching in terms of a particular ministry project. God has opened the way to preach pre-evangelistically on prime-time secular television each New Year's Day. Our biggest competitor is the remote control! Our biggest challenge is to get secular stations to approve programs that feature the name of Jesus. Read on to grasp our strategic assumptions and tensions in the pre-evangelistic enterprise. This less-than-perfect illustration may also give you ideas for ensuring that unbelievers are present in your evangelistic preaching events.

Strategic Assumptions

1. The telecast is classified as a pre-evangelistic curtain-raiser on Jesus—exposing people to Jesus. The purpose is not evangelistic, though the results will likely be evangelistic for many.
2. Our intended audience is neither Christians nor nominal Christians, but pre-Christians, non-Christians. Christians

may benefit from it, may take courage from it, but they are not our intended audience. I am nonseeker sensitive.

3. Our aim is to expose large numbers of individuals to Jesus—changing the way they *think* about Jesus. We will pursue a large number of viewers and draw large numbers of registrants to our website.
4. Sinners respond with less than perfect motives. We offer incentives to bring them to our website. Incentives are hooks not for the message but for motivation to go beyond watching a program to registering on our site for follow-up. God uses these imperfect motives to give us the opportunity to further present Christ.
5. We don't get viewers to accept Christ with incentives. Using incentives to draw people is not a high-class version of making "rice Christians." Our opinion-leader audience made up of English-speaking and Internet-active people does not *need* any of the small incentives we give—unlike rice Christians, who need rice. Further, it is an affront to consider opinion leaders as not discerning enough to identify and reject inducements.
6. While the three phases explained on pages 210–11 form one project, we do *not* mix the three phases. For instance, phases 1 and 2 have to be kept distinct for the sake of this project. Phase 1 "hooks" them to register on the website and may not be the same as the promise of follow-up materials to help them grasp the gospel in phase 2.
7. We count responses, not results. Registrations are measurable—because drawing people to the website is somewhat under our control. Conversions are anticipated by follow-up cultivation, but they are not predictable.
8. Follow-up is more critical and needs greater attention from us than the initial telecast. Active, frequent, creative dialogue needs other sharp evangelists with a heart for nonbelievers, a temperament for frequent dialogue, and a mind for creativity in evangelistic approach. We have to provide basic theological preparation and practical training so they can reinforce the message, present additional truth, discern level of interest, and grow relationships toward conversion.

9. Our work is substantially concluded at phase 2. For the sake of phase 3, we undertake pastoral training thrusts. There is a seamless connection from the first introduction (the point of entry of the name of Jesus) to reception (the salvation of Jesus) to incorporation (the local church).
10. We will present Jesus on the telecast in the best way we can for the least cost we can to the most people we can within the standards and policies of secular host stations. The long version of the telecast with a clearer message of the gospel, Jesus's substitution, and an invitation to believe on him can be seen instantly downloaded from the website in text, audio, or video formats. We will take viewers through the climatization process for registration, the evangelization process for conversion, and the incorporation process for spiritual growth.

Strategic Tensions

1. Retention of viewer through entire program
    a. Competing with remote control
    b. Competing with other programs
    c. Competing with environment—family conversation, etc.
    d. Competing with spiritual forces—Satan
  Solution and Action
  - One hearing of the message is not enough
  - Drive them to the website to register
  - Instant .pps version emailed to them of fuller message, longer talk, and clearer gospel presentation than the telecast
  - Download first talk on MP3 player when sending it to them—with questions to answer
  - Download full transcript of talk upon registration
2. Grasping content
    a. Unusual accent
    b. Longer words
    c. Rapid speech
    d. Difficult thoughts

Solution and Action
- Questions on website for comprehension with incentive to win grand prize
- Opportunity to email us for conversation and debate

3. Incentive philosophy

Solution and Action
- Incentive is not to convert people but to register them—that is, there are no ongoing incentives
- Organizational or program sensitive incentives—pens with website information, books with spiritual content, MP3 players on which they download messages, grand prize of a computer will keep audience communicating with us via the Internet but only after they answer the questions on the talk
- In post-registration conversation, mention that we have not and will not sell them anything
- Put "FREE" (the best word in the English language) on the website and follow through efficiently
- Post other talks and transcripts on the web each month
- Three-phase, six-month, twenty-one-step follow-up dialogue for simple, free, and clear offer of the Good News around midyear

A Three-Phased Philosophy and Strategy

1. Pre-evangelism

Key Word: *climatization*

Purpose: lifting up Jesus for God to draw people, introducing people to Jesus

Strategy: casting the net wide and long, announcing the name of Jesus, drawing people to a follow-up channel for cultivation

Content: the news of Jesus—proclaiming the name

Harvest Metaphor: preparing soil, planting seed

Action Steps:
1. Annual telecast
2. Use telecast to invite people to register on evangelistic website

3. Hooks embedded in the television program as incentives
   4. Immediate attention and follow-through of promised incentives

Measurable Result: number of hits, unique user sessions, and registrations

2. Evangelism

Key Word: *evangelization*

Purpose: cultivating interest toward salvation, offering Jesus to people

Strategy: facilitating reception of salvation among those registered on website, dialoguing, relationship building, offering salvation

Content: the person of Jesus—proclaiming the gospel

Harvest Metaphor: watering and fertilizing the implanted seed

Action Steps:
   1. Viewer accesses fuller version of the telecast, which includes a more complete presentation of the gospel. Correctly answer questions on the transcript to be enrolled for grand prize.
   2. Begin frequent and creative six-month-long dialogue, a three-phase, twenty-one-step follow-up process—mass emails inviting discussion of spiritual condition (e.g., Bible study in John).
   3. Send follow-up materials with clear presentation of the gospel—e.g., weekly "spiritual prompter" emails.
   4. Continue active dialogue with midyear invitation (sixteenth step of follow-up) to trust the Lord Jesus.
   5. Send ongoing contextualized materials to nurture interest.

Anticipated Result: enrollment in weekly Bible study, checking "conversion" option

3. Post-evangelism

Key Word: *incorporation*

Purpose: nurturing decisions into discipleship

Strategy: reinforcing conversion by introducing spiritual life

Content: the life of Jesus—proclaiming the spiritual life

Harvest Metaphor: harvesting and growing

Action Steps:
1. Find their interest in meeting a local believer in their city
2. If interested, and socio-political-cultural context permitting, make connections with like-minded believers and churches

Desired Result: membership and leadership in a local church

Hand-Off Procedures: We consider this telecast project as pre-evangelistic moistening of minds and fertilizing of hearts in setting up a toehold for Christian neighbors of enquirers to present the Good News. We are working with more than 70 percent non-Christians in responses and are pursuing innovative methods of presentation and follow-up. Ultimately, presentation must precede conversion and result in incorporation. We cannot go beyond inviting them to trust Christ by email dialogue with a very "soft" offer to introduce them to like-minded people (Christians and churches) in their locale.

Appendix 4

A Sample Pre-evangelistic Sermon

I invite you to read this sample talk with a "homileticized" mind on the basis of my discussion of a topical evangelistic sermon. I look forward to hearing your comments and critique so I can learn from your experience and perspective. Again, you may write me at proclamation@rreach.org. Let me make this sermon more interesting for your reading. Can you pick up my theme and thrust? Let me know.

Unmasked: Facing the Mystery of Evil

A juvenile story of "unmasking" comes from the South Pacific. The local city zoo had run short of gorillas. They hired a young man to wear a gorilla costume and sit in the cage. The young man decided to add some fun to this rather uninteresting job. In order to get some attention, he asked for a blackboard and white chalk. He wrote out "$2 \times 2 = 4$." That stopped a few people. He went back to the board and wrote "$4 \times 4 = 16$." Now everybody was amused. Word got around about this amazing humanlike gorilla, the long-awaited proof of evolution.

That Saturday, a huge crowd gathered in front of the gorilla's cage. People with families and journalists with cameras climbed over each other. In good stride the gorilla walked up to his blackboard and wrote 16×16—do you know what the answer is? 256! (I learned the answer for this story.) The people erupted in applause.

The gorilla decided to add to his repertoire of *human* tricks. In the next cage lived an old but quiet lion. Arched over the lion's cage was a tree with a long branch. The gorilla reached for the branch and swung across the lion's cage. He made it to the other side but heard the branch crack on the way. Nobody else heard the noise of the crack. The crowd urged him to do it again, to come back to his cage. He was afraid, but pride got the better of him. He leapt to the branch in order to come back to his cage. Unfortunately, the branch broke. He fell into the lion's cage. Immediately the lion got up. Not knowing what to do, the man was filled with terror. Each step he took backwards, the lion walked toward him. He took a step to the left, and the lion moved to his right. He took a step to his right and the lion moved to the left. As he eyed the door, he looked for help. Locked in with the lion and filled with desperation, he shouted, "Help! Help! Help!" and the lion whispered to him, "Shut up, or both of us will lose our jobs."

"Unmasked: Facing the Mystery of Evil" is our subject. Evil unzips the masks we wear to hide our identities. It exposes the difference between appearance and reality, and it shows how we fool ourselves by what we know, what we do, or what we have. Evil forces us to identify ourselves, and it discloses our humanness. Facing evil's mystery is an authentically *human* experience.

Some of you are facing *personal* evil. You may be sitting on a hospital bed waiting out your days to die. Or maybe someone you love or someone who hates you has raped you or even attempted to get rid of you.

Others are facing *communal* evil. Riots may have broken out against minority communities. Or maybe the majority has begun an ethnic cleansing campaign to rid the world of your people.

Yet others are experiencing *social* evil. Whole continents are affected by the crises of epidemics. A country in southern Africa may lose its entire male workforce over the next ten years because of AIDS. Once sturdy, stable economies in South America are collapsing under the weight of their debt while hoping for international monetary funds to help them out. Then there is the specter of war. Thousands of men stare at each other across warring borders, not knowing if they're going to live or die.

There is also *natural* evil. Volcanoes, tornadoes, earthquakes, and other apocalyptic weather—the same region might be affected by both flood and drought within just one year!

Humans face the mystery of evil—that's the human question, the human predicament, and the human experience. We ask hard questions as we try to solve the problem of evil. We look for hope and feel the intellectual, moral, emotional, and physical anguish of pain.

Think with me about how evil unmasks who we are—about how evil reveals our humanness.

First, evil tells us we're not animals. You may act like a brute, but humans are not mere animals. For instance, animals don't possess the privileges of self-consciousness or historical consciousness or self-recognition or self-identity. They don't look into a mirror or into a television camera wondering if their hair is uncombed. When a horse breaks its leg on a race course, it is put out of its misery. But if the jockey breaks his leg, doctors bring him care and healing. The horse lacks the self-consciousness of the human.

Only human beings enjoy the gift of language and possess the ability to think reflectively, even abstractly. The distinct power of reflection drives humans to experience intellectual pain over the problem of evil. We ask questions like, why do good things happen to bad people? and why do bad things happen to good people?

The power of reflection helps us grasp the status of evil, which cannot boast independence—evil is abstract in concept, but in reality it is always embodied and concretized. We can have evil persons, evil things, or evil actions but not evil on its own. Take a sheet of copy paper, a perfectly good sheet of paper, fold it in half, tear a hole in it, and then open it full length. The paper has become tainted, bad, unuseable—or evil. Now take away the borders of that tear, and you have . . . nothing. Philosophers use this famous illustration to lay bare the impossibility of evil's existence without the good. If you take that hole out, you have a completely good sheet of paper. Evil can only exist in the context of good—not by itself.

In fact, evil is not a thing in itself. So when we say, "God created all things," it does not imply that God created evil, because evil is not a thing in itself. Your power to reflect confirms that you are not a mere brute.

Second, evil discloses that we're not machines. Machines are different from human beings, though sometimes you may feel like you're like a replaceable component in an organizational machine, or even worse—a cog in the cosmic machine. When matters are mundane, when there's nothing creative about life, you may feel like an automaton. Yet you are much better and matter much more than engines, machines, and computers.

How can we be better than machines, considering the sound beating that a computer program, IBM's Deep Blue and its successors, gave to Gary Kasparov, the Russian chess genius and his successors? Machines are only as good as their last development, software only as good as its last version, and computers only as good as their last program. Did you know that Deep Blue was programmed by *humans*? A very sophisticated human Deep Blue team programmed the supercomputer. They studied all of Mr. Kasporov's games and then programmed the machine to eventually beat him. The contest merely showed that several bright human minds wielding a supercomputer are together better than one gifted human without a computer. Machines can only perform the same play over and over again under the same conditions. When a machine is set up to execute the same play, that's what it will and must do. A machine can only choose between options; it *cannot* choose against an option like we can. Even the most advanced artificially intelligent machine can choose against a bad option if it's programmed to choose a good option, but it cannot choose against a good option if it's programmed to choose that option. *You*, however, can choose evil options at will, desire, and temptation—that's the power of human choice.

In our human choice, we locate the origins of earthly evil. When God created human beings, he didn't make us machines. He gave us the privilege to choose against him, and we exercised that choice. It was not unlimited choice, for humans are not unlimited beings, but it was true, real choice. We decided that we would choose evil against good. When creatures began to choose against God, the ultimate good, that act unleashed a comprehensive and disastrous consequence. We got landlocked in a killing field of explosive mines affecting us and everything around us. That original choice affects natural evil—we face volcanoes and earthquakes. It generates personal evil—the reason why we do evil one to another. It affects moral evil—we still regularly choose bad options over good options, knowing that we choose those options.

So when you question why God gave you the power to choose, why he didn't make humans without choices, you are asking him why he didn't make you a machine. (But if he made you a machine, you would not have the privilege of asking the question in the first place!) The gift of freedom makes evil possible, but it does not make evil necessary. Just like an airline company is not held responsible for a hijacker taking a good plane and using it for destruction, we cannot hold God responsible for making evil actions possible. The airline company is not held responsible for manufacturing an airplane, nor is it responsible for pilot error. The company is responsible for a good original product. Your freedom is part of a wonderful original "product"—your humanness. But we've hijacked freedom and used it for evil. Evil unmasks who we are.

Third, evil tells us we're not demons. Some believe in neither demons nor Satan. I heard of an English-language student learning about the forms of government. He noted that a theocracy is ruled by God, an aristocracy is ruled by aristocrats, a plutocracy is ruled by wealth, and a democracy is ruled by demons! Your husband may act like a demon, but he's not a demon. He can be possessed by a demon—a demoniac. We even know individuals who worship demons, but people are not demons. Demons have no moral capacity to serve—they don't possess the ability or inclination to do good.

They don't have the capacity to show moral sympathy, experience empathy, and serve compassionately in anguish over pain. Demons cheer when evil happens. I once saw a woman falling on the street. Immediately three or four people rushed to help her up. However, in the spiritual realm, the demons stood by, cheered, and clapped their hands because the lady fell.

Demonic attempts to dismiss or downgrade the problem of evil include attempts to deny the reality of evil. Satan wants you to think that the fault does not lie with reality, that the problem of evil is really with your mind—however, weeping at the funeral of a prematurely dead loved one is reality and not simply in your mind. The demons also want you to deny that evil is universal. You may be aware of sophisticated philosophical systems, sometimes called postmodernism or postcolonialism, which hold that all truth is created by, confined by, and construed by language interacting with local historical and cultural realities. Now, those claims reek of a universal affirmation—something that postmoderns and postcolonialists decry. A hundred thousand people dead in an earthquake or another hundred thousand people dead in a tsunami are not locally interpreted realities. The whole world knows that those evils are indeed true anywhere and anytime—everywhere and at every time. The problem of evil provides for the possibility that an event can affect all people (metanarratives)—everywhere, regardless of space and time.

Actually, Satan tries to get you to deny that there is a God on the basis of the existence of evil. That argument, however, does not serve its proponents well. I was flying with a Hungarian businessman, a self-proclaimed atheist, who asserted his belief that there is no God because of all the evil in the world. I asked, "What do you mean by evil?" He replied, "Don't you think catching babies at the end of bayonets is evil?" I responded, "Most definitely, yes. I think that is horrific evil, but why do *you* call it evil?" As he was groping for an answer, I pressed him with the moral argument for God's existence. "For you to call something evil, sir, is to assume a standard, an ultimate standard of morality and justice and good; and only if you assume an ultimate standard of good can you call something evil. If you don't assume an ultimate standard of good, you don't have a good case to make evil's presence counter the existence of God." He understood, looked at me, and remarked, "Apparently, I've assumed that ultimate standard." Unless you have an ultimate standard of good, you don't have evil.

Fourth, evil also tells humans that we are not angels. Your wife may act like an angel on occasion, but she is not an angel. A rather large gap exists between angels and humans. Angels live in heaven, where there are no tears, no death, and no anxiety, while we live on the earth, where we face the mystery of evil. Angels don't feel physical pain. We do. We mourn, we groan, we cry, and we die. The biggest difference between angels and humans in terms of evil, however, is that we still hold the power to err—to do wrong, to sin, and even to destroy. Did you notice that the most "advanced" of all centuries, the twentieth century, also turned out to be the bloodiest? The twenty-first century has begun, but it's not very promising that it will eradicate evil. Why? Because the whole world and all of history is made up of people like you and me who can do wrong. Nobody taught us to do wrong. There's a nature inside us that differentiates us from angels. Evil exposes human sinfulness. It asks us to identify ourselves as ones who can do and have done wrong.

Finally, in exposing our humanness, evil tells us that we are not God. A judge once dismissed a man's appeal to change his name to "God." Instead, he changed it to "I Am Who I Am," with "I Am" as his first name and "Who I Am" as his last name! Some people think such grandiose things about themselves and expect others to worship them.

Yet we are certain that humans are not God. To many, he seems to be sitting in his heaven oblivious to the human situation. He doesn't appear to care about us. He seems impotent and therefore unable, immoral and therefore unconcerned, ignorant and therefore vague in addressing the mystery of evil. He is distinct from us and therefore distant.

For God to resolve the *human* predicament, he'd have to become one of us and somehow provide meaning in the middle of chaos. If God were to become man, live among us, experience evil, and show us the way to a permanent solution, perhaps we could start to make sense in the face of evil's mystery. Yet that seems impossible.

This is where I have some extraordinary news for you.

Evil not only unmasks who we are. Evil unmasks who God is. In this regard, may I point you to the Lord Jesus Christ as the God whom evil unmasks? I direct you to him for your personal consideration and embrace. He not only claimed to be God, but he went through the full range of human experience as man. Unlike an *animal*, Jesus faced and dealt with intellectual pain. When his disciples pressed him to answer why a particular man suffered, he did not point to the man's wrongs or his parents' sins but rather viewed the pain as resulting in the glory of God. Unlike a *machine*, Jesus was confronted with and chose from moral options. He was tempted and tested at every point of our human weakness, but he lived a perfect life by the public confession of his allies and his adversaries. He lived a sinless life. Unlike a *demon*, Jesus experienced and tackled emotional anguish. At the tomb of his beloved friend, he snorted in anger over death's intrusion into the human situation. God did not create human beings to die, yet humans chose against God's desire, thus ending up in physical death and eternal separation from God. Jesus wept in sorrow when his dear friend died—but then he raised him from the dead. Unlike an *angel*, Jesus endured and suffered physical pain. Brutalized on a cross, he died in the most atrocious form of capital punishment then known to man. Without protest he underwent tremendous physical pain.

For God to live the ordinary human life is an excruciating limitation, a shocking condescension, and a painful humiliation. The fact that God chose to familiarize himself with human pain magnifies the extremity of the suffering. One painful incident would have been enough to comprehensively affect the God-Man adversely. Jesus endured all of this to solve the credibility problem for the invisible God from the perspective of evil's presence once and for all. He was not some kind of abstract, generic, monotheistic, distant God against whom you can levy charges of irrelevance, imperfection, ignorance, and impotence. Had God not come down to be one of us in Jesus, he would have been subject to your complaints, charges, and criticisms. Yet to counter your charges, disarm your criticism, and address your complaints, he experienced the humanness of pain and the pain of humanness. Thereby God established his credibility, reliability, and trustworthiness in the Lord Jesus Christ. Nothing is impossible with God.

The issues, however, go further and deeper for us. Jesus not only brought credibility to God in the face of evil, he gained the ultimate human victory to provide the guarantee of a permanent death-free, tear-free, pain-free environment for humanity. How did Jesus do that? He raised himself from the dead in the only verifiable self-resurrection in all of history, and he offers his life as a free gift for those who receive him in faith.

In experiencing pain, Jesus gained credibility with us. Because he raised himself from the dead, we can place our full confidence in him. He experienced extreme pain so that you and I will never accuse God of being unconcerned or irrelevant. He won an unequaled victory over death so that you and I will never have to be resigned to this life alone in all its suffering and limitations. Evil unmasks who we are as humans. But evil also unmasks who God is pointing us to—the Lord Jesus Christ.

Imagine a global earth summit, not to discuss sustainable development or environmental protection or the AIDS crisis, but to discuss the problem of evil in all its awful mystery. Presidents and prime ministers, moral and religious leaders, philosophers and economists all attired in their beautiful African robes, Indian saris, and pinstriped suits meet in closed-door meetings, make speeches, and finally present a global declaration on the problem of evil.

The chairman of the summit begins his final pronouncements on the problem of evil on live television, watched by billions of people. Since the subject is weighty and his declaration sober, his throat becomes dry. He asks for water, takes a gulp, and climaxes with a succinct summary of the problem of God and evil. He mixes soft voice with hardened heart to ask, "Why does God have the privilege of judging humanity while he's sitting in his heaven? He's irrelevant! He's impotent! He's imperfect! He's ignorant of everything that is happening here on this distressed and depressed earth! How could God ever judge us if he does not know what it means to be born in a third-class city where people have no place to lay their heads? What does God know of racial and ethnic prejudice? What does God know of being abandoned and alone? What does God know of being tortured and tormented to death?"

Just at that moment, the waiter who replaced the chairman's pure, microbe-free bottled water, whispered into the speaker's ear, "Sir, I've got something to tell you." Immediately the cameras cut away to shots of the crowd, not allowing the waiter to show off on global TV. He leaned to the chairman and said, "There is a God who does know what it means to experience evil in the ways you have just stated."

Shaken by the waiter's impudence, the chairman's trembling hand accidentally knocked his open bottle off the table. With quivering voice, he continued to read his proclamation, "If God really wanted to sentence humanity to evil, he has to go through the sentence of evil himself. Here are the primary conditions our globally representative committee has put together, the criteria that God must meet to be a credible judge in the eyes of the human race: (1) Let God be born on this earth—not in a legacy of wealth, but of a poor family. (2) Let him experience the social ostracism of a bastardized child. (3) Let him be betrayed by those whom he loves—including his family, his closest friends, corrupt governments, and popularity-seeking judges. (4) Let him be abandoned so completely that he knows what it means to be dreadfully alone. (5) Let him be brutalized without trying to numb his pain with drugs and narcotics, even if concerned people offer him pain killers. (6) Let him die a tortuous, torturous death. In this way he would have experienced the problem of evil in humanity all the way from his birth to his death. (7) Finally, let him give us some verifiable indication that he survived evil and death to give humanity hope in facing evil, even a way to survive his sentence. Then, and only then, will he have the right to judge humanity."

The janitor who had arrived to clean up the water spill couldn't stand it any longer. He jumped out from under the table, mop in hand, and bellowed, "Mr. Chairman, there is a God who has met all the criteria of your sentence already and won. You may want to consider him, Your Excellency. His name is Jesus."

Aghast at this unplanned public declaration, the media quickly moved into news, sports, and movies. But the whole world had heard that God had met the sentence that humanity had placed on him. God, in the Lord Jesus, experienced evil to give himself credibility with us, and the Lord Jesus raised himself from the dead to give us hope in facing the dastardly mystery of evil. You can have hope right now, in the present, as you face the full spectrum of intellectual, moral, emotional, and physical pain. But you can also have hope forever when you can embrace the Lord Jesus as your only God and Savior. You can permanently live without evil and death in eternity. You would have survived God's sentence on humanity.

Evil unmasks who we are. It shows us that we are humans. Evil unmasks who God is for you, for me, for the whole world. The Lord Jesus experienced humanness. He was born, he bled, and he breathed his last for you and me so that we could have eternal life. He rose again in order to give us the confidence of an eternity without evil. He welcomes you to embrace him as your only God and Savior. If you want to know how to embrace the God whom evil has exposed as humanity's only Savior, please visit and register on our website at www.rameshrichard.com. We will be glad to dialogue with you and lead you into life's ultimate decision concerning the mystery of evil.

Appendix 5

The Evangelistic Invitation

A Preparation Checklist

Following is a checklist to help you determine the integral connection of your evangelistic invitation to the theme or to the entire central proposition of the sermon. This list will also assist you in checking on the clarity of your presentation in gospel content in the invitation and response mechanism. Please consult chapter 10, "The Evangelistic Invitation," as you read through this list. Once you get some practice, you will be able to quickly run through the list in your mind each time you get to preach evangelistically.

Preparation

1. Have I prayed over (and raised prayer for) the invitation segment—its content and everything surrounding the event?

2. Have I intentionally prepared an evangelistic invitation?
3. Am I including the purpose of the talk in the invitation as well?
4. Will I focus on a single audience—unbelievers to turn to Christ?
5. Would I also be giving backslidden believers an opportunity to return to Jesus?
6. Have I provided adequate time to present a good invitation?
7. Have I set out a need for personal response from early in the talk?

Transition from the Sermon's Conclusion to the Invitation

1. Is there smoothness in the wording of this transition?
2. Is there a genuine connection to the theme or the central proposition or purpose of the sermon?
3. Have I kept from introducing new ideas or incidental thoughts that would distract and detract from the theme or central proposition or purpose of the sermon?
4. Is my verbal expression of the transition clear?

Content of the Invitation

1. Is the central proposition of the sermon rehearsed or reviewed?
2. Is the content of the gospel introduced in short form?
   a. Is the root problem of human sin clarified as that which separates God from humanity?
   b. Is God's provision of salvation through the death, burial, and resurrection of the Lord Jesus spelled out?
3. Is the centrality of salvation by grace rather than by works apparent?
4. Is the exclusivity of the Lord Jesus as one's *only* Savior obvious?

5. Is the sole condition of personal faith for eternal salvation clear and lucid?
6. Do I communicate an urgent appeal without coercion to respond?
7. Do I convey compassion without weakness in the invitation?
8. Am I promising only what can be unconditionally given at salvation and not promising too much?
9. Am I concealing any implications of "eternal salvation by grace alone through faith alone in Christ alone" without adding to those criteria?
10. Am I communicating a measure of salvation assurance for those who respond?

Mechanism of the Invitation

1. Do I know the physical options and limitations of the evangelistic setting?
2. Do I know how long the invitation segment of the sermon should or could last?
3. Do I know the audience culture enough to use a comfortable but straightforward method of responding to the invitation? (For example, what local practice and tradition of invitation is practiced by evangelists and pastors there?) And how much may I depart from it without violating or distracting the audience?
4. What method would be most appropriate and winsome in this setting for both the response and recording of responses?
5. Will I stick with one method or mix-and-match methods in gaining a response?
6. What else will be happening during the invitation? Will it be quiet? Will there be music? Visuals? Singing? Praying?
7. Have I made clear what will happen when people respond—the availability of counselors, literature, collecting names and other data, etc.?
8. Have I decided what will happen after the time of response?

9. What part of my follow-up strategies do I disclose so that respondents will not be surprised—means of further contact by phone, website, friends, etc.?
10. Have I given maximum room for people's response to the Holy Spirit's inner conviction rather than counting on other factors like peer pressure, or promise of incentives?

Appendix 6

A Checklist for Evaluating the Textual or Topical Evangelistic Sermon

As in *Preparing Expository Sermons*, I borrow from the homiletical laboratories and preaching faculty of Dallas Theological Seminary to lay out this list for self-evaluation. These are exactly the forms I use in evaluating students in my evangelistic preaching courses.[1] Ponder every new heading and subheading below as you prepare, deliver, and evaluate your sermon. You have probably known me to say that there are no consistent A grade sermons (those are for heaven), but you can consistently preach A- sermons and occasionally preach A sermons! God can use B and C sermons, but don't use that as an excuse for lack of solid preparation, effective delivery, and careful evaluation.

Textual Evangelistic Sermon Evaluation Form

    I. Textual Faithfulness
        A. Central proposition: Does it accurately reflect the subject, proposition, and context intent of the original author in the text or context?
        B. Validation: Is it exegetically, theologically, or logically appropriate?
        C. Anchor: Does the speaker direct you to where he is in the text?
    II. Content and Organization
        A. Introduction
            1. Need
            2. Attention
            3. Purpose
            4. Orientation
            5. Subintroduction
        B. The Central Proposition of the Sermon
            1. Relevance to unbeliever's understanding
            2. Connection to unbeliever's language
        C. Development
            1. Outline sketch: simple and memorable?
            2. Effectiveness of rhetorical strategy
        D. Conclusion
            1. Summary: connection to sermon's purpose and theme
            2. Invitation
                a. What are you calling for?
                b. Are the terms clear?
                c. Is the response mechanism or process clear?
    III. Style and Delivery
        A. Voice: speed, volume, pitch, expressiveness
        B. Delivery: facial expressions, gestures, bodily movement

  C. Style: grammar, word choice, articulation, straightforwardness
  D. Support materials: adequate, appropriate, credible
   1. Appropriate to the experiences of the lost?
   2. Use of humor
   3. Explanation of biblical and theological terms
   4. Is the support material adequate?
  E. Presence: rapport, eye contact, personality, friendliness, mood
 IV. Relevance
  A. Interest level
  B. Concrete understanding of the relevance of Jesus's salvation and how this truth may be appropriated

Topical Evangelistic Sermon Evaluation Form

While content and organization in topical evangelistic sermons will substantially differ from textual evangelistic sermons, style and delivery issues remain the same.

 I. Content and Organization
  A. Introduction
   1. Need
   2. Attention
   3. Purpose
   4. Orientation
   5. Subintroduction
  B. Topic
   1. Choice of topic for relevance to the nonbeliever
   2. Clarity of topic in presentation
   3. Correlation of topic to the gospel
   4. Communication of biblical and theological concepts
  C. The Central Proposition of the Sermon
   1. Specific?
   2. Relevant to unbeliever's understanding?
   3. Devoid of Christian jargon?

4. Stated, reviewed, restated by speaker?
   5. Restatable by audience?
   6. Within range of biblical texts and/or canonical meaning?
   D. Development
   1. Outline sketch—simple and memorable?
   2. Effectiveness of rhetorical strategy
   E. Conclusion
   1. Summary: concrete understanding of the relevance of Jesus's salvation
   2. Invitation
      a. What are you calling for?
      b. Are the terms of the gospel clear?
      c. Is the response process clear?
II. Style and Delivery
   A. Voice: speed, volume, pitch, expressiveness
   B. Delivery: facial expressions, gestures, bodily movement
   C. Style: grammar, word choice, articulation, straightforwardness
   D. Support materials: adequate, appropriate, credible
   1. Appropriate to the experiences of the lost?
   2. Use of humor
   3. Is the support material adequate?
   E. Presence: rapport, eye contact, personality, friendliness, mood
   F. Interest level

A Concluding Challenge

A Preaching Audit

We have considered the calling of the evangelistic preacher, laid some foundations, provided a method for evangelistic preaching, and considered some pertinent issues. In conclusion, I invite you to conduct an audit of your preaching in general, and especially to audit your preaching for evangelistic faithfulness. We will regard this as a self-audit, a sort of pre-audit, before a public audit by your earthly audiences and the final audit by the heavenly Judge.

The more obvious infractions occur where

- you have preached through biblical passages with someone else's outline
- you have robbed from other preachers by way of illustration or the Internet without disclosing your sources
- you have passed off as true or personal what was neither without giving anyone a clue that you lied
- you have cheated your people from the pulpit by not working hard at preaching and teaching

- you have neglected opportunities to introduce the gospel in your sermons or in preparing and delivering a textual evangelistic sermon, thus betraying biblical values in proclamation

Upon such discovery, any independent auditor worth his professional membership would write you up. His notes would call for total disclosure of errant habits, deceptive practices, and neglect of acceptable pulpit requirements.

You are not a mere member of a professional society paying annual dues, receiving newsletter updates, and attending trade shows. In fact, in deed, and perhaps in blood, you have signed a sacred covenant with your God (inner calling) and a social contract with your hearers (outer calling). The sovereign Savior authorized you to accurately reflect his life-giving and life-building message upon entering the proclamation ministry. That obligatory agreement included a symmetry between public persona and private life (1 Thess. 2:3–13), priority work in prayer with hard work in sermon preparation (Acts 6:4; 1 Tim. 5:17), and integrity of character (1 Tim. 4:16).

That covenant and contract also included your delivery of the Good News of Jesus's salvation as clearly, widely, urgently, and boldly as possible.

Perhaps your self-audit shows a major deficit in your preaching. You are flying like a one-winged bird. You have slanted your proclamation ministry to building Christians and have neglected the ministry of rescuing non-Christians. You have wavered from the total mission of God's church. You have betrayed your authorization. You have fallen short of your duty, Christ's commission, and your calling, with people's eternal destinations at stake.

Fortunately, only you know about this departure. Voluntary professional societies, like in public accounting, can articulate minimum standards for excellence, but they cannot formally certify giftedness or calling. They can only informally encourage members to meet those standards. Congregations, however, vote for you with regular attendance, with their giving, *and* with the introduction of non-Christian neighbors to your ministry. Church members (present and prospective) evaluate your preaching, but if they do not reach non-Christians or don't have special opportunities to bring them to

A Concluding Challenge

church, you have just read their private audit notes and must take action from the platforms God has created for you.

We asked the pastor of a rather fine congregation to announce my upcoming evangelistic event for six weeks, as is our practice. He did. I preached my evangelistic heart out to about 150 people that morning. Not a single one acknowledged trusting Jesus at the invitation. Later the pastor assured me, "That was a powerful, clear evangelistic talk. If I hadn't been a Christian, I would have become one today. The reason you didn't have any responses is because not a single nonbeliever was present. No one brought a non-Christian acquaintance or relative to this event. I am sorry."

I was sorry too. Not because no one had responded but because I had possibly spent an evangelistic sermon and energy on a bunch of spiritually lazy, inward-looking, selfish, and busy believers. I encouraged myself in that some believers would appreciate God's salvation in a new way after the talk.

Yet the problem did not lie with the people, whom the pastor held responsible for not having brought non-Christian friends. You guessed it. We place the blame on the pastor himself. If he did not bring a nonbeliever to the event, why would they? He himself did not model evangelism—either personally or in the pulpit—so why would the sudden presence of an itinerant evangelist motivate people to reach out? He hardly preached evangelistically, so they didn't know this church existed for the world of unbelievers too. This pastor did a great job in showing the profit of Scripture to believers, but he hadn't lived out his own authorization in practicing, facilitating, and preaching salvation. Culpability for such squandered opportunities lies squarely upon a pastor who hasn't cast a vision for the lost, incarnated the reality in his personal life, or cultivated the mission of his people.

The only way out for this man was to pursue a self-audit, a pre-audit of his preaching. It was between him, God, and his hearers to address the evangelistic neglect, to work hard at evangelistic preaching and teaching, to pay attention to his evangelistic self and teaching, to preach the evangelistic Word in and out of season, to do the work of an evangelist. For each time he preached, the whole congregation came together for one event, and his words translated into their conversation for the week. He would have to change his planning and preaching strategy to provide for evangelistic preaching.

There are two pre-audit, self-audit issues: accuracy and authorization.

Accuracy

Ask yourself, Did I accurately reflect biblical priorities in my preaching? Did I primarily engage in life-building with Christians, or did I also pursue life-giving preaching toward non-Christians? When *Preaching Expository Sermons* was released in Spanish, I got to meet its gifted and careful translator. She remarked, "I have translated thirty or forty books, but you are the first author I have met. I have always wanted to meet authors. I hope I have been faithful to your intent and content in my translation." I assured her that I myself was a translator in my preaching ministry, seeking to reflect the intent and content of the Author and the authors of Scripture.

So with the pre-audit, you might realize that for the most part you preached the Bible. You studied and structured a text and arrived at its central proposition. You constructed a textually faithful and audience-relevant purpose on your way to your homiletical proposition. You structured and preached the biblical sermon with much power and clarity. But this pre-audit question remains: Did you mirror the Author and the author's intent, content, and extent accurately?

As pointed out in this book, evangelistic preaching reflects God's intent, content, and extent in the Scriptures. While all the content of Scripture is profitable for the Christian life (2 Tim. 3:16–17), the Scriptures carry the intent of making people wise to salvation (2 Tim. 3:15) and often can be extended into evangelistic preaching. You have probably passed the test for *accuracy* of pulpit content for the Christian life, but do you pass that test when it comes to preaching evangelistically, laying the path for a person's salvation? Look over your last month's, six months', or year's preaching. How much of your preaching includes the following?

- evangelistic intent
- evangelistic planning
- evangelistic appeal
- evangelistic footnotes to sermons otherwise preached to Christians
- evangelistic extension of passages primarily related to believers
- exclusively evangelistic messages in content, intent, or extent
- evangelistic clarity
- evangelistic invitation
- evangelistic response mechanism
- evangelistic follow-up

I know your rejoinder: "Most of my audience is Christian. My spouse, my kids, even my dog—they are all Christians. Ninety-nine point nine percent of my audience are Christians. I don't want to waste an evangelistic sermon on believers. And I don't know that I am gifted in evangelism." You are absolutely right. There's nothing redemptive in preaching redemption to the redeemed, nothing more wasteful than casting salvation pearls before saved swine, and nothing more discouraging than when the saved don't respond even at the thirteenth verse of the invitation song.

That brings us the second pre-audit question: Was the expense properly authorized?

Authorization

If you are a pastor ministering mostly to believers, I concur that the majority of your sermons, as well as your time in preparation, must relate to Christians. And if you don't see people trusting Christ, the lack of recognition by unbelievers of your evangelistic gifting would cause you self-doubt.

However, questions remain. Is preaching to believers all that your ministry consists of? Don't you do weddings, funerals, and social functions where you can squeeze in the Good News? Aren't there Sundays where non-Christians sneak into your service and squirm while your worship team repetitively sings unfamiliar songs while the nonbelievers stand with heart and mouth disengaged the whole time? Do you ever meet or greet a non-Christian—a postman, a dry cleaner, a doctor, a golfer, a young man or woman, a banker—and do you seek, see, and seize opportunities for gospel presentation? What makes you think that preaching to believers will ever help you recognize evangelistic gifts? And if you don't have unbelievers present, how will you practice and improve your evangelistic preaching?

A major part of your divine authorization for proclamation—the evangelistic mandate in preaching—is left unused, unspent, and undeveloped. Just like a board of directors would throw out budget items that consistently did not show activity and expense, your desertion of evangelistic preaching as originally authorized by God is now abandoned for lack of activity or expenditure. Evangelistic ennui has set in, and evangelistic preaching is gone from your pulpit.

Instead, if you live by Christ's mandate, by apostolic authorization, by Pauline calling, by Petrine example, and other biblical directives on preaching, you will hardly stay away from evangelistic preaching. You would seek to incorporate

- evangelistic thrusts in your church's programmatic launches so that nonbelievers will be present;
- evangelistic motivation by exhortation, illustration, and personal example so that believers will reach nonbelievers as a lifestyle; and
- evangelistic sermons in your annual calendar for personal reminders of divine authorization and people's reminders to reach and bring nonbelievers to these specialized services.

Remember, the expense has already been authorized. There are unlimited resources in the divine budget for evangelistic preaching. Your pre-audit may reveal dishonesty on your part. It may reveal lack of heart, weak initiative, deficient perspective, and inadequate development of people to fulfill your ministry. Soon the budget item will be removed, and you will have compromised and watered down the preaching mission of the church.

Your pre-audit could prompt you to immediately resign from leadership for not fulfilling your position description. If you were your boss, you would probably de-hire yourself for ongoing underperformance. Or you may re-sign the preaching covenant and decide to stand between heaven and humanity as an ambassador begging people to be reconciled to God. Then you can set about passing the divine audit of your ministry. You will be authenticated by the divine Auditor as worthy of carrying on the ministry of biblical proclamation. You will more accurately reflect the intent and content of Scripture. You will live under God's authorization for the extent of Scripture toward reaching unbelievers. You will expend already authorized resources for the ministry. People who become saved will co-sign your audit report. You will come out clean before heaven, rejoicing with the angels over anyone who repents.

This book has addressed you, my dear prodigal preacher. You may have wandered with your inheritance, away from the Father's heart, to do your own thing in the pulpit. We have explored the calling and the work of evangelistic preaching. I have outlined the theological values that undergird evangelistic preaching and explained the homiletical processes that help you unleash the Good News from the pulpit. If these values and processes are understood, accepted, and practiced in your ministry, you can live out your authorization accurately in view of the only audit that counts.

In the presence of God and of Christ Jesus, who presently audits you for authorized and accurate fulfillment of calling, and who will appear in kingly power to finally audit your ministry implementation, preach the Word—when ready, convenient, suitable, with great results or not—do the work of an evangelist (2 Tim. 4:2–5), and you will fulfill your ministry.

You may not be a preaching evangelist, but you ought to preach evangelistically. Will you intentionally preach to evangelize the unbeliever even as you preach to equip believers to grow enough to reach unbelievers? In this way, all will be pleased at the final audit.

NOTES

Introduction

1. Five months later I spoke at another similar event in a quick stopover in Buenos Aires. Enrique was there. He listened. His face and eyes beamed in agreement. From salvation's side of spiritual enlightenment, he understood its content and scope. His eyes had been opened. He seemed to appreciate this second talk much more than what I recall of our first encounter.

2. First published in 1995 with a revised and expanded edition, *Preparing Expository Sermons* (Grand Rapids: Baker, 2001). The Scripture Sculpture method provides a preaching process applicable across cultures, biblical genres, audience needs, and literacy levels.

Chapter 1: The Inner Calling of the Preaching Evangelist

1. The comparison between "the saving work" of *designated* ministers in this passage allows me to launch this chapter and book on evangelistic preaching—which is our saving work in the divine economy. By all means, to *save* some (cf. 1 Cor. 9:22)!

2. Summarized from Ashley's (no last name identified) radio interview on KRLD in Dallas, Texas, during the week of September 8–15, 2002. She added, "You are grateful for whatever you get, because your dream is being fulfilled. Six hundred people apply, and I tried out three times before being chosen."

3. I begin with this unusual calling because any profession can be viewed as calling in a secular sense. Some sense callings in the altruistic sense. My friends are consumed with making a difference for people who suffer with AIDS in Africa, orphans in Russia, young black musicians in the art of jazz, etc. These callings may reflect a love of humanity, while others are pursued in the name of Christ. Common constituents of the called include a strong awareness of identity (who they are—spiritual or otherwise); gifting (what they have—talents, spiritual gifts, resources, relationships, etc.); and vision (what they like to see changed—often based on personal sensitivities).

4. Biblically speaking, calling almost always refers to the spiritual dimensions of salvation, holiness, and glory rather than in the sense of vocation. Vocational calling is a "subordinate application" of the word "to God's summons and designation of individuals to particular functions and offices in his redemptive plan" (J. I. Packer, "Call, Calling," in Walter A. Elwell, ed., *Evangelical Dictionary of Theology* [Grand Rapids: Baker, 1984], 184), and simply applies the theological use of the word in *contemporary* reference (cf. Acts 13:2).

5. Ramesh Richard, *Soul Vision: Ensuring Life's Future Impact* (Chicago: Moody Press, 2004), 127–30.

6. The word *ought* originally was the preterite form of *owe*, "to be held or bound in duty or moral obligation," s.v. "ought" (*The New Webster Encylopedic Dictionary of the English Language*).

7. "Mustness" in doing God's will can be derived from the Greek word *dei*, "as an expression of necessity grounded in the will of God" (Walter Grundmann, s.v. "dei," *Theological Dictionary of the New Testament*, vol. 2, ed. Gerhard Kittel, trans. and ed. Geoffrey W. Bromiley [Grand Rapids: Eerdmans, 1976], 24).

8. For additional discussion on the broader needs and strategies of an intentional life, you may want to consult the author's trilogy on the intentional life published by Moody Press (2003–2004).

9. The first entry under *kaleō* in W. Bauer, F. W. Danker, W. F. Arndt, and F. W. Gingrich, *A Greek-English Lexicon of the New Testament and Other Early Christian Literature*, 3rd edition (Chicago: University of Chicago Press, 2000), 502–3, carries the "identification" nuance, followed by the second meaning of "invitation," which informs a latter part of our reflection on this equation.

10. Summarized from *apostellō*, ibid., 120.

11. One use of *tithēmi*, "to place or put," is to appoint or assign to some task or function as found in 1 Tim. 1:12.

12. There's another point: if you bring a self-sufficient, "can-do" spirit to God's work, he will have to break you down first.

13. "Apostleship is the only spiritual gift in connection with which the word 'call' is used. . . . However, from another perspective he [Paul] regards all spiritual gifts as equally the work of one and the same Spirit, and he gives them to each one, just as he determines (1 Cor. 12:11)" (Stephen Motyer, "Call, Calling," in *Evangelical Dictionary of Biblical Theology*, ed. Walter A. Elwell [Grand Rapids: Baker, 1996], 81).

14. *Kaleō*, "to call," has worked itself into the dominant, figurative sense of God's calling to salvation.

15. Stephen Kinzer, "Lilly Heir Makes $100 Million Bequest to Poetry Magazine," *New York Times*, November 19, 2002.

16. Jim Collins, "Is the Economy Just Built to Flip?" *Fast Company*, October 2002, 94.

17. Or as someone else told me about creators and reactors, if C stands for Christ, a called person moves Christ from the mix and muddle of life to being the head of his life! Of course, we want Christ at the head and center of our lives, because evangelists are creator-reactors but creators first. They operate out of oughtness, by sentness, with willingness.

18. We could possibly add other aspects of calling, "nowness" (or urgency) and "boldness" being two of them, but those are the benefits and results of "oughtness."

19. http://www.christcenteredmall.com/stores/art/dicianni/legacy.htm.

Chapter 2: The Outer Calling of the Preaching Evangelist

1. Dag Hammarskjöld, *Markings*, trans. Leif Sjöberg and W. H. Auden (New York: Alfred A. Knopf, 1966), 155.

2. I obtained this illustration from a hope-giving article: Nicholas Thompson, "Self-adjusted Glasses Could Be Boon to Africa," *New York Times*, December 10, 2002.

3. Ibid.

4. See my manuscript and method for clarifying and surmounting worldview, religious, and cultural filters in effective evangelistic and apologetics presentation in the author's upcoming work on engaging international neighbors exploring worldview apologetics and cross-cultural evangelism.

5. For an extended exegesis of this passage, especially in critiquing inclusivist assertions, see my *Population of Heaven* (Chicago: Moody Press, 1994), 57–60.

6. C. S. Lewis, *The Problem of Pain* (New York: Macmillan, 1944), 106.

7. Jeffery L. Sheler, "Hell Hath No Fury," *U.S. News and World Report*, January 31, 2000, 47.

8. Jonathan Edwards, *Sinners in the Hands of An Angry God*, www.jonathanedwards.com/sermons/warnings/sinners.htm.

9. For instance, see Edward W. Fudge and Robert A. Peterson, *Two Views of Hell: A Biblical and Theological Dialogue* (Downers Grove, IL: Intervarsity Press, 2000).

10. Wesley L. Gerig, "Reward," in *Evangelical Dictionary of Biblical Theology*, 686. For my convenience and yours, I use this standard dictionary as a resource over the next pages of treatment of pertinent biblical subjects.

11. "Pots of Promise," *Economist*, May 24, 2003, 69–71.

12. G. F. Hawthorne, *Dictionary of Paul and His Letters* (Downers Grove, IL: InterVarsity Press, 1993), 321–22.

13. *Common Ground*, November 2002, vol. 20, no. 11.

14. See chapter 8 of the forthcoming work on engaging people across worldviews and cultures.

15. Merrill F. Unger, R. K. Harrison, Howard F. Vos, and Cyril J. Barber, eds. *New Unger's Bible Dictionary* (Chicago: Moody Press, 1961), s.v. "evangelist."

16. "In other words, God does not hand out literal crowns, but offers the acknowledged honor of the presence of this characteristic in the believer for eternity" (Darrell L. Bock, "Crown," in *Evangelical Dictionary of Biblical Theology*, 138). Every writer on crowns appropriately points out that Christ wore a crown of thorns and one day will wear a crown of triumph. There may be a pattern for our own crown expectations: a crown of hardship now for a crown of joy later.

17. P. H. Davids, "Crown," in *Evangelical Dictionary of Theology*, 288.

18. "What he [Paul] means is that some Christians will be saved but with little, if anything, to show for their years on earth. Whether because of wrong motives or laziness or misplaced priorities, they will conclude their lives with very little of any eternal worth to show" (Wesley L. Gerig, in "Reward," commenting on 1 Corinthians 3:15 in *Evangelical Dictionary of Biblical Theology*, 685).

19. "'Baywatch' It Isn't for Lifeguard Recruits," *New York Times*, May 21, 2003.

Chapter 3: A Theological Framework for Evangelistic Preaching

1. Christina Burbank, "Humor in Uniform," *Reader's Digest*, November 2002, 64.

2. John D. Hannah, "Evangelicalism, Conversion, and the Gospel: Have We Sold Our Heritage for Relevance?" in *The Coming Evangelical Crisis: Current Challenges to the Authority of Scripture and the Gospel* (Chicago: Moody Press, 1996), 162.

3. There is much scholarly discussion on the content of κήρυγμα, but the meaning of εὐαγγελίζομαι is not complex in Paul or the apostles—to proclaim Jesus to non-Christians. For seminal discussions see C. H. Dodd, *The Apostolic Preaching and Its Developments* (London: Hodder and Stoughton, 1936); J. I. H. McDonald, *Kerygma and Didache: The Articulation and Structure of the Earliest Christian Message*, Society for New Testament Studies Monograph Series 37 (Cambridge: Cambridge University Press, 1980); P. Stuhlmacher, "The Pauline Gospel," in *The Gospel and the Gospels*, ed. P. Stuhlmacher (Grand Rapids: Eerdmans, 1991), 149–72, and other summary discussions in New Testament lexicons or theological dictionaries.

4. Sri Lankan bishop D. T. Niles's definition of evangelism as "one beggar telling another beggar where he found bread" finds biblical grounding in this story. Evangelism is one liberated prisoner, one redeemed slave, one healed from blindness, one resurrected man pointing others so spiritually imprisoned, enslaved, blind, and deadened to the source of liberation, light, and life. Since our focus is on evangelistic *preaching* rather than evangelism, I borrow these metaphors and motivations of evangelism as framing strategy in evangelistic preaching.

5. The bold young man continued, "While forgiveness is given, restitution is still required." And then speaking to her family, he said, "A lot of you will all have phone calls, letters and visitation. We don't have any of these anymore. We would like to say we are sorry for your loss as well." Dave Levinthal, "Mallard Handed 50 Years," *Dallas Morning News*, June 28, 2003.

6. For a useful and retainable method of personal evangelism (easier with those sharing a Christian worldview) in personal evangelism see Randy Raysbrook, "One-Verse Evangelism," *Discipleship Journal* 34 (1986): 28–32.

7. I present the apologetic of life more fully in the future volume on cross-cultural apologetics and worldview evangelism.

8. Howard W. French, "Japanese Pastor Reaches Out with Suicide Line," *New York Times*, May 31, 2003. With the limitations a reporter faces in narrating a ministry in a secular newspaper, the underlying biblical convictions of this pastor can easily be discerned. He most likely treats this pre-evangelistic ministry as paving one's road to Jesus.

Chapter 4: A Definition of Evangelistic Preaching

1. William Willimon, *Peculiar Speech* (Grand Rapids: Eerdmans, 1992), 89.

2. Moody Adams, *The Titanic's Last Hero* (Columbia, SC: Olive Press, 1997), quoted in Charles Colson, "Twice Saved—A True Titanic Hero," *BreakPoint Commentary,* Wednesday, April 14, 1999.

3. Fred B. Craddock, "Preaching," *The Anchor Bible Dictionary*, ed. D. N. Freedman (New York: Doubleday, 1996), 5:451.

4. "The Gospel of Jesus Christ: An Evangelical Celebration," *Christianity Today*, June 14, 1999, 51. This theological definition of the gospel, if left alone in the preamble, would have been unambiguous. Actually, the rest of that statement is well thought out, biblically grounded, and expressed in near credal form. But the latter discussion, "What's the Good News? Nine Evangelical Leaders Define the Gospel" (*Christianity Today*, February 7, 2000, 46–51), opens up an assortment of opinions mostly desirous of including the theological *framework* (see chapter 3) and scope of the gospel (especially in discipleship)

into its essential and vital content. While you are looking up the definition of *preaching* in your dictionaries, be sure to look up *gospel* as well.

5. In order to provide freedom to the evangelist in contextual situation and audience sensitivity, I recommend a four-movement sequence in personal presentation and public proclamation of the gospel: God, Humanity, Jesus, Faith. Somehow and somewhere I must disclose God's expectation, humanity's situation, Jesus's provision, and salvation's condition to the unbeliever, preferably in sequence. The four-part movement can be grouped in two sections, (1) God—Humanity, 2) Jesus—Faith, to constitute the theological atmosphere of the gospel. I will refer to this four-part, two-section movement throughout this work. As in personal conversation, so in effective pedagogy, there is repetition and overlap for emphasis, understanding, and hopefully, the personal embrace of Jesus.

6. Deborah Baldwin, "In Search of the Perfect Cup, The Old Coffee Pot is Passé," *New York Times*, July 7, 2003.

7. James Daane, *The Freedom of God* (Grand Rapids: Eerdmans, 1973), 118.

Chapter 5: Textual Evangelistic Preaching

1. Charles Osgood, "Osgood on Speaking: How to Think on Your Feet without Falling on Your Face," *American Way*, August 15, 1988, 23, 25–26. Excerpted from Charles Osgood, *Osgood on Speaking: How to Think on Your Feet without Falling on Your Face* (New York: William Morrow and Company, 1988).

2. Washington State Crop Improvement Association, home page, http://Wscia.com/dw_certified_seed_HotBot.htm.

Chapter 6: Sources and Samples of Textual Evangelistic Preaching

1. Craig A. Loscalzo, *Evangelistic Preaching That Connects: Guidance in Shaping Fresh and Appealing Sermons* (Downers Grove, IL: InterVarsity Press, 1995). Chapter 4 of Loscalzo's work entitled, "Preaching Good News from the Old Testament," carries practical hints and helpful samples in interpreting Old Testament genres for preaching.

2. See the excellent comments by Sidney Greidanus, "Preaching Christ from the Old Testament," *Bibliotheca Sacra* 161, no. 641 (January–March 2004): 3–13; and "Preaching Christ from the Creation Narrative," *Bibliotheca Sacra* 161, no. 642 (April–June 2004): 131–41. Evangelistic preaching from the Old Testament shows up critical hermeneutical presuppositions between "continuity and discontinuity" theological systems. I suggest you do not follow a christological hermeneutic of the Old Testament. To put it in a simple but pregnant way, pursue a grammatical-historical *hermeneutic* of the Old Testament but a christological *homiletic* in all Old Testament preaching.

3. Hugh Litchfield, *Visualizing the Sermon: A Guide to Preaching without Notes* (Sioux Falls, SD: self published, 1996) suggests a practical way from IDEA PICTURE IMAGE as a helpful format to develop and deliver sermons without notes.

4. Bryan Chapell, *Christ-Centered Preaching: Redeeming the Expository Sermon* (Grand Rapids: Baker, 1994), 40–41. While the "Fallen Condition Focus" provides a theological focus and framework for preaching to Christians primarily, it is even more easily and fully utilized for preaching to nonbelievers.

5. J. L. Mays, *Harper's Bible Commentary* (Harper & Row: San Francisco, 1996), on Romans 5:1ff.

6. Thomas G. Long and Neely Dixon McCarter, eds., *Preaching In and Out of Season* (Lousiville, KY: Westminster John Knox, 1990), 83.

7. For advanced students of homiletics (and hermeneutics), an excellent grappling of issues relating to preaching Christ from the Old Testament (thus the possible connection to evangelistic preaching) in *textual exposition* along with a model highly compatible with the Scripture Sculpture process is found in Sidney Greidanus, *Preaching Christ from the Old Testament: A Contemporary Hermeneutical Method* (Grand Rapids: Eerdmans, 1999). See especially his method, examples, and summary in chapters 6–8. A practical resource of texts, doctrines, events, words, etc., for the Old Testament in evangelistic preaching (not as hermeneutically well-grounded as in Greidanus but well worth browsing) is Faris D. Whitesell, *Evangelistic Preaching and the Old Testament* (Chicago: Moody Press, 1947).

Chapter 7: Text-Driven Topical Evangelistic Preaching

1. "Topical preaching has a venerable place in the history of the craft. Its legitimacy is seen in the validity of biblical and systematic theology. While this should not be the first choice of the pastor-teacher, every pastor will preach topically on occasion. . . . Because the topical sermon can be more relentlessly unitary, one discovers that any list of the ten sermons which have most decisively influenced world culture and society consists mostly if not entirely of topical sermons" (David L. Larsen, *The Anatomy of Preaching: Identifying the Issues in Preaching Today* [Grand Rapids: Kregel, 1999], 31).

2. I make these prepositional distinctions to preserve the text from being used as an illustration of a greater principle carrying a theological referent not embedded in the intention of the author in the text.

3. Roger E. Van Harn, *Pew Rights: For People Who Listen to Sermons* (Grand Rapids: Eerdmans, 1992), 134. While the book is oriented to Christianized audiences, I like the author's summary on preaching that transfers to our subject: "The Spirit's order that creates the expectation that we will hear the Word of God is this: an appointed person speaks an intended message from a Bible text to the world and life of the listeners" (p. 135).

4. For those desiring exegetical structural grounds, we derive these from clauses following ὥστε and ἵνα.

5. There is scholarly discussion on whether οὕτως should be regarded as extent (the depth and breadth of God's love) or manner (i.e., this way of God's love). Hence, the *degree* of God's love.

6. I tease pastors all over the world that *The Thompson Chain-Reference Bible* often rescues them at the last moment before preaching because they haven't prepared their own meals for their people. Nevertheless, this significant work contains thousands of topics that can be quickly put together into sermons for sudden opportunities. If we use this reference regularly, we will be preaching someone else's structure (Dr. Thompson's) rather than our own (topical) or the text's (textual) structure. "They really don't need you for spiritual food. Just give them their own copy and you can take off on Saturday too as believers in Sabbath!"

Chapter 8: Audience-Driven Topical Evangelistic Preaching

1. Van Harn, *Pew Rights: For People Who Listen to Sermons*, xi.

2. I borrow this phrase from Ninian Smart, "The Philosophy of Worldviews—That Is the Philosophy of Religion Transformed," *N. Zeitschr. f. syst. Theologie* 23:2, 1981.

3. See Charles Kraft, *Christianity in Culture: A Study in Dynamic Biblical Theologizing in Cross Cultural Perspective* (Maryknoll, NY: Orbis Books, 1979), 33–37.

4. Daniel C. Dennett, "The Bright Stuff," *New York Times*, July 12, 2003.

Notes 251

5. I have explained a method of exegeting audiences in *Preparing Expository Sermons* and more extensively in a future volume tentatively entitled *Wisdom toward Outsiders: A Manual on Cross-Cultural Apologetics and Worldwide Evangelism.*

6. More sophisticated scales of the spiritual awareness of an unbeliever toward conversion and maturity began in contemporary evangelism with the Spiritual Segmentation linear model of V. Søgaard, *Everything You Need to Know for a Cassette Ministry* (Minneapolis: Bethany, 1975), 27–53, and the Engel Scale (from awareness of supreme being and no knowledge of the gospel all the way to Christian stewardship), in James F. Engel and H. Wilbert Norton, *What's Gone Wrong with the Harvest* (Grand Rapids: Zondervan, 1975), 45. Many suggestions for refinements are suggested on the Internet (type "Engel Scale" on your search engine). The Gray Matrix, http://www.thegraymatrix.info/, adds the critical component of *attitude* (antagonism/enthusiasm) to prior Christian knowledge (in communication effectiveness).

7. I used to give away a fine short book, Josh McDowell's *More Than a Carpenter*, but then I noticed that many people were not asking the academic questions about Jesus as their *first* questions. After looking around for a preliminary gift, I decided to write *Mending Your Soul: The Spiritual Path to Inner Wholeness*. I still keep copies of *More Than a Carpenter* as a second book to lead people into a further consideration of Jesus.

8. All three headlines appear in the same section of "The Science Times," *New York Times*, July 8, 2003. Each day I find more topics to turn into evangelistic themes and thrusts.

9. In a more technical series, I explored the hermeneutical range of meaning: (1) *statement*, (2) *implication* for *continuities* between them and us—the human author's intention, and (3) *extrapolation* for *discontinuities* between them and us—based on the divine author's intention. See my articles from a series on "Methodological Proposals for Scripture Relevance": "Selected Issues in Theoretical Hermeneutics" *Bibliotheca Sacra* 143 (January–March 1986): 14–25 and "Levels of Biblical Meaning" *Bibliotheca Sacra* 143 (April–June 1986): 123–33.

Chapter 9: Support Materials

1. Do a search for "illustrations" on any Internet bookseller's website, and you will find innumerable sources for illustrations, especially books on preaching and books of sermon illustrations. Most of these works will also give you instruction on the brief subjects I address below in this chapter. I encourage you to read those works for additional input. This textbook is not on preaching per se; it is on evangelistic preaching, and I attempt not to repeat or review material introduced elsewhere by myself or others on the matter of illustrations.

2. Robert Aunger, *The Electric Meme: A New Theory of How We Think* (New York: The Free Press, 2002), borrows a metaphor from biogenetics—genes—and transfers them to neuroscience—memes—to show how evolutionary biology propagates ideas with lives of their own. While the evolutionary premises for memetics are doubted, we do know the power of ideas and contagious stories to stick in people's heads and hearts to shape lives and culture.

3. Ramesh Richard, *Preparing Expository Sermons* (Grand Rapids: Baker, 2001), 122–23.

4. Numerous sources can help you understand your own and others' learning styles. Your understanding enables choices of support materials. You can begin with the index of learning styles found at http://www.ncsu.edu/felder-public/ILSpage.html.

5. From W. E. Sangster, *The Craft of Sermon Illustration* (Philadelphia: Westminster Press, 1950), 27–43.

6. Missionaries have found that storytelling is a universal form of communication across cultures, religions, and styles of learning and that it really emulates the Master storyteller, our Lord Jesus. (Tom Steffen, "Story Telling: Why Do It? Is It an Essential Skill for Missionaries?" in *Missions Frontiers Bulletin* [March–April 1997], 10–12, a reprint of *Reconnecting God's Story to Ministry: Cross-cultural Story-telling at Home and Abroad* [Pasadena: William Carey Library, 1996]).

7. Annette Simmons, in *The Story Factor: Inspiration, Influence and Persuasion through the Art of Storytelling* (Cambridge, MA: Perseus Books, 2001), writes, "Story is your path to creating faith" [meaning "credibility for your presentations"]. She identifies six types of stories: (1) the "Who I Am" story that reveals something about who you are; (2) the "Why I Am Here" story to reassure audience that you have good intentions; (3) the "Vision" story to promise them a future; (4) the "Teaching" story to cut down the teaching time; (5) the "Values in Action" story to provide an example of the value you want to teach; and (6) the "I Know What You Are Thinking" story to identify and address potential objections to your message.

8. Refer to David Rees, "Being Serious about Humor," *Clergy Journal* 73, no. 5 (March 1997): 4–7, for ways to use humor in good taste. For a serious treatment of humor in the pulpit, especially the theological, ethical, and practical objections, with insights into the "comic sermon" genre, see Joseph M. Webb, *Comedy and Preaching* (St. Louis: Chalice Press, 1998).

9. Sent by a member of the Japan Mission by email on April 30, 2000, and sourced from the *Yomiuri* newspaper.

10. Richard, *Preparing Expository Sermons*, 121–26.

11. It is good, if possible, to keep complete sources for your illustrations. I had to spend extra effort in finding bibliographic details for this summary from Barry Bearak, "Sounding the Alarm on Deadly Wells," *New York Times*, December 8, 1998. In my case, I can find the source at our local library if I really need the information.

12. Stephen Kinzer, "Long Dead, Possibly Mad, Bavaria's Royal Enigma Still Fascinates," *New York Times*, August 28, 1995.

13. James Gorman, "How a Forest Stopped a Fire in Its Tracks," *New York Times*, July 22, 2003.

14. "Giving of Yourself, Literally, to People You've Never Met," *New York Times*, July 27, 2003.

15. Denise Grady, "Donor Mix-Up Leaves Girl, 17, Fighting for Life," *New York Times*, February 19, 2003.

Chapter 10: The Evangelistic Invitation

1. The evangelistic invitation moves the hearer from a crisis of understanding to a crisis of decision. Some homiletical resources, strategies, and texts to *seize* (especially in topical exposition) in inviting people to come to Christ in the "crisis" of the evangelistic invitation are found in Joseph R. Jeter, *Crisis Preaching: Personal and Public* (Nashville: Abingdon), 1998.

2. J. D. Douglas, ed. *The Calling of an Evangelist: Second International Conference for Itinerant Evangelists, Amsterdam, the Netherlands* (Minneapolis: World Wide Publications, 1987), 173.

3. Greg Laurie, "Whatever Happened to the Clear Invitation?" in Rick Warren's Ministry Tool Box, #15, June 27, 2001, http:www.pastors.com/RWMT/?id=15&artid=485&expand=1.

4. A helpful treatment of evangelists and invitations through Christian history is found in chapter 4 of R. Alan Street, *The Effective Invitation: A Practical Guide for the Pastor* (Grand Rapids: Kregel, 1984). Billy Graham's "Use of the Public Invitation" in chapter 5 is also useful. This fine book is oriented to a Baptistic environment in North America.

5. Clarence E. Macartney, *The Greatest Questions of the Bible and of Life* (New York: Abingdon-Cokesbury, 1948), 55–56.

6. Annie Dillard's comments on writing resonate with our frailty in preaching: "Write as if you were dying. At the same time, assume you write for an audience consisting of terminal patients. That is, after all, the case. What would you begin writing if you knew you would die soon? What could you say to a dying person that would not enrage by its triviality?" (*The Writing Life* [New York: Harper & Row 1989], 68).

Appendix 1: Relevant Terms in Evangelistic Preaching

1. For example, see David B. Barrett, *Evangelize! A Historical Survey of the Concept* (Nashville: Broadman and Holman, 1987).

Appendix 6: A Checklist for Evaluating the Textual or Topical Evangelistic Sermon

1. For a comprehensive checklist for evaluating and applying the Scripture Sculpture process, see *Preparing Expository Sermons*, appendix 12, "Sermon Evaluation Questionnaire."

About the Author

God has permitted Ramesh Richard to become a global spokesman for the Lord Jesus Christ. Dr. Richard is a professor at Dallas Theological Seminary, where he teaches courses credited across three academic departments. He also serves as president of Ramesh Richard Evangelism and Church Health (*RREACH*).

A global proclamation ministry, the vision of *RREACH* is to change the way one billion individuals think and hear about the Lord Jesus Christ. Its mission is to proclaim the Lord Jesus Christ worldwide with a strategic burden for strengthening the pastoral leaders and evangelizing the opinion leaders of developing economies.

From his platform at *RREACH*, Dr. Richard travels throughout the world, clarifying the message of the Bible through lectures and preaching. His audiences are wide-ranging—from non-Christian intellectuals at Harvard to poor pastors in Haiti, from gatherings of a few hundred to a hundred thousand. The Lord has given him the opportunity of training thousands of church leaders in over seventy countries to preach, live, and think biblically. He also has the privilege of exposing society's "opinion leaders" to the Good News of Jesus Christ.

A theologian, preacher, philosopher, evangelist, and author, Dr. Richard holds a Th.D. (in systematic theology) from Dallas Theological Seminary and a Ph.D. (in philosophy) from the University of Delhi. He previously served as the pulpit pastor of the Delhi Bible

Fellowship in New Delhi, India. He founded and chairs the Trainers of Pastors International Coalition (TOPIC)—an international coalition of pastoral training organizations accelerating the training of large numbers of pastoral leaders where the church is growing.

Dr. Richard, his wife, Bonnie, and their children, Ryan, Robby, and Sitara, live in the Dallas area.

For clarification or information, you may write the author at Dallas Theological Seminary, 3909 Swiss Avenue, Dallas, TX 75204; at *RREACH*, 5500 W. Plano Parkway, Plano, TX 75093; or at www.rreach.org.